Fairness and Justice in Environmental Decision Making

'A clear and compelling case for fairness as a foundation for resource sharing. Catherine Gross' book is essential for those wanting to understand the role of fairness and justice in preventing social conflict.'

Paul R. Ehrlich
Bing Professor of Population Studies, Stanford University, USA

'Building on real-world examples of environmental conflict over wind power and water access, the author clarifies what fairness and justice mean to those affected. She then argues the need for a theory of justice to guide environmental decision-making and to optimise fairness, as understood and seen. A timely book, as environmental tensions mount.'

Professor Tony McMichael
Australian National University, Australia

By crossing disciplinary boundaries, this book uniquely connects theories of justice with people's lived experience within social conflicts over resource sharing. It shows why some conflicts, such as local opposition to wind farms and water disputes, have become intractable social problems in many countries of the world. It shows the power of *in*justice in generating opposition to decisions. The book answers the question: why are the results of many government initiatives and policies not accepted by those affected?

Focusing on two social conflicts over water sharing in Australia to show why fairness and justice are important in decision making, the book shows how these conflicts are typical of water sharing and other natural resource conflicts experienced in many countries around the world, particularly in the context of climate change. It tells the stories of these conflicts from the perspectives of those involved. These practically based findings are then related back to ideas and constructs of justice from disciplines such as social psychology, political philosophy and jurisprudence.

With a strong practical focus, this book offers readers an opportunity to develop a deep understanding of fairness and justice in environmental decision making. It opens up a wealth of fairness and justice ideas for decision-makers, practitioners, and researchers in natural resource management, environmental governance, community consultation, and sustainable development, as well as people in government and corporations who interface and consult with communities where natural resources are being used.

Catherine Gross is engaged in research on the application of fairness and justice principles to resolve natural resource conflicts as a Visiting Fellow at the Fenner School of Environment and Society, The Australian National University. Catherine is also Vice Chair of the Frank Fenner Foundation, an Australian NGO.

Routledge Explorations in Environmental Studies

Nuclear Waste Management and Legitimacy
Nihilism and responsibility
Mats Andrén

Nuclear Power, Economic Development Discourse and the Environment
The case of India
Manu V. Mathai

Federalism of Wetlands
Ryan W. Taylor

Governing Sustainable Urban Renewal
Partnerships in action
Rory Shand

Employee Engagement with Sustainable Business
How to change the world whilst keeping your day job
Nadine Exter

The Political Economy of Global Warming
The terminal crisis
Del Weston

Communicating Environmental Patriotism
A rhetorical history of the American environmental movement
Anne Marie Todd

Environmental Justice in Developing Countries
Perspectives from Africa and Asia-Pacific
Rhuks Temitope Ako

Climage Change and Cultural Heritage
A race against time
Peter F. Smith

A Global Environmental Right
Stephen Turner

The Coming of Age of the Green Community
My neighbourhood, my planet
Erik Bichard

Fairness and Justice in Environmental Decision Making
Water under the bridge
Catherine Gross

Carbon Politics and the Failure of the Kyoto Protocol
Gerald Kutney

Fairness and Justice in Environmental Decision Making

Water under the bridge

Catherine Gross

Routledge
Taylor & Francis Group
LONDON AND NEW YORK

earthscan
from Routledge

First published 2014
by Routledge
2 Park Square, Milton Park, Abingdon, Oxon, OX14 4RN

and by Routledge
711 Third Avenue, New York, NY 10017

Routledge is an imprint of the Taylor & Francis Group, an informa business

British Library Cataloguing in Publication Data
A catalogue record for this book is available from the British Library

Library of Congress Cataloging-in-Publication Data
Gross, Catherine.
Fairness and justice in environmental decision-making : water under the bridge / Catherine Gross.
pages cm. – (Routledge explorations in environmental studies)
Includes bibliographical references and index.
1. Environmental policy–Moral and ethical aspects. 2. Natural resources–Management. 3. Social justice–Environmental aspects. 4. Environmental justice. I. Title.
GE170.G76 2014
179'.1–dc23
2013026654

ISBN13: 978-0-415-83389-9 (hbk)
ISBN13: 978-0-203-48899-7 (ebk)

Typeset in Times New Roman
by Cenveo Publisher Services

Contents

Photographs

Figures

Tables

Acknowledgements

Many people have contributed to this book. First, I am indebted to the scores of people I talked to, mainly from rural Australia, whose experiences form the bed-rock of the book. These people, with their stories, ideas and understanding of unfairness, fairness and justice, were my inspiration. Second, I thank many friends and colleagues at the Fenner School of Environment and Society at the Australian National University. Three people in particular made a significant difference: David Dumaresq for his encouragement and crystal-clear perspectives from the outset, and for many discussions about this book; and Val Brown and Steve Dovers for their guidance and assistance. I also thank Sue Holzknecht; Clive Hilliker for diagrams and cartography; and Steve Leahy and Karl Nissen for technical assistance. Thanks to Elsevier for permission to use text extracts and Figure 1.1 from my 2007 *Energy Policy* paper, and Stephen Boyden for permission to use Figure 3.1. I thank Murray May for editing, and Rob Dyball, Patrick Troy, Ben Gross and other readers for their constructive suggestions. There are many others who have helped; in particular, Stephen Boyden for discussions about the bigger picture and Kaye Devlin for looking after Roly. Finally, I thank my family, especially my parents, Peter and Barbara, for support, ideas and distractions along the way.

Glossary, abbreviations and terms

Australian government: three levels in a federal system There are three elected levels of Australian government: federal, state and local. Federal government is primarily responsible for national affairs, including foreign affairs, trade, taxation, social security, etc. State government responsibility includes justice, health, education, public transport, land administration, including water and natural resources. Local government responsibility includes local road maintenance, garbage collection, development applications, building regulations and land subdivisions. Elected members of the public who sit on the local government council are called councillors. Friction and policy disagreement occurs frequently between these three levels of government.

Cap A limit imposed on water that can be extracted or diverted from a system.

Carry-over water Carry-over water enables a water allocation to be carried over from one water allocation year to the next allocation year for use at a later date. Carry-over water refers to the water allocation, not the physical water. The carry-over water mechanism is an adaptive management tool that enables irrigators to manage their water allocation from one season to the next.

Catchment A land area from which rainfall run-off combines into one river system.

Councillor An elected member of a local government council

Deniliquin Deniliquin is a small regional town in the Murray Irrigation Area in south-western NSW, Australia. It is well-established as a long-standing regional service centre for dryland and irrigated agriculture. Murray Irrigation Ltd, the largest irrigation infrastructure company in the region, is based in Deniliquin. The population is approximately 8000.

DNR Department of Natural Resources, NSW Government

DSE Department of Sustainability and Environment, Victorian Government

Dryland farming Dryland farming depends on natural rainfall for crop and pasture production.

Gigalitre One billion (1,000,000,000) litres, or 1000 megalitres

Inflows Water that flows into a water storage or river system.

Managed investment scheme In a managed investment scheme (also known as 'MIS') investors contribute to a common enterprise to produce financial gains. The scheme is managed by a responsible entity and investors usually acquire interests in the scheme through their investment rather than direct ownership of the resources. Investors can gain tax advantages by investing in managed investment schemes.

Megalitre One million (1,000,000) litres

Melbourne Melbourne is the state capital of Victoria, Australia. The metropolitan area of Melbourne has approximately 4.1 million people.

NIMBY Not-in-My-Backyard. NIMBY is an explanation used to describe people who are against a development in their local area, but who may support that type of development elsewhere, or use the services it provides.

NSW New South Wales (NSW) is a state in the east of Australia. It has a population of approximately 7.3 million people.

Over-allocation Refers to situations where the total volume of water able to be extracted by water users exceeds the environmentally sustainable level of extraction.

Shepparton Shepparton is a well-established regional city located on the floodplain of the Goulburn River in the northast of Victoria, Australia. It services the Goulburn Valley irrigation area and is the region's agricultural and manufacturing centre. The population of the urban area is approximately 38,000.

Sleeper and dozer water licences A sleeper licence is one which has not recorded any water use at all. A dozer licence is one which has had some recorded water use but not up to the full amount available.

Stranded assets In an irrigation system the term 'stranded assets' refers to irrigation infrastructure assets that are used less when water is traded out of the system, because the overall amount of water used in the system is reduced. As a result, the irrigation system becomes less financially viable. The term stranded assets can be used more broadly to include other social and material infrastructure.

Victoria Victoria is a state in the south-east of Australia. It has a population of approximately 5.7 million people.

Wind farm A wind farm is a renewable energy development that harnesses wind for electricity production. A wind farm comprises infrastructure including a number of wind turbines, an access road to each turbine, electricity substations, and power lines to transmit the energy to the electricity grid.

Introduction

Why do our social institutions seem to get so many decisions wrong? Why are the results of many government initiatives and policies not accepted by those affected? Our institutions struggle to deliver outcomes that are perceived by those affected as fair, even though many decision-makers *think* they have made fair decisions and the decisions may indeed be fair. This book addresses two questions that help us find answers: why are fairness and justice important, and how can fairness and justice principles be put to better use in day-to-day decision making? As individuals, many of us have a clear idea of what fairness means and why it is important. But achieving a general understanding of what fairness means in the practice of resource sharing is much more difficult. In environmental decision making we do not talk the language of fairness and justice and we do not apply fairness and justice principles routinely. For example, the continuing conflict over renewable wind energy and the placement of wind turbines shows that we need to address fairness and justice in decision making if we are to make progress in implementing alternative solutions to energy production. By understanding the fairness issues and genuine concerns that underlie people's reluctance to accept decisions, we can make our decision-making processes better. This book shows that there are different forms of justice which influence people's behaviour within a decision-making process. It shows how institutions can achieve *greater* acceptance of decisions by the broader community through the application of fairness and justice principles.

Ideas of fairness and unfairness are intrinsic to human nature. At an early age children learn about the importance of getting along with each other and how good relations with family and friends contribute to happiness and well-being. As individuals, we know how we want to be treated and we know when we are treated unfairly. 'But that's unfair!' is a heartfelt reaction known to all. We know that fairness is important.

Fairness is embedded in societal arrangements, yet at the institutional level these notions often seem to get lost. As human culture has evolved from hunter–gatherer communities through to modern-day civilisation, implicit fairness principles have been incorporated into a range of formal and informal societal activities. These enable people to get along with each other and avoid friction and disputes when people interact in close proximity.

But fairness in these areas can be fragile. Longstanding arrangements work well where there are constant conditions, where people understand the rules and where inconsistencies and anomalies have been ironed out over time. But in rapidly changing conditions where expanding urban populations put pressure on the supply of land, water and other amenities, then arrangements fall short, and tension and conflicts follow. Those affected who feel they have no alternatives use protests to draw attention to the issue. Protesters are often derided as being emotional, irrational and lacking in objectivity. This is where societal arrangements break down and fail to deliver 'fair treatment' for those affected by changing circumstances and decisions. It is in situations such as these that ideas and theories of injustice, fairness and justice can be used, first in showing what has gone wrong, and then in showing how arrangements can be improved.

My aim is to show how theoretical ideas about fairness and justice from a variety of disciplines, combined with people's lived experience of fairness and justice, can be put to use in the day-to-day social conflict over natural resources. How can we avoid social conflict around resource sharing? We are all familiar with terms associated with sharing and allocation, including the words fairness, justice, equality, need and equity. But, in the realities of day-to-day decision making, what do these terms really mean, and how can we really achieve fairness when there are apparently not enough resources to go around and when it seems some will inevitably lose out? It is not my intent to lay blame on those who must make the difficult decisions. The intent here is to improve decision making through the use of principles that derive from justice theory.

This book works in the middle area between the practical reality of resource sharing, and the less tangible principles, ideas and goals of justice theory. The book does not set out to be a text on justice and fairness alone nor environmental decision making alone. It brings these two areas together in the pursuit of improving how we go about sharing resources. Although the context here is natural resources, such as water and wind within the frame of environmental decision making, these principles apply broadly to decision making about the full range of societal issues.

I have not taken a traditional approach in structuring this book. For example, I do not provide definitions of fairness and justice in the opening pages, and then apply them to environmental decision making. Since the entire book is about increasing our understanding of what people think about fairness and justice, an early definition would set artificial boundaries and limit the exploration. It would perpetuate the very closed-ness that the book endeavours to open up. The approach I take is to find out from people who have a role to play in resource conflicts what they think about fairness and justice. In other words, an important goal of the book is to see how people understand and use these concepts.

Another way in which this book takes a non-traditional approach is in the flow of the chapters. Many readers might expect the first chapter to lay out the bones of an argument and subsequent chapters to flesh out the overall body of the work. This book follows a different path. It is structured around a journey in which an *understanding* of fairness and justice is developed. The objective is to deepen our understanding of fairness and justice in environmental decision making, because there are many conflicts in resource sharing, and finding ways to resolve or mitigate these is crucially important for society. So the approach I take is to look at some current conflicts to see what issues of fairness there might be. Thus, case studies of social conflicts in natural resource management are used as 'carriers' that I explore for themes of fairness and justice. Understanding the *substance* of the social conflict is *not* the objective of the book. It is a useful and important by-product, and is a necessary step on the way to understanding fairness and justice themes. The objective of the book is to develop an understanding of fairness and justice that is common within many, or perhaps, all, resource-sharing conflicts. While I have chosen to explore natural resource conflicts in Australia, this is on the basis that underlying fairness issues in conflicts about sharing are universal around the world. Once this fairness and justice understanding has been developed, it can then be used in any conflict or decision-making episode, whether this is environmental, social, political or in the workplace.

So this book is a journey of *understanding*. There are three interconnected levels of understanding that are important. On the first level are the differing viewpoints, interests and perspectives of people involved in a resource-sharing conflict. These vary according to the nature of people's involvement in the issue and how they perceive decisions and outcomes. On the second level are the substantive facts and details of the resource issue: who stands to gain or lose; how the resource is shared, and how decisions are made in changing circumstances. The third level is an understanding of the fairness and justice issues and themes that emerge from each conflict or resource-sharing episode. The first two levels are specific to each situation, although many similar themes are likely to emerge from multiple conflicts. It is the understanding from these two levels that gives rise to the third level, which is why many chapters in the book are concerned with the substantive details of these carrier conflicts.

The sequence of chapters takes the reader on a path in which different aspects of these levels of understanding are built as the story progresses. This is not to say that readers should not 'dip' into the book to follow their particular interest. There are many audiences for this book, ranging from students and academics in environmental or governance disciplines, to policy makers, natural resource management practitioners, water professionals and those generally interested readers with a conflict in or close to their community. Some will be interested in the stories of the two Australian water conflicts in Chapter 4 and the discussion of water sharing in irrigated agriculture in Chapter 7, to compare with water sharing arrangements in different parts of the world. Others will be interested in the review of renewable energy in Chapter 1 to see what fairness and justice themes have emerged from research on the social acceptance of renewable energy. Many readers will find the review of theories of justice in Chapter 2 useful as a window into this complex and expanding area. Readers interested in the application of justice theory to present-day conflicts can gain insights from the detailed justice analyses of the two water conflicts in Chapters 5 and 6.

Those involved in policy development and decision making will be interested in Chapter 8 which provides a synthesis of the findings and describes how justice principles can be applied to environmental decision making. But, for those readers interested in developing a deep and real understanding of fairness and justice in environmental decision making, one option is recommended, and that is to follow the chapters sequentially.

The terms justice and fairness do have areas of similarity but there are also areas where they are distinct. I do not use these terms interchangeably, but for the sake of brevity I do not always use both terms together. Readers should note that where I talk about justice, particularly in the final chapter, I take justice to include elements of fairness, as I believe it is useful to bring them together to help resolve resource conflicts. But this is to prefigure where my book leads and the journey that I am taking the reader on.

I came to the topic of fairness and justice while studying a bitter social conflict over a proposed wind farm. I felt the chill wind long before any turbine was built. The acrimony and distress experienced by some of the people I talked to was an eye-opener to me. This was not an objective and factual exercise: it was raw emotion and a lasting legacy. Loss of trust, loss of hope and broken relationships can leave as much damage as a flood or a fire. My purpose is to show the impact of perceived injustice, derive some insights, and show why fairness and justice matter.

Book outline: from injustice to justice as a means and an end

This book tells the story of injustice and the search for justice. Chapter 1 begins with a reflection on the deep roots and far reaches of fairness and justice in society, as an experience of life and as an exploration of the mind. From these reflections some questions arise. Why is it the case that fairness is well understood in everyday interactions yet is not a routine consideration in more formal aspects of decision making? Is this because the nature of fairness and justice is hard to define in day-to-day terms, and most writing about these topics tends to be in the academic literature? Is it because ideas of fairness and justice are too abstract, encompassing moral feelings, emotions, desires and values from a range of life experiences?

A better understanding of fairness and justice as it relates to people's everyday lives is needed. Chapter 1 sets the scene by showing the importance of fairness and justice in the broad context of renewable wind energy, an area that has generated social conflict in many countries. This is a good starting point because renewable wind energy appears to be a benefit to society, but local opposition to wind farms seems ubiquitous. There are also many studies that explore different aspects of renewable energy, including the underlying reasons for local resistance. So what can we learn about fairness and justice from these studies? An important conclusion from this renewable energy investigation was that while it was recognised that fairness and justice are critical considerations in these disputes, they were not central concerns for either researchers or decision-makers. So it appears that the full case to include fairness and justice in both environmental research and environmental decision making still needs to be made, despite its widespread appearance in the academic literature.

This is where new research is required, the main subject of this book. Chapter 2 looks at the literature to see how academics and writers deal with theories and ideas of justice and fairness. What fairness and justice principles and constructs do they use and could these be helpful in understanding conflicts in environmental decision making? The chapter explores justice from a societal and individual perspective including questions about why people care about justice and the experience of injustice. Distinctions are drawn between the concepts of justice and injustice, and justice and fairness. The chapter summarises ideas and constructs of justice that could be useful in environmental decision making.

The next step is to find out from people themselves how they understand fairness and justice in their day-to-day lived experience. Chapter 3 shows how theory can be used to help us understand the practical reality of lived experience. Using constructs and principles from the preceding chapter, an investigative framework is developed to structure and organise an empirical investigation. The idea of 'adaptive theory' is introduced; this enables a researcher to work at the interface between theory and practice, developing insights from each area as the research progresses.

In Chapter 4 the story turns to two water conflicts in rural Australia. Readers should note that water conflict is being used here as a carrier for this discussion about fairness and justice. The first water conflict takes place in an irrigated agricultural area in the state of New South Wales (NSW) and concerns a dispute over irrigation water cutbacks as a result of dry conditions. The second takes place in two agricultural areas in the state of Victoria. It concerns a dispute over water being diverted from agricultural use to the state capital, Melbourne, for household consumption and industrial use. The aim in this chapter is to find out what people think about fairness and justice from within their local social conflict, using the investigative framework developed earlier to guide the exploration. The chapter begins with the background context for the two studies, including biophysical features, the cultural significance of water, and an outline of the history of water development in Australia. A selection of photographs is placed between Chapters 4 and 5. Some photographs are directly related to the Victoria protest while others provide a visual illustration of the context for the case studies.

Chapters 5, 6 and 7 examine these conflicts and the themes that emerge from a justice and fairness perspective. Injustice emerges in both conflicts, as a social harm, not only to individuals but also to the community. Chapter 5 analyses how people understand and react to notions of fairness and justice and whether they distinguish between these concepts. It investigates why people engage in issues of justice and their motives for justice. Calls for justice include remedies to fix perceptions of harm. Connections between theories of justice and practical experiences of social conflict are made. Chapter 6 considers broader perspectives of fairness and justice in decision-making processes and outcomes at a community level. The experience of injustice can be separated into different areas of justice theory that deal with how people are treated, the processes by which decisions are made, and the decisions themselves. These insights show us why different aspects of justice are important in the different stages of decision making. Such insights bring intangible ideas about fairness and justice into sharp focus so that tangible actions can be taken to make decision processes fairer. Chapter 6 explores how perceptions of fairness and justice in decision-making processes can contribute to gaining greater acceptance of outcomes and how better outcomes can be achieved.

Chapter 7 considers some broader aspects of fairness and justice in resource sharing at a societal level. It explores some historical aspects of sharing resources in Australian irrigated agriculture. Again, water is the carrier of the discussion, not its subject. The aim is to understand from a societal perspective how fair and equitable solutions can be achieved, and to learn from those who have been involved in resource sharing. There are lessons to be learnt from past water sharing arrangements considered to be fair and equitable by the communities involved. Stories and narratives about water sharing in irrigated agriculture show how theories of justice have been used in practice, and provide insights into successes as well as challenges. The chapter provides examples of initiatives that have been seen to work well. It identifies 'model' fairness characteristics of resource sharing that includes the initial distribution of the resource and how adaptive arrangements accommodate changing conditions. The chapter shows why a 'rationale' for resource reforms is required and why decision-makers must be explicit about how fairness is to be achieved in reforms that disrupt well-established resource sharing arrangements.

At this point we have developed an understanding of why people care about fairness and justice and what they consider important in decision making about natural resources. Chapter 8 provides a synthesis of the findings from the social conflicts and shows how fairness and justice can be considered a means and an end. From this understanding of *why* justice is important to people, decision-makers (including politicians, policy makers and government agencies) can then develop decision-making processes that are more likely to gain people's acceptance of decisions. One might argue that gaining acceptance of decisions is unlikely when resources are scarce, and when some are likely to win and some are likely to lose. This is a valid viewpoint. But decisions *do* need to be made and decision-making processes *can* be seen as fair and just if fairness principles are used. This is the goal: how to bring fairness and justice principles into decision-making processes and bring the language of justice into everyday use. The chapter shows the importance of *in*justice in understanding why people will resist decisions that they perceive as unfair. It presents a decision acceptance framework that helps explain how and why people accept or not the outcome of a resource allocation decision. The chapter makes the case for decision making in natural resource management to routinely operate within a theory of justice. The chapter concludes with a reflection on the critical importance of fairness and justice in resource sharing at a global scale.

1 A global concern

Seeking fairness in resource sharing

Fairness and justice: conflicts, scale and scope

Fairness, justice and injustice are critical when considering the practical realities of resource sharing and environmental decision making. Resource sharing has a long history of conflict. Many would argue that the central issue in resource conflicts is the wielding of power and the clash of interests between those involved. Self-interest is a recurring and dominant theme in explanations for resource-sharing disputes. For example, Not-in-My-Backyard, or NIMBYism, is a well-known explanation based on self-interest that describes local opposition to infrastructure such as roads, energy facilities, waste dumps and other types of large development. Those accused of being NIMBYs are often seen as selfish and not wanting to share their local amenity with public infrastructure that others view as vital for the common interest. The sharing of resources and the way decisions are made about infrastructure planning, siting and building is the domain of fairness and justice. The way in which people think about their families and livelihoods, their future security and their communities is intimately connected with their interests in the natural resources on which they depend. To be labelled a selfish NIMBYist when one has the perspective that one is protecting one's family and livelihood may well be perceived as an injustice in itself. The NIMBY explanation needs to be thoroughly examined. No doubt there are people who fit the NIMBY description ('I support it somewhere else but not in my neighbourhood'), but on the other hand there are many who are *called* NIMBYs who are not. They have genuine concerns that underpin their opposition to a proposed development. Name-calling and accusations about hidden agendas, such as 'who' is funding 'what' group, are prevalent in resource conflicts around the world. But these claims are largely irrelevant when real – and universal – concerns are routinely glossed over by opposing campaigns. The remedy for the NIMBY claim is that local questions and concerns must be answered and put to rest before decisions about the public interest are made. Such matters of injustice, fairness and justice have a broad reach, from local contexts through to how societies are organised for the common good.

My goal is to bring the concepts of injustice, fairness and justice to life through a close exploration of several social conflicts and people's lived experience within those conflicts. Another underlying goal is to show that there are different perspectives within each context and that these need to be understood. As outlined in the introduction, there are three levels of understanding that are important in resource conflicts. The first involves the differing perspectives held by those people affected by resource decisions. The second concerns the substantive facts and details of the decisions and processes by which decision-makers allocate or share the resource. The third level of understanding concerns the fairness and justice themes that arise from the first two levels (a goal of this book). But the journey starts at the first level. It is here that viewpoints and interests are frequently intertwined with each other and difficult to understand or tease apart. As the saying goes, 'beauty is in the eye of the beholder', but so, one could say, is justice. On the one hand many perspectives share common ground but there are also situations where people living in a community have entirely different and frequently opposing ideas about the same issue or proposal. These differing perspectives need to be understood, not only by the resource decision-makers, but also by different groups within each community and onlookers outside the community. Decision making thus becomes a shared enterprise between those affected by the decision, those implementing the decision, and the decision-makers. Onlookers play their part in the democratic process. They do this either by tacitly nodding their approval of the way people in the community have been treated and by the outcomes reached, or by joining protest groups if they think that an injustice has been done. Another saying speaks to this, 'justice must be done and must be seen to be done'.

However, there is currently no requirement in most decision-making processes about resource sharing to specifically articulate whether and how a particular proposal can be seen to be fair or just, or that justice was done in the decisions made. Rather, the language typically used in these types of processes tends to be technical and based on the specifics of the proposal, with some localised considerations of social or environmental impact. Ideas and statements about perceived fairness to different stakeholders are not on these types of agenda. Where there is perceived unfairness, or injustice, then conflict is likely to follow. Social conflicts take many forms. They range from one-off local protest marches that do little to change the perceived injustice, to the formation of well-organised long-standing protest groups which gather momentum and generate a ground-swell of support in the broader community. The Environmental Justice movement which originated in the USA in the 1980s is a good example of a localised social conflict model which has spread around the world (Walker 2012). Another example of what has become a globalised and hard-fought conflict is the widespread local opposition to renewable energy infrastructure, such as wind farms. A confluence of forces put wind farms on the global map when governments around the world wanted to encourage the rapid uptake of renewable energy to decrease reliance on high carbon emissions-based power. A central issue became one of perceived common interests at a societal level trumping local interests at a landscape level (Haggett 2008). A loosely connected network of opposition groups formed, frequently with the words landscape or country guardians in their title, and these have played their part in polarising the debate on wind farms (see, for example, Hindmarsh 2010; Keane 2012; and Parkinson 2013 for viewpoints).

Issues of fairness and justice scale up from small local conflicts through national government policies and on to large-scale global issues of climate change and the fair distribution of global resources. Fairness and justice considerations are also important aspects in the distribution of public goods, such as subsidies for higher education, or any type of public dis-benefit, burden or harm, such as pollution or hazardous waste. Understanding the range of fairness and justice implications in these distributions can often be difficult. While there may be clearly obvious instances of actual and potential injustice, there can also be many nuanced and indirect implications. For example, in higher education research, a report questions the real public benefit from tuition subsidies to graduates in Australia, arguing that the graduates themselves are winners, and that public money could be better spent elsewhere (Norton 2012). Along similar lines D.A. Brown (2008) examined ethical issues of allocating public research funds to technology for carbon capture and storage, when the technology is not proven to be completely viable and where there are still many unknowns about future impacts of storing gases underground. D.A. Brown (2008: 1) suggests that every proposed solution associated with decreasing carbon emissions needs to be examined for the 'enormous ethical issues' it raises in the context of anthropogenic climate change. Time scale is an additional factor in considering fairness: can (and should) past injustices be attributed to current people or institutions; can they be put right and how far does one take the notion of responsibility? Indeed, the *scope* of justice is still a much-debated idea or ideal with some arguing that justice applies only on a human scale whereas others extend the scope further to animals, nature, biodiversity and the environment (Schlosberg 2007; Bosselmann 2008). Many of these issues are contentious and disagreement is a common thread in discourses and public debate about matters of justice. But there *is* agreement that justice does matter and that fairness is an essential component of human affairs!

Many people develop a sharply defined sense of fairness, justice or injustice from their early experiences. Some are drawn into public service careers to play their part in instilling fairness and justice into societal arrangements, such as laws and policies. For others it is the concepts of justice that count. Ideas about justice can be developed through research in academic disciplines. People wanting to contribute to rights or justice-based causes from a more practical perspective are drawn to groups that advocate human rights or environmental causes. Examples include Amnesty International, Greenpeace and the anti-whaling group Sea Shepherd. A sense of fairness or justice, or an understanding of what is right or wrong, is a common motivating factor in people's choice of what they get involved in and this is underpinned by people's values, beliefs and lived experiences. This sense of fairness or justice is also important in determining whether people participate in or *accept* decisions made by authorities and large-scale social institutions, even up to the global scale of the United Nations. Gaining social acceptance is a critical aspect of planning and development.

The pervasiveness of fairness and justice is also reflected across the academic disciplines. For example, the study of 'social justice' can occur at a societal level within political science (see, for example, Barry 2005) but it can also occur within the more focused discipline of social psychology. Here social justice becomes a study at an individual level concerned with a person's perspectives about what they perceive as right or wrong (see, for example, Tyler *et al.* 1997). From the disciplines of social psychology and organisational science has emerged the field of 'organisational justice' which focuses on justice in the workplace (Ambrose 2002). These different roots and changing use of the term social justice are evidence that justice research is continually evolving in a number of fields. Another example is 'environmental justice' which has developed beyond its origins of a grassroots movement in the USA and now describes a field of academic research as well as various political movements and campaigns on a global scale (Walker 2012). The term 'ecological justice' was introduced in part to extend the scope of justice from human-centred justice to include the environment (Low and Gleeson 1998; Bosselmann 2008). Also more recently introduced is the idea of climate justice which is concerned with past, current, and future inequities of human-induced climate change (see Brown 2013). Underlying all these different but related areas is legal justice and jurisprudence, the philosophy of law (Meyerson 2006).

With this wide range of disciplinary roots it is not surprising that justice research has been subtly shifting from isolated strands in each discipline to a type of research that draws on multiple disciplines. The emergence of transdisciplinary research (see Ramadier 2004 and Mobjörk 2010) has enabled justice research to go beyond these academic disciplines to investigate challenges facing society. By its nature, transdisciplinary research operates within but also beyond disciplinary boundaries to include people with direct experience of the topic being studied. The research described in this book takes a transdisciplinary approach to investigating justice issues in natural resource conflicts. It does this by including people who have been personally involved in or affected by social conflicts in a natural resource context. It is here that ideas about injustice, fairness and justice turn into tangible red-hot issues with impacts and outcomes that are both observable and experienced.

An investigation of fairness and justice in environmental decision making covers a lot of ground. From the academic disciplines there is a huge and continually expanding literature on ideas and concepts of justice, and from the environmental disciplines there is also a good deal written about environmental decision making (see, for example, National Research Council 2008; Harding *et al.* 2009). However, studies in which justice concepts have been both applied and explored at the practical level within a decision-making context are still relatively few. Even though planners, implementers and researchers do recognise the importance of having people actively involved in planning processes to gain their consent or acceptance of developments (Syme and Nancarrow 2005), there is still a limited amount of contextual research that applies justice frameworks teasing out the specific issues of fairness and justice, for example in renewable energy (Walter and Gutscher 2012). There is even less research explaining *why* different aspects of fairness and justice are important to those involved in decision-making processes. This book aims to fill this knowledge gap by providing insights on why justice is important to people, why they get involved in protest groups, and on the importance of fairness and justice in developing decision-making processes and outcomes.

I have found the controversy over renewable wind energy to be a useful and enlightening way of getting into the nuances about fairness and justice. This is because wind farms have become such a deeply polarising issue in many close-knit and seemingly homogenous communities in many different places across the whole planet. From a wind farm study I carried out (discussed on p. 12), I learnt that while fairness was an important undercurrent in the community, fairness issues were not specifically articulated or acknowledged either by the people affected or by the decision-makers. The issues of wind power and wind farms remain contentious and unresolved. Communities around the world continue to struggle with decisions about wind farms and their actual and potential impacts. The issue of wind power, seen as both a benefit and a burden, shows no signs of going away in the near future. Thus a discussion of renewable energy at this point is a good way to introduce the reader to justice and fairness in resource conflicts.

A global and local issue: the social acceptance of renewable energy

Wind turbines are a familiar sight in many countries around the world. Many people see them as graceful symbols of development harnessing the wind for the common good. Others see them as spoiling the landscape and as an unwanted disruption to the environment. There is a seemingly endless stream of commentary in the media (for example, Seccombe 2012; Lloyd 2012). Accusations and finger-pointing are commonplace and reasonable commentary is lacking. Why is this debate so polarising? For governments around the world the implementation of renewable wind energy has been a major challenge (Jacquet 2012; Bergek 2010; Hindmarsh 2010). Wind energy is seen as an important strategy in the shift away from high greenhouse gas production energy sources. Other renewable energy sources such as biomass, hydropower and tidal energy are also significant initiatives. But instead of the anticipated widespread social acceptance of these types of developments as being for the public good, governments have been surprised by the extent of opposition, often at a local level. There is a range of questions here. Is this purely self-interest at work? Is the local opposition due to the Not-in-My-Backyard NIMBY syndrome? Or are there other factors to consider? How can social acceptance of an energy source that is perceived to be for the greater good be achieved in the face of local resistance? Are these sorts of social conflict intractable and generally unsolvable? If so, how is social acceptance of change that is seen as necessary in the bigger picture of human-induced climate change to be achieved?

It is at the local community level that much of the controversy over wind farms has been generated. A variety of local stakeholders are affected by wind farm infrastructure, directly or indirectly and positively or negatively. There is a long list of potential and actual impacts. These include physical and visual intrusion on the landscape, low-frequency noise and infrasound caused by turbine movement, light reflection from the turbines (shadow flicker), physical impacts on the environment and wildlife, safety for people working in the area, and potential impacts on human health and domestic animals from the longer term effects of living close to turbines. However, much local opposition has been attributed to the Not-in-My-Backyard syndrome and local people have been branded NIMBYs as a result. This broad-brush explanation has been soundly dealt with in the academic literature as being both derogatory and inaccurate because there are very many reasons for local opposition which are valid and need to be addressed (Wolsink 2007; Haggett 2010; Devine-Wright 2011b). Irrespective of whether wind turbines have a temporary or permanent health effect or not, the concerns of those living in proximity to wind turbines cannot be ignored. These concerns are real to those who are bearing what they perceive as a local burden of wind farms in their locality. Local acceptance will not be achieved until local views are respected and local concerns are taken seriously.

Research that explores the 'social acceptance' of renewable energy has generated a significant body of work, following the publication of a special issue of *Energy Policy* in 2007 (Wüstenhagen *et al.* 2007). This special issue was the outcome of a conference in Switzerland in which researchers discussed the concept 'social acceptance' in the context of renewable energy. The concept includes three areas of acceptance: socio-political, community, and market (see also Horbaty *et al.* 2012). Exploring a specific case study is useful because it introduces ideas about fairness and justice in a decision-making process and shows how different aspects of fairness are important to different groups within a community.

A justice approach to community perspectives: the Taralga wind farm

My involvement in this research area began when a wind farm was proposed near Taralga, 140 km north of my home town of Canberra in the Australian Capital Territory. I had heard that there was some local discontent with the proposal and was interested in investigating why this was so, given the importance of renewable energy. Rather than look at the pros and cons of the wind farm, I decided to investigate the fairness implications from the perspective of the local residents. Some meetings between the developer and the community had taken place and the public had been invited to participate by sending in their comments on the proposal as part of the New South Wales state government environmental impact assessment process. Since a decision on whether the wind farm would be built was still unknown it would be interesting to find out what individuals in the community thought about the fairness of the wind farm decision-making process, and how that related to their views about the wind farm. For the full report of this case study see Gross (2007).

The town of Taralga sits snugly in a hollow surrounded by the wind-swept hills of an Australian agricultural landscape. It is a small community in the fertile plains of the Southern Tablelands of New South Wales. With a population of less than 400, Taralga inhabitants are proud of their pioneering pastoral heritage and town, which has many houses of architectural interest. Cattle and sheep farming in the district date back to 1840 when the region's rich fertile soils were discovered by European settlers. Residents have strong attachments to the town and the landscape. The area is also popular with tourists and retirees from the New South Wales state capital, Sydney. A wind farm proposal was submitted in 2004 by RES Southern Cross, a wind energy development company. The proposal comprised 69 turbines in rows along the ridges to the east of the town with many being visible from the town. A development application had been lodged and people in the community submitted their feedback during the submission period of the planning process. Concern about community division over the proposed wind farm was an important issue as shown in many submissions to the enquiry.

The research approach focused on developing an understanding of fairness issues and how the community had been involved. This included the fairness of the decision-making process as well as what people thought about the outcome itself, the wind farm. In order to explore a full range of attitudes people with differing perspectives of the wind farm were interviewed. These largely fell into the three groups of being in favour, neutral or opposed to it. A justice framework was developed which acted as a guide in the interviewing process. Elements of the framework focus on two key aspects of a decision-making process: the process and the outcome. Processes can be separated into components such as being able to participate in the process; being able to ask questions, express opinions, and have questions answered; being respected as a stakeholder with an interest in the process and outcome; being given adequate information about the proposal; and having a decision-maker who is impartial. These components contribute to the fairness of a decision-making process. In terms of the decision, or outcome, there are two key concepts: outcome fairness and outcome favourability. Outcome fairness is whether an outcome is considered fair when compared to some societal standard. Outcome favourability relates to whether an outcome is perceived as favourable or unfavourable to individuals who have an interest in the outcome. These justice concepts are explored further in Chapter 2.

So what happened in Taralga? The community had become divided into 'winners' and 'losers' around those who stood to gain from the placement of turbines on their land and those who stood to lose from the proximity of turbines and other indirect consequences of the wind farm. Tensions arose between those who stood to gain (and those who supported them) and those who stood to lose and opposed the wind farm. Some neighbours stopped talking to each other and others became guarded in their conversations and would not engage in discussion about the wind farm. So even before the decision had been announced, there were tangible social impacts caused by the proposal and the process: the community lost some social cohesion and many were unhappy with the whole process. This early community division is often seen with proposed wind turbine developments, a more recent example being King Island in Tasmania (Twomey 2013).

In Taralga there were major concerns about the secrecy of discussions between the wind farm developer and landholders, as well as about what people perceived to be a lack of detailed information. An opposition group formed, the Taralga Landscape Guardians, and this group loudly voiced its opposition to the wind farm. Other voices became more muted with some people not wanting to show their support for the wind farm because they felt drowned out by the opposition group. They were concerned about a distorted representation of the community's views being given to the decision-maker caused by the loudness of the protest group.

Attitudes to the wind farm changed as time progressed and this influenced people's perceptions of fairness of the process and the outcome. Some explained how they had been in favour of a wind farm at the start, but had become concerned about the community division and the way people had been treated, and had changed their views. Some became neutral and others became opposed to the wind farm. Of these, some thought that the process had not been fair because of the lack of information and what they perceived as an untrustworthy proponent and lack of impartiality demonstrated by the decision-making authority (initially the local government and then the state government).

Three main areas of concern were described by interviewees in rating the fairness of the process and attitudes towards the legitimacy of the outcome. These were secrecy, insufficient community discussion, and the inequitable distribution of the benefits and burdens of the wind farm (the fact that winners and losers had emerged). Interviewees had their own ideas as to what would confer greater legitimacy on the outcome and these were related to the things that they thought were inadequate or unfair in the process they had experienced. For example, some suggested a more open consultation process that started earlier in the negotiation, conducted by an entity that was not closely connected to the wind farm developer. Others were more concerned about having every question and issue responded to and a better debate and discussion within the community.

Several themes can be drawn from these findings that are relevant to other case studies and social conflicts. The first is that local communities cannot be treated as homogenous entities. Rather, different groups within communities have differing perspectives, experiences, and fairness needs in decision-making processes. For example, in this case study several groups emerged: winners, losers, people opposed to the wind farm on a moral basis (called here moral opponents), people who strongly supported the wind farm on a moral basis (moral proponents), people who were neutral, and people who did not express their opinions.

A second theme is that fairness of process and fairness of outcome are clearly important to those involved, but which one is more important will be different for each group. Which area of fairness will have the greatest influence on each of the groups within a community, and therefore on social acceptance can be investigated. Those who stand to gain or lose are more likely to be interested in the favourability of the outcome to themselves than in the overall fairness of the process and outcome. However, those who do not stand to gain or lose are more likely to be concerned about fair processes, because a fair process is more likely to result in a fair outcome for the whole community, through better decision-making processes.

From this a third theme emerges: outcome fairness is important for the general social well-being of a community, and process fairness is important in leading to a fair outcome. Thus groups within communities can be structured in a framework according to process fairness and outcome fairness. In the Taralga case study a community fairness framework emerged from these findings (Figure 1.1). The

Fairness perception influenced by	Group affected	Primary reason
Outcome favourability	'Winners'	Personal benefit from positive outcome/decision
	'Losers'	Personal loss from positive outcome/decision
	'Moral proponents'	Overriding belief in outcome
	'Moral objectors'	Overriding belief in outcome
Outcome fairness	'Neutrals' no strong belief either way	Prefer outcome to be fair for everyone in community in order to maintain social well-being
	'Silent majority' who may or may not have an opinion	
Process fairness	Whole community where fair outcome desired for health of community	A fair process is more likely to result in a fair outcome

Figure 1.1 Community Fairness Framework.

key point from this is that a fair process is more likely to result in a fair outcome, and social acceptance can be increased as a result of fair processes. This idea about the influence of fair processes originated in the field of social psychology and is described further in Chapter 2.

Justice research: learning from the Taralga study

The Taralga case study has two clear implications for justice research. First, it demonstrates that a justice approach to understanding a complex social problem *does* develop good insights into matters of fairness and social acceptance. Such an approach is the basis for the discussion of fairness and justice using water conflicts as the case studies described in this book. Second, it describes different aspects of the fairness of process and outcomes in a social conflict. These fairness themes have relevance in other situations as well.

The Taralga case study has been drawn on in different ways by numerous researchers since it was published in 2007. In reviewing some of these studies it is interesting to note the great diversity of research projects around social acceptance. It is worthwhile taking a brief look at some of these studies to see how themes of fairness and justice emerge in other countries, landscapes, social contexts and institutional settings. In parallel it is interesting to explore how researchers from a variety of disciplines reflect on and deal with these themes. The following brief review describes some themes, strands and threads in which fairness and justice issues arise. The purpose is to explore some of the substantive issues that arise in renewable energy and to see where fairness and justice themes arise. Recalling the three levels of understanding (outlined in the introduction and at the start of this chapter) that are required by decision-makers, this review operates at all three levels, with the objective of identifying fairness and justice themes. In other words, this review of some aspects of renewable energy is used here as a carrier to further our understanding of fairness and justice.

Fairness and justice themes: a review of renewable energy research

The diversity of research projects that seek to understand different aspects of opposition to renewable energy reflects a growing global phenomenon. This is the conflict of interest between renewable energy being seen as a common good at a national level but a burden at a local level (Bergek 2010; Newman 2012). Research studies exploring social aspects of renewable energy implementation have taken place across the globe, including England, Wales, Scotland, Sweden, Belgium, Denmark, the Netherlands, Germany, Switzerland, Italy, Greece, Crete, the USA, and Australia. Although these studies have one area in common – public involvement and social acceptance – they have a wide range of research goals and interests. These include:

- Exploring specific local case studies, such as biogas (Magnani 2012); greenhouse clusters (Rogge *et al.* 2011), wind energy (Fisher and Brown 2009), tidal energy (Devine-Wright 2011a) and hydro storage (Steffen 2012)
- Reviewing government policies and planning procedures for public involvement and community engagement (Newman 2012; Kerselaers *et al.* 2013)
- Exploring psychological factors (Huijts *et al.* 2012) and emotion (Cass and Walker 2009) in renewable energy conflicts
- Investigating a range of barriers to social acceptance (Valentine 2010) and predictors for increasing social acceptance (Jones and Eiser 2009)
- Investigating concepts of justice in specific contexts, such as ethical dimensions of underground carbon dioxide storage (Gough and Boucher 2013); whether process fairness matters in offshore wind power (Firestone *et al.* 2012) and a framework of procedural and distributive justice in wind energy and bioenergy (Walter and Gutscher 2012)
- Building frameworks that draw on theoretical and empirical research to understand the impacts of social interactions and institutional variables on siting outcomes for high-voltage transmission lines (Cain and Nelson 2013)
- Exploring green consumerism in relation to wind power (Thøgersen and Noblet 2012)
- Exploring the benefits of different research methodologies in assessing public participation and conflicts (Strazzera *et al.* 2012)
- Exploring the potential of new tools such as information technology visualisation to enhance information provision and public participation (Berry and Higgs 2012)
- Exploring the pros and cons of community benefits in wind energy development (Cass *et al.* 2010; Cowell *et al.* 2011)

- Understanding local opposition in the context of the Not-in-My-Backyard (NIMBY) syndrome (Devine-Wright 2009, 2011c; Haggett 2010)
- Increasing understanding of the 'public' in the context of public engagement (Barnett *et al.* 2012)
- Understanding people's attachment to landscape, including rights, identity and disruption (Devine-Wright 2009, 2011a; van der Horst and Vermeylen 2011)
- Exploring support for university campus approaches to sustainable energy use (McComas *et al.* 2011)

Many of the studies that explored specific case studies acknowledge the vital importance of public participation in planning processes. In a study of rural planning processes in Flanders, Kerselaers *et al* (2013) found that farmers could not understand why they were not involved in planning processes as they were clearly affected by the outcomes. The authors suggest that the principles of procedural fairness described in the Taralga case study also apply to the difficulties encountered in this rural planning study. They conclude that these are needed to 'counteract uncertainty and the perception of unfairness' (Kerselaers *et al.* 2013: 205). Another study explored the perceived fairness of process in determining the acceptance of offshore wind power in the USA. Firestone *et al.* (2012: 1398) found 'the more a person perceives the process as just – involving fairness, a local voice and a transparent developer – the more likely they are to move from opposition to undecided to support.' They conclude that 'a fair planning process ... may produce outcomes that feel more satisfying even if they do not please all the stakeholders'(Firestone *et al.* 2012: 1399).

Haggett (2011) recognises the critical importance of fair processes in gaining support for outcomes in her general discussion of public engagement in renewable energy decision making. She advocates an approach in which local people's concerns can be understood, rather than prevailing attitudes where local residents are treated as being generally uninformed and creators of needless opposition. She also notes the contrast between the tangible local impacts on local residents in comparison with the apparently obscure global benefits of renewable energy projects.

Some authors point to the lack of theoretical input to increase our understanding of what is happening in local conflicts. For example, Walter and Gutscher (2012) point out the lack of theory-guided research, and develop a framework of distributive justice (concerned with outcomes) and procedural justice (concerned with process) theories (see Chapter 2) to explore controversies in renewable energy projects in Germany, Austria and Switzerland. They concur with the findings from the Taralga case study that these justice theories are valuable in understanding the controversial aspects of renewable energy. Gough and Boucher (2013) also use a framework approach to develop a list of potential ethical concerns for carbon capture and storage technology. They consider ethical principles of intergenerational justice; social justice; environmental justice and financial justice in relation to well-being; the benefits of the technology; and the prevention of harm to those involved.

Two studies are noteworthy in their use of frameworks to organise information concerning different aspects of public engagement or opposition in the context of renewable energy. Both studies draw directly on the empirical findings from the Taralga case study. One develops a framework of psychological factors that influence energy technology acceptance (Huijts *et al.* 2012). People's experiences of trust, process fairness and outcome fairness are key areas included in a 'comprehensive acceptance framework'. The authors propose that this model can be widely used in different contexts to explore other technologies, such as gene technology and nanotechnology, where there are perceived benefits as well as potential risks. The second study investigates opposition to high-voltage transmission lines needed for renewable power. This study by Cain and Nelson (2013) operates in the middle ground between theoretical and empirical research. They develop an extensive framework that draws on planning, social psychology and political science theories. Empirical data from the Taralga case study is used as one part of a framework to show the importance of a sense of fairness regarding the decision-making process. The authors put this framework to use in a Californian case study. They are very clear about the importance of fair processes: '[I]n a range of contexts, if individuals perceive that the siting process is fair, they are more likely to participate' and '[i]f there is a sense of trust in the process, participants will be more likely to accept results that are counter to their perceived interests' (Cain and Nelson 2013: 212). These studies offer direct evidence that fairness is important: fair processes lead to greater participation in the decision-making process as well as greater acceptance of the outcome. This gives us a hint as to where we might go in pursuit of greater understanding.

In addition to exploring justice themes, these studies also demonstrate the effectiveness of frameworks to gather, organise and analyse information on a topic, particularly when there are many related constructs and influences, covering cognitive and behavioural areas. In a study of stakeholder attitudes towards greenhouse clusters in Flanders, Rogge *et al* (2011) use a theoretical scheme to explore community opposition. They note that the Not-In-My-Backyard explanation frequently touted is too simple a concept to explain the opposition to the greenhouse clusters. Their study demonstrates the utility of a framework to explore deeper nuances. They compare their findings with the Taralga case study and discuss the similarities in the two studies in that 'conflicting perspectives on values are frequently at the basis of divisions in local communities' (Rogge *et al.* 2011: 340). Another comprehensive framework to understand public engagement with renewable energy projects has been developed by Walker *et al.* (2011). It was the outcome of a broad-based multidisciplinary study and has four distinctive characteristics. First, it gives equal attention to both the public (i.e. those affected) and the organisations involved in promoting renewable energy; second, it recognises the importance of people's expectations in decision-making processes and outcomes; third, it is dynamic in that it acknowledges that projects and attitudes change over time; and finally, it recognises the importance of differences in local context for each renewable energy project. A key point here is the emphasis on people's expectations. As will be discussed later in the book, people do *expect* to be treated with fairness and this is why consultation processes are vital in delivering what people expect.

The importance of the Not-in-My-Backyard explanation in the context of opposition to renewable energy projects is highlighted in the title of the book *Renewable Energy and the Public: From NIMBY to Participation*, edited by Devine-Wright (2011c). Devine-Wright has written extensively about the concept of NIMBYism, why it is an unsatisfactory and destructive way of thinking about local opposition, and how the cycle of NIMBYism needs to be broken (Devine-Wright 2009, 2011b). The authors review a range of social science research and deal with both conceptual approaches and empirical research to public engagement with renewable energy. Interestingly, although the NIMBY explanation receives broad coverage, much less attention is given to theories and ideas of fairness and justice. As discussed above, Haggett (2011) gives value to the importance of fair and just processes in public involvement, and the framework developed by Walker *et al.* (2011) acknowledges that people have fairness expectations. However, there is only one index entry in the Devine-Wright book for fairness (and none for justice), which is surprising given the importance of fairness and justice at both the local and global scale of renewable energy. This is not a criticism of the book: the conclusions firmly call for a broadening of social science research to move beyond NIMBY explanations in public engagement. Rather, this is more likely a reflection of the state of play in the social science research scene. It also reflects a lack of justice researchers in social science who routinely apply ideas and concepts of justice to these complex societal challenges.

The bigger picture: from social acceptance to social justice

From this review of research on fairness and the social acceptance of renewable energy, it is clear that the *full* case for justice research in a social context has not yet been made. Even though there are many isolated strands of justice and fairness themes, and associated undercurrents, such as the unjust labelling of people as NIMBYs, there are no loud and clear calls for fairness and justice explanations of social conflicts concerning resource allocation. The goal now becomes one of showing why a major transition needs to be made, from understanding social conflict and resource allocation challenges in terms of NIMBY-like explanations to a much more far-reaching and all-encompassing understanding of fairness and justice.

A fairness and justice basis is required for decision making in which NIMBY-like explanations can be put in perspective. A social conflict gives us glimpses into what is going wrong from various people's perspectives and their experience of unfairness or injustice. But this is only part of the picture. The full picture of what people need and expect for their well-being within a just and fair society is required. Decision making about resource allocation is just one part of this bigger picture: we need to consider environmental decision making as one aspect of how we want to structure a fair and just society. In this picture fairness and justice constitute an important societal goal as well as underpinning the well-being of a group or one particular aspect of a dialogue between a developer and community. In other words, fairness is within, above, underneath and beyond each of these studies. It is a societal aspiration as well as a part of a decision-making process.

People want to live in a just and fair society. Fairness extends from the local to the global. NIMBYism has become a prominent explanation because the motivation of self-interest seems to be ubiquitous wherever there are conflicts over territory and landscape. Putting NIMBY into perspective, it is but one element in a number of issues about landscape and place disruption. Devine-Wright and colleagues have moved the discussion from NIMBY to participation. Now it is time to put justice and fairness theory 'fair and square' in the foreground of environmental decision making. In this approach to decision making, community engagement and participation processes become delivery vehicles for what people expect in all aspects of their lives: fair treatment, fair processes and fair outcomes.

A major problem for society is how to share benefits and burdens and remain cooperative. This fundamental issue was tackled by John Rawls, a leading political philosopher of the twentieth century, whose major work *A Theory of Justice* was instrumental in bringing justice to the foreground of debate in the 1970s. In the following quotation Rawls articulates the vision, the problems, the means and the ends that bring together the notions and concepts of injustice and social justice:

> [A]lthough a society is a cooperative venture for mutual advantage, it is typically marked by a conflict as well as by an identity of interests … There is a conflict of interests since persons are not indifferent as to how the greater benefits produced by their collaboration are distributed, for in order to pursue their ends they each prefer a larger to a lesser share. A set of principles is required for choosing among the various social arrangements which determine this division … These principles are the principles of social justice: they provide a way of assigning rights and duties in the basic institutions of society and they define the appropriate distribution of the benefits and burdens of social cooperation.
>
> (Rawls 1971: 4)

Rawl's view is apt here because this book is concerned with the sharing and distribution of natural resources at a societal level: how can resources be shared and allocated in ways that are perceived as fair and just?

Searching for fair and equitable solutions: water in Australia

Having established the bigger picture of fairness and justice as a societal aspiration, we now turn to the practical area of natural resource management and the way in which fairness and justice are applied in resource sharing. So far we have seen that although fairness has been shown to be important in gaining acceptance of renewable energy projects, the full case for fairness still needs to be made. To deepen our understanding of fairness in natural resource management we turn to water allocation, an area in which solutions can appear to be unforeseeable and difficult to attain. Where better to look than Australia, which is well-known as the driest inhabited continent, as well as a land of climate extremes with its cycles of droughts and floods. But water disputes are a global concern: communities all over the world face water shortages and future water insecurity. What we can learn from Australia is relevant in many countries facing ecological water crises brought about by over-allocation, expanding populations, and changing climatic conditions.

Water management in Australia has a long and complex history. This primarily involves upstream–downstream disputes and clashes of viewpoints on how water should be shared and used. These conflicts are further exacerbated by a highly variable climate and pattern of rainfall. Even though Australia is seen from a global perspective as a leader in water management (Howe and Ingram 2005) major disagreements still take place (Mercer *et al.* 2007; Crase 2008; Owen and Ackerman 2009). This is despite water issues having been high on the national agenda for decades and the subject of much focused research (Smith 1998; Hussey and Dovers 2007b; Syme and Nancarrow 2008; Connell and Grafton 2011). Governments recognise that there are different social perspectives and positions about how water resources are shared and use phrases such as 'fair and equitable' (NSW Government 2010) and 'fairness of outcomes' (National Water Commission 2008) to describe their approaches and desired solutions. However, these phrases are often expressed as visions or goals rather than as practical statements as to how the resources are to be shared.

Although government agencies and practitioners call for fairness in decision making, most would agree that current practice falls well short of this general vision of fair and equitable solutions. Long-time Australian justice researchers Syme and Nancarrow (2008: 242) are blunt in their assessment: 'Fairness is largely ignored despite the development in Australia of techniques to include it in a transparent fashion'. Indeed, Syme and Nancarrow (2005, 2008) have spear-headed fairness research in natural resource management in Australia. They led a series of studies that used social psychological theories of justice to investigate fairness in decision-making processes and outcomes. They concluded from these studies: 'Fair decision-making processes are of paramount importance to community acceptance of water allocation decisions' (Syme *et al.* 1999: 67). They found that people have a range of fairness criteria which include personal beliefs or philosophical positions about how water should be used and shared. Their research showed that there was strong support for water rights to be assigned to the environment, that water trading and water markets were largely not perceived as fair approaches in water allocation, and efficiency of use was important in fairness considerations (Syme *et al.* 1999).

The research undertaken by Syme and Nancarrow and their colleagues has established that fairness in natural resource management is important and that people have well-developed ideas about fairness and justice in relation to the allocation of resources. But they also recognise that there are significant challenges that impede implementation of the findings of justice research and the incorporation of fairness principles into decision-making processes (Nancarrow and Syme 2001; Syme and Nancarrow 2008). These challenges include the way in which self-interest motivations can be pervasive and obstructive in fairness discussions; the need for people to be able to interact and co-operate in the development of solutions, and the extent to which decision-makers will adopt such solutions; and the relatively low profile of justice-based research (Nancarrow and Syme, 2001).

Environmental decision making: from a fairness and justice basis

The next step is to understand environmental decision making from a basis of fairness and justice. This is within a context where water policy is high on the national agenda, and drought conditions put pressure on water supplies. In addition, there is a solid foundation of fairness research and two controversial water conflicts on our doorstep. There are several specific aims in this book. The first is to find out how people understand and react to fairness and justice, or the lack of fairness and justice, in environmental decision making. The second is to find out how people perceive fairness and justice within the social context of a decision making-process, and how their perceptions contribute to their acceptance of an outcome. A third aim is to find out how better outcomes can be achieved.

We have already seen that widely differing positions, interests and attitudes exist within social conflicts, so gaining an understanding of these is a good starting point for understanding perspectives of fairness and justice in decision-making processes. The review of the social acceptance of renewable energy has shown that common themes within the conflicts are likely to emerge, even though each is set in a local context and each has roots in different social and institutional arrangements.

2 Theories of justice and the search for fairness

This chapter considers how a range of disciplines concerned with justice theories have dealt with justice and fairness. The aim is to provide a broad overview of theories of justice and to describe specific ideas and constructs of justice that could be relevant in natural resource sharing. While much has been written about justice, and the topic receives a good deal of attention in a variety of disciplines, there are some key themes of particular interest in the context of resource sharing. The chapter starts with some definitions of justice and how these relate to different aspects of society. It then explores justice in the way people are treated; justice in decision-making processes; and justice in decisions about sharing. This is followed by a section on why people care about justice, motivations for justice and how people become engaged in matters of justice. The discussion then considers distinctions between justice and injustice, and between justice and fairness, followed by thoughts about why theories of justice are important. Finally, the chapter summarises several key justice themes that could be useful in developing an understanding of fairness and justice in environmental decision making.

What is justice?

> All I would suggest is that justice is not something you can see. It is not temporal but eternal. How does man know what is justice? It is not the product of his intellect but of his spirit. The nearest we can get to defining justice is to say that it is what the right-minded members of the community—those who have the right spirit within them—believe to be fair.
>
> (Denning 1955: 4)

The meaning of the term justice has been debated for centuries. Scholars, philosophers and ordinary folk alike have debated and described their view of what justice means to them. This review begins with Sir Alfred Denning's perspectives on justice. Denning's description of justice in the quotation above reflects what he perceives as a general difficulty in coming up with a solid and unambiguous definition. For Denning, justice is more about the 'spirit' than the 'intellect', and justice is also about people deciding what is 'fair'. In his book *The Road to Justice*, Denning clearly distinguishes between the law and justice, arguing that the law can be 'inadequate for the needs of today' and that lawyers have an obligation to see that justice is done. He suggests that on the 'road to justice' there are two 'great objects to be achieved: one is to see that the laws are just: the other that they are justly administered' (Denning 1955: 6). For Denning, adhering to the letter of the law can lead to an injustice being done and lawyers should therefore not assume that the law is an end in itself. He argues that the reason why people obey the law is because they have an obligation to obey the law but in turn, 'the law must correspond with what they consider to be right and just … [i]n other words, it must correspond, as near as may be, with justice' (Denning 1955: 3). Denning thus leaves us in no doubt as to his position on lawyers, justice and the law: law should deliver justice and lawyers should do what is 'right' to ensure that justice is done. To Denning, impartiality in interpreting and dealing with the law is not enough: 'you can be impartial in distributing injustice as well as justice' (Denning 1955: 5).

Distinguishing between justice theories

Denning's perspective is a good starting point because conceptions of justice are wide-ranging, and the overall concept itself is still being actively explored. Many theories are considered inadequate (Schlosberg 2004), lack conceptual clarity (Greenberg 2001a) and are too inward-looking (Ambrose and Arnaud 2005). Denning (1955), as outlined above, talks about justice in simple terms: justice in relation to the law; justice as what is fair or right, and injustice that can arise when justice is not done. Wissenburg (1999) makes the distinction between '*moral* justice, the normative or evaluative concept, and *legal* justice, which is more or less synonymous with positive law' (Wissenburg 1999: 19 emphasis in original). This distinction is useful here because this book addresses the normative rather than legal aspects of justice. What is also relevant is how many distinctions can be made between justice concepts, such as between different types of justice. Related concepts that are discussed in this review include distributive justice, procedural justice and interactional justice; fairness and justice; and injustice and justice.

Society, distributive justice and fairness

The justice debate has various strands. Justice can describe a quality that is displayed by individuals in the way they go about their business and treat fellow individuals. It can also be about how society itself is organised. Wissenburg (1999) compares the theories of Aristotle (1959), Nozick (1974) and Rawls (1971) which respectively accord the primary property of justice to the individual, to social interactions between individuals and to the structure of society. Although there are many differing approaches to justice, Wissenburg (1999: 21) suggests that modern conceptions of social justice have been concerned with two main aspects: distributive justice and impartiality. Distributive justice is concerned with how goods are distributed in society and impartiality is concerned with lack of bias on the part of the distributor or decision-maker (Wissenburg 1999). In his seminal text *A Theory of Justice*, Rawls (1971) connects these two concepts by suggesting that a so-called 'veil of ignorance' can be invoked in the interests of impartiality and fairness in order to distribute social goods in a way that could be perceived as fair. Rawls (2001: 5) in his later book *Justice as Fairness* proposes that 'the idea of society as a fair system of social cooperation' can be 'regulated by a public conception of justice'. Rawls (2001) outlines three points for his conception of a well-ordered society: first, that such a society is based on the common knowledge and agreement of a conception of justice; second, that a society's political and social institutions conform to that conception of justice; and finally that citizens understand and apply these principles of justice (Rawls 2001: 8,9). While Rawls (2001: 11) clarifies that his theory of justice is a political one, and not a moral or general one, it is clear that he recognises the important role of individuals, and the notion of fairness within the basic structure of society.

Theories of justice in which distributive justice is the primary organising idea of justice, such as that advocated by Rawls (1971), have been criticised as being too narrow in scope (Fraser 2001; Schlosberg 2004). Schlosberg (2004: 518) describes a conception of justice that includes three specific elements: 'recognition, distribution, and participation'. These are 'three interlinking, overlapping circles of concern', in which the notion of cultural recognition is not incorporated or 'subsumed' into a theory of distribution (Schlosberg 2004: 521). He argues that the notion of recognition has been neglected and that justice should be a balance of these three elements (Schlosberg 2004).

The notion of recognition includes respectful treatment of individuals and the importance of dignity as a condition in a just society (Honneth 2001). Honneth (2001: 48) suggests that 'moral injury' and perceptions of injustice arising from a lack of recognition are a 'starting-point' for a concept of recognition. Whether recognition is an issue of justice or of ethics is discussed by Fraser (2001). She argues that it is clearly an issue of justice, in part because repeated 'patterns of disrespect' can 'impede parity of participation, just as surely as do distributed inequities' (Fraser 2001: 27). Thus it can be seen that for some justice theorists matters of distribution are uppermost, whereas for others matters of process and recognition or interpersonal treatment have equal weight with distribution. This leads to the concepts of distributive and procedural justice as two specific entities.

While Miller (1999: 1) acknowledges that social justice is to a large degree concerned with distribution, such as how 'the good and bad things in life' are distributed, his conception of justice includes the social context in which the question of justice is raised. He argues that people must understand their relationships with others and describes three theoretical types of community relationships in a pluralistic approach. These are: first, a 'solidaristic community' where people share a common identity, such as in a village community or kibbutz; second, an 'instrumental association' where people collaborate together in the pursuit of their individual goals, such as in a government department or company; and third, 'citizenship' such as in membership of a society (Miller 1999: 26, 27, 30). Miller's focus is on distributive justice and the three principles of distributive justice that he identifies, namely, need, desert and equality. Miller's proposal is that for each of these types of community one of these three principles will apply as the substantive principle of distribution. In a solidaristic community the primary principle of distribution is to distribute according to need; in an instrumental association the principle is distribution according to desert or contribution; and in citizenship the principle of distribution is equality, recognising the equal status of citizens. Justice researchers frequently refer to these three principles of distributive justice, but the principle of desert described here by Miller is also commonly referred to as the principle of equity in which allocation is according to merit or input (Montada 2003; Fortin 2008).

In setting out these three structures with their associated justice principles Miller (1999) is showing that different situations require different principles of distribution, which is a reflection of the dilemmas faced in current societies. With such dilemmas or conflicts, guidance is required for decision making.

Theories of justice and empirical research: a gap or a partnership?

That there is a disconnection between justice theorists, such as political philosophers, and empirical researchers, such as social psychologists, is acknowledged by both Miller (1999) and Wissenburg (1999). The latter comments that 'philosophers of justice hardly ever use data from empirical research' and that 'empirical scientists ... seldom or never use philosophical material' (Wissenburg 1999: 25). Miller (1999) devotes a chapter to this conundrum and argues that these two areas are interdependent: he proposes that theories need testing empirically and that empirical research into justice needs theories to help distinguish what are genuine justice issues. He suggests that theory and empirical research can work together.

Outcomes, processes and interpersonal treatment

> Justice is not just a set of principles derived from objective sources ... [i]t is also an idea that exists within the minds of all individuals. This subjective sense of what is right or wrong is the focus of the psychology of justice.
>
> (Tyler *et al.* 1997: 4)

Procedural justice and distributive justice

Procedural justice, concerned with the perceived fairness of decision-making processes, has been researched by social psychologists since the mid-1970s (Colquitt *et al.* 2001). Researchers of that period realised that it was not only distributive justice, or decisions, that were important to people: it was also the processes by which those decisions came about. This was a departure from the dominant distributive justice paradigm of the time. As indicated in the quotation above, social psychologists take the research approach that justice arises from an individual's subjective evaluation of what is fair or just (Tyler *et al.* 1997). Fair decision-making processes have been shown to have a positive effect on the acceptance of outcomes (Tyler 2000; Greenberg 2001b). Some social psychologists claim that processes are more important to people than outcomes in their evaluations of what is fair (Lind and Tyler 1988; Skitka *et al.* 2003). Procedural justice involves several criteria that together constitute the fairness of processes. These criteria include such items as the ability to participate in the process and be heard (voice); receiving adequate and accurate information; the trustworthiness and neutrality of decision-making authorities; the ability to raise issues and have these responded to; and being treated with respect and dignity (Tyler 2000; Colquitt 2001).

The fair process effect and construct distinctiveness

Much research has focused on the relationship and interactions between two constructs: procedural justice and distributive justice. A key question is which one of these processes or outcome dimensions has a stronger effect or matters more when, for example, the outcome is negative (Lind 2001). Empirical studies have shown that people are more satisfied with outcomes if the decision-making process is perceived to be fair; for example, if they have been given an opportunity to have their say (Fortin 2008). Further, people will accept decisions that have a negative impact on them if they perceive that the process has been fair. Researchers identify this as the 'fair process effect' (Skitka *et al.* 2003: 310; MacCoun 2005; Brockner *et al.* 2007).

However, Greenberg (2001b) advises caution in how the fair process effect is approached. He suggests that fair procedures matter more in situations when the decision or outcome is negative because, where an outcome is positive, participants are less concerned about fairness of procedures. A second caution is that there must be sincerity in the way procedures are conducted by the decision-maker: if there is perceived insincerity, there is a risk of the 'frustration effect' taking place and lower acceptance of outcomes by participants (Greenberg 2001b: 257). A further caution is described by Skitka *et al.* (2003). They point out that there is a difference between the perceived fairness of a decision and the degree to which the decision or outcome is perceived as favourable. Outcome fairness relates to whether an outcome is considered fair against some societal norm or standard whereas outcome favourability confers a positive result on an individual or group with an interest in the outcome. Skitka *et al.* (2003) suggest that researchers have tended to fuse these two constructs into one, thereby not recognising the distinctions, or have used them interchangeably in studies that compare procedural justice and distributive justice effects. However, there is a difference between the two terms which can be important in a particular setting, thus they should be considered as distinct.

The two- and three-factor models of justice: introducing interactional justice

Just as research shifted from a focus on distributive justice to procedural justice, another later shift took place to include the interpersonal aspects of procedures. For example, the value perceived by participants in being able to take part in a decision-making process and express their voice had already been shown to be important in early research and was included in the principles of procedural justice (Tyler and Blader 2003). Other relevant interpersonal matters included respectful treatment, such as whether people's issues were listened to by decision-making authorities. Research into interpersonal treatment showed that the quality of such treatment was important in people's perception of their 'standing' or their 'status recognition'. This was seen as distinct from other fairness criteria for a decision-making process (Tyler and Blader 2003: 351). Some researchers were of the opinion that interpersonal treatment issues were important and distinct enough to be identified in a separate justice construct; thus the construct interactional justice was introduced (Cropanzano *et al.* 2001). This three-factor model of justice, in which interactional justice became a construct distinct from procedural justice, itself distinct from distributive justice, was introduced in the 1980s by Bies (2001). Bies (2001: 90) describes the roots of this rather controversial proposal as originating in the notion of interactional injustice: 'The truth is that … when people talk about justice, their narratives are in terms of the injustices they experience'. He goes on to describe the harm to 'one's psyche and identity' and suggests that the human aspect of harm is 'underemphasised and underappreciated in organisational justice theory' (Bies 2001: 90).

Bies (2005) strongly defends the validity and the conceptual distinctiveness of interactional justice. For example, the way people are treated may be quite separate from a decision-making process, which is a central part of procedural justice. This means that interactional justice can stand on its own, outside a process concerned with a decision (Bies, 2005). Bies (2005: 101) describes this as 'justice as encounter versus justice as exchange', whereby the exchange context is concerned with specific decisions or allocations. The encounter context is more of a separate everyday occurrence where people may be concerned with 'abusive bosses, broken promises, disclosure of confidences and secrets … [and] insults' which are viewed by the receiver as '*harmful* and *wrong*, the bases for feeling unjustly treated' (Bies 2005: 101, emphasis in original). He suggests that there is a difference between interactional *justice* and interactional *injustice*, as there is between justice and injustice, and that these should be methodologically distinguished in empirical studies (Bies 2005).

Why people care about justice

There are three broad groupings of theories and proposals that justice researchers use to explain why people care about justice. These are: first, theories that generally hold that self-interest is the central motivation in the way people deal with each other; second, theories that propose that people care about fairness and justice because this is an indication of their status or worth within a community or group; and third, theories in which morality or justice as an end in itself is the primary motivation for behaviour and interactions (Cropanzano *et al.* 2001; Montada 2003; Skitka 2009).

Why people care about justice: self-interest

Perhaps the single most influential theory put forward as an explanation for why people care about justice is the theory of self-interest (Tyler *et al.* 1997; Tyler and

Blader 2003). As Miller and Ratner (1996: 25) describe it 'self-interest is the cardinal human motive, or so many of the most influential theories of human behavior would have us believe'. A self-interested individual or group operates for material gain, whether this is at a personal level or at a community level. Indeed, self-interest could be used to explain a wide variety of activities or motivations, for example, to increase social well-being through membership of an exclusive club or a desire to be seen to be altruistic to promote one's image in a community (Montada 2003). On the surface some community activities could seem to have nothing to do with self-interest, being concerned with the welfare of others, but as Montada (2003) points out, an underlying self-interest motive could be found for a whole range of apparently unselfish actions. This may explain why the self-interest theory is so firmly entrenched as the dominant explanation for why people care about justice. Social psychologists have labelled it the 'myth of self-interest' because, although it is a widely held view, there are many other explanations for human motivation about justice that do not include the self (Tyler and Blader 2000: 70).

Why people care about justice: group engagement and identity

The group engagement model is focused on the motivations exhibited by people when they join and become involved in groups. In describing their model Tyler and Blader (2003) review the contribution made by earlier research into the effects of procedural justice on people's motivation and behaviour. This includes the significance of interpersonal treatment, such as the importance of voice in people's evaluations of how they were treated. Interestingly, Tyler and Blader (2003) chart the progress of the character of justice research as it moved from 1960s considerations of allocation rules for the distribution of resources towards the more recent view being more about 'quality of treatment issues'. They suggest that early justice research was focused on showing that 'justice matters' and that 'people's thoughts, feelings, and behaviors are shaped by their justice judgements', which suggests that 'information about justice is central to people's evaluations of social situations' (Tyler and Blader 2003: 352). This demonstrates the strong connection between the notion of justice and people's feelings and behaviour.

The key point to be made about Tyler and Blader's group engagement model is the importance of procedural justice and interpersonal treatment in shaping people's social identity within groups. Membership of a group provides an individual with a way of forming a social identity and that co-operation within the group is in part shaped by a common identity. Aspects of identity include 'identification, pride and respect' (Tyler and Blader 2003: 356). While cooperation includes the sharing of resources, the importance of procedural justice and interpersonal treatment in this model is not so much related to making decisions about resource allocation as it is about the security of people's identities within the group, or as Tyler and Blader (2003: 358) describe it 'identity security'. Identity security is important because it provides a sense of self-worth for group members. Many research studies in this relational type of model have highlighted the importance of procedural justice and its effect on an individual's sense of identity and self-esteem (Ambrose 2002).

Why people care about justice: morality and justice as an end in itself

Cropanzano *et al.* (2003: 1019, emphasis in original) argue that justice 'includes treating others as they *should* or *deserve* to be treated by adhering to standards of right and wrong'. They suggest that 'justice is in part a judgment about the morality of an outcome, process, or interpersonal interaction' and not just about a person's identity or gain (Cropanzano *et al.* 2003: 1019). Folger (1998: 32) is also concerned with the inclusion of morality in justice considerations and suggests that procedures have a role to play in 'preserving human dignity', and should not be considered merely as a means for seeking outcomes or as ends in themselves. Along the same lines, Montada (2003: 538) suggests that justice is 'a moral imperative for social life. It is not a means to achieve personal aims, but rather an end in itself'. For Montada (2003) justice comes with an obligation as well as an entitlement: obligation to deliver justice as well as an entitlement to receive justice from others. Similarly justice can be claimed on behalf of others as well as for oneself (Montada 2003).

Justice as an end in itself is a central element of Belief-in-a-Just-World theory which Lerner (1998) describes as having roots in a childhood need for a stable environment and the belief that good prevails over bad. In this theory people have a need for justice and get what they deserve. If an injustice takes place then their belief in a just world is challenged. Lerner (1998: 261) suggests that it is part of human nature for people to 'develop a commitment to justice' in part, because people's lives are concerned with creating stability in their environment. He strongly refutes the dominance of self-interest, suggesting that justice is 'an omnipresent and sanctified part of people's lives'. He maintains that the principles of justice are part of the fabric of institutional arrangements and that 'people remain exquisitely sensitive and continually responsive to issues of deserving and justice' (Lerner 1998: 260). Finally, for Lerner, justice is about people's need for the structure and stability of their world and injustice is about threats to that stability (Lerner 1998).

From competing models to a complex mosaic in a social context

Skitka (2009: 102) has described the three groupings outlined above (self-interest, group identity and justice as an end in itself) respectively as '*homo economicus*', '*homo socialis*' and '*homo moralis*'. She calls these groupings 'perspectives or frames of reference' but also suggests that these could be regarded as 'contingencies' because which perspective or frame of reference is adopted will depend on how people see their current situation: in terms of their self-interest, in terms of their membership of a community or in terms of what they see as right and wrong (Skitka 2009: 99). These groupings have traditionally been seen as 'competing explanations for why people care about fairness, and therefore what shapes fairness judgments' (Skitka 2009: 104). In her view a contingency model of justice would recognise that people have different perspectives about fairness depending on their current situation and concerns. Social context is therefore important in understanding people's perspectives about justice and fairness. As Skitka suggests, the contingency model could be useful in examining current situations in which interactions between groups or communities and disagreements or conflicts are taking place. In other words, rather than having a single motive as a dominant explanation, as these theories imply, there are likely to be many reasons and motivations underlying concerns about fairness and justice. Ambrose (2002) also takes the view that there are many reasons why people care about justice and theories should not be seen as competing but rather as 'different parts of a complex mosaic' (Ambrose 2002: 807). Having considered the three groupings of why people care about justice, we now turn to the next question: when do people become concerned about justice?

When and how do people become engaged in matters of justice?

Understanding *when* and for what reason people become engaged in issues of justice is an important area of justice research. As suggested above, there are many reasons *why* people care about justice and specific instances of these will depend on the social context. Skitka (2003: 286) developed her 'Accessible Identity Model' as a tool to understand more about when and why people become engaged in issues of justice. The model proposes that people have three primary layers of identity that are organised around material, social and personal identities. People will determine whether an action or decision is fair or not fair according to which layer of identity is more actively engaged at the time. The material identity is largely concerned with livelihood, family and possessions; the social identity is concerned with social relationships, status and belonging within groups; and personal identity is concerned with personal values, beliefs and concerns with what is right or wrong. If any one of these three areas is threatened then the Accessible Identity Model suggests that people will engage in thoughts about justice and fairness from that threatened identity perspective. For example, the Accessible Identity Model suggests that when a person's livelihood or material interests are threatened then their justice concern will be associated with the fairness of outcomes. This model can also apply to a group's perspective of justice, and a group can also engage in issues of justice at these three identity levels (Skitka and Bravo 2005). Platow *et al.* (2003: 267) highlight the importance of a *shared* social identity and propose that this shared social identity is important in people's consideration of fairness.

Justice judgements and two fairness theories

How people form justice or fairness judgements is another area of enquiry that has generated several theories. These have their roots in the early equity theory developed by Adams (1965), which is concerned with the perceived fairness of what people receive as an outcome in relation to their inputs (Cropanzano *et al.* 2001). More recent theories such as fairness theory developed by Folger and Cropanzano (2001) and fairness heuristic theory developed by Lind (2001) are concerned with the process by which the judgement is made as well as the actual fairness judgement (Cropanzano *et al.* 2001). Taking fairness theory first, this is concerned with accountability in fairness judgements and the assignment of blame onto the entity causing the perceived unfair treatment. Fairness theory has three components: first, an action or situation which is unfavourable to the perceiver; second, the action or situation must have been voluntarily caused by an entity that is therefore seen to be accountable; and third, the action or situation must be perceived to be wrong or violate some ethical code or principle (Folger and Cropanzano 2001: 3). The perceiver can make distinct fairness judgements about these three components (Cropanzano *et al.* 2001).

In contrast, Lind's fairness heuristic theory is concerned with fairness judgements where there are 'repeated encounters' between, for example, managers and employees in organisations (Lind 2001: 61). Central to the theory is what Lind (2001: 61) calls the 'fundamental social dilemma' of competing demands between group interests and individual interests. Lind suggests that people develop impressions of fair treatment over time, but in episodes. For example, an individual will make a fairness judgement at the outset of a relationship which will then be used as a guide as the relationship progresses. The fairness judgement will be updated from time to time. Therefore the first impressions of fairness are important and these can be process or outcome related. Lind (2001: 73) argues that the general fairness judgement becomes 'an anchor and a context used to understand and interpret justice-relevant experiences'. Importantly, the fairness heuristic theory suggests that there is a 'substitution effect' whereby the fairness impression of a process can substitute for the fairness impression of an outcome, if the latter is missing or an outcome has not yet been reached in the relationship (Lind 2001: 75). This accounts for the 'fair process effect' because an earlier fairness assessment will influence a later fairness judgement of an outcome (Lind 2001: 74).

These explanations and themes show that there are many reasons why people care about justice and many ways in which justice judgements are formed. Theories which aim to answer these questions should be seen as *alternatives* that depend on the context rather than being in competition with each other to provide a single explanation. There may be more than one explanation that is applicable at any particular time and for any particular context.

From theories of justice to a theory of injustice

> Justice is not a collection of principles or criteria … justice is the active process of the preventing or repairing of injustice.
>
> (Cahn 1967: 381)

Distinguishing between justice and injustice

Cahn decided to write his book *The Sense of Injustice* because he realised he had been talking about 'justice' for 18 years and yet could still not 'explain intelligibly what I meant by the word … I could not explain the one word that made sense of my professional life' (Cahn 1964: 188). His book is about establishing that there is a 'sense of injustice' which he describes as 'an indissociable blend of reason and empathy' (Cahn 1949: 26). Reason provides 'observation, analysis and science' and empathy provides 'warm sensibility': both are required for the sense of injustice (Cahn 1949: 26). Whereas justice gives people a sense of security, the sense of injustice is an active part of the day-to-day operation of the legal system, driving it towards justice. For Cahn the term justice had come to signify a 'static condition' whereas he thought justice should be seen more as an '*active process* of remedying or preventing what would arouse the sense of injustice' (Cahn 1949: 13, emphasis in original).

Also concerned with making a clear distinction between justice and injustice is the philosopher Wolgast who observes that a common, but incorrect, conception of justice is that it is 'an ideal or standard from which injustice departs' (Wolgast 1987: 125). She looks to the derivation of the word injustice, and how people speak about justice in common usage. She points out that the word *injustice* derives from the Latin word *injuria* which means injury (Wolgast 1987: 133). An injury is not a negative state; it is an active event that has happened. In day-to-day terms people generally speak about justice as correcting a wrong that has already happened: the wrong is in the past. Thus, to Wolgast, 'Justice appears then as an indefinite corrective to injustice rather than something definable in its own right' (Wolgast 1987: 146). In a similar vein, writing from the perspective of political theory, Shklar (1990: 15) criticises philosophy and art in her book *The Faces of Injustice* because they 'seem to shun injustice' and they 'take it for granted that injustice is simply the absence of justice'. Shklar is concerned that the 'sense of injustice' and 'the difficulties of identifying victims of injustice' are not taken into account (Shklar 1990: 15). These include victims who are recognised as such and those who would not normally be recognised as victims of injustice, for example, people who have been the subject of fraud.

Simon (1995: 11) also develops an argument for separating the terms justice and injustice 'to show that a theory of injustice does not have to depend upon a theory of justice'. He argues that injustice can exist and be defined without a definition of justice and that injustice 'has its own dynamic, apart from justice' (Simon 1995: 14). He suggests that injustice takes 'priority' over justice in four ways: 'empirically, temporally, psychologically, and morally' (Simon 1995: 16). By priority, Simon means that injustice comes first. Thus an unjust event results in a call for justice. Empirically, injustice takes priority because it is more concrete and connected with real-life events than justice, which is more abstract. Similarly in psychological terms, injustice arouses passion, anger, outrage and action in contrast to justice, which is felt and discussed in less emotional ways. In moral terms, injustice arouses a psychological response which then invokes a sense of injustice (Simon 1995: 18). In claiming this priority of injustice over justice Simon (1995: 24) argues that a theory of injustice should first look at 'what is wrong before embarking upon a program based on what is right' and that this theory of injustice can occupy the middle ground between theories of justice and day-to-day experiences of injustice.

The experience of injustice

> From a psychological point of view, there is no objective justice. It is the subjective perceptions of justice and injustice that matter.
>
> (Mikula 2005: 199)

Social psychologists call attention to the subjective nature of justice and injustice. It is the individual's evaluation of interpersonal treatment or perception of justice or fairness that counts. As Mikula (2005) points out, in social conflicts it is the differing perceptions and viewpoints of what is just or unjust that lies at the heart of the conflict or disagreement. In a social conflict there is no such thing as objective justice: a conflict revolves around differing views about processes and outcomes and is often a result of perceived injustices (Mikula and Wenzel 2000).

Having clarified this distinction between the notions of subjective justice and objective justice, we now turn to perceptions of injustice and the experience of injustice. Mikula *et al.* (1990) found that the daily events which people considered unjust were spread across a broad range of distributive, procedural and interpersonal concerns, with interpersonal treatment accounting for a significant amount. Further, the importance of interpersonal treatment in their results supported the proposal to recognise interactional justice as a justice construct in its own right. In a similar study Clayton (1992) investigated the experience of injustice from people's own perceptions of unjust situations and found that these varied considerably according to the social context of the perceived injustice.

Lupfer *et al.* (2000: 405) investigated what they call 'folk conceptions' of fairness and unfairness and found that how people experience fairness and unfairness in everyday events is consistent with categories used by social scientists, namely distributive, procedural and interactional. They found that people react more strongly to events that are perceived as unfair, than they do to events perceived as fair. Importantly, in making judgements of unfairness, people used criteria from all three justice constructs: distributive, procedural and interactional. This is in contrast to their finding of the predominance of procedural justice criteria when people make judgements of fairness. Thus they suggest 'the standards people use in judging events to be fair versus unfair are not symmetrical and complementary' (Lupfer *et al.* 2000: 424). They note that this supports Shklar's (1990) assertion that injustice is not simply the absence of justice (described above) and conclude that 'true fairness requires that all three be satisfied' referring to the three justice constructs (Lupfer *et al.* 2000: 426).

In a review of research into the experience of injustice, Mikula (1993) suggested that there are different perspectives involved in assessments of injustice which can be grouped into three areas: perspectives of the victim; perspectives of the individual or group held to be responsible for the injustice; and perspectives of bystanders who observe the incident but are not directly affected by it. Mikula (1993) also identified three basic components of injustice judgements in which the notion of *entitlement* is critical. These were the perceived violation of entitlement; the attribution of responsibility to an agent causing the injustice; and attribution of blame to that agent (Mikula 1993: 240).

It is well recognised that notions of entitlement and corresponding violations of entitlement are key elements in the formation of justice or injustice judgements (Mikula and Wenzel 2000). Lerner (1987) proposed a framework in which rules of entitlement are a major feature of the social structure within which people live. Such entitlements are expressed through general day-to-day activities in which people understand 'who is entitled to what from whom': these have a psychological basis and are embedded into daily decision making (Lerner 1987: 108). Entitlement is not only concerned with tangible aspects of daily life, such as property rights, but is also concerned with the way people are treated, such as the right to be treated with respect, to be provided with explanations and to be able to participate and have a voice (Miller 2001).

In a review of research on disrespect, and the experience of injustice and entitlements, Miller (2001) suggests that there are two main areas in which people have a sense of entitlement. These are interpersonal sensitivity (including respectful treatment) and accountability (including explanations relating to processes or outcomes in which an individual is involved). However, the difficulty in describing what constitutes respectful treatment is acknowledged: people recognise disrespectful treatment but find it hard to articulate what would be respectful treatment. Miller (2001: 532) suggests that disrespectful treatment can 'compound the injustice created by an undeserved outcome and constitute an injustice of its own'. In seeking explanations for why people perceive disrespectful treatment as an injustice Miller (2001: 533) comes up with two rationales: disrespectful treatment first 'deprives people of something to which they are entitled' and second 'subjects people to something they do not deserve'. Such explanations of why people consider being treated with respect is important are critical in gaining an understanding of how people interpret and react to issues of justice.

Justice and fairness: interchangeable or distinct?

> Social scientists advance knowledge by finding facts and grounding theory on them. But that advance is impeded, I submit, by confusion and inconsistency over how the concepts of justice and fairness are understood, related, and used.
>
> (Finkel 2001: 43)

Finkel (2001: xiii), in his quest for 'the unearthing of commonsense unfairness' first sets to work to seek clarification about the terms justice and fairness. As the quotation above clearly shows, Finkel's (2001: 55) position on the topic is that there is 'an ever-present confusion' over the use and meaning of these two terms. Once this confusion has been pointed out, it is indeed quite striking, particularly in the social psychology of justice literature, that the terms justice and fairness are used interchangeably. Few authors seek to clarify their use of these two terms although some do acknowledge that they use them interchangeably (for example, Lind and Tyler 1988; Brockner and Wiesenfeld 1996; Greenberg and Colquitt 2005). Although many researchers use the terms justice and fairness interchangeably, there are also those who make distinctions between the terms and where they are used. For example Reis (1984) states:

> Indeed, the notion that outcomes and procedures demand separate consideration is so well recognized in philosophy that the term *justice* is usually reserved for outcome distributions, whereas *fairness* is applied to procedural matters.
>
> (Reis 1984: 27, emphasis in original)

Similarly Wissenburg (1999: 34, 35) points out that fairness has been seen as 'a procedural rather than a substantive ideal' and 'treating like cases alike' whereas the idea of justice is more about 'giving each his due'. Finkel (2001) devotes considerable attention to the distinction between fairness and justice and how these terms have been used in the literature. He identifies three patterns of use, namely identity, conjugate and subset (Finkel 2001: 43). In the first pattern, identity, the two terms are used interchangeably. In the second pattern, conjugate, the terms are paired as in 'just and fair'. In the third pattern, subset, either of the terms can be seen as a subset of the other. Finkel adds his own fourth category 'overlapping and separate' in which the two terms have distinctions as well as areas that overlap (Finkel 2001: 44). In a broad review of literature in which distinctions are made, Finkel finds that there is a frequent distinction in which fairness is seen as process and justice is seen as outcome, but also finds support for his fourth category, overlapping and separate. He found that fairness had three different meanings: 'fairness as reciprocity, fairness as outcome and fairness as a moral response' (Finkel 2001: 57). Interestingly, he decides from his review to focus on the topic of *unfairness* as a fruitful field of research, also in part drawing on the distinctions between justice and injustice made by Shklar (1990) and Wolgast (1987).

Why theories of justice and injustice matter

> The absence of an explicit conception of social justice in political life has the result that arguments about public policy are made without any attempt to explain from the ground up what is their justification.
>
> (Barry 2005: 10)

The quotation from Barry's (2005) book *Why Social Justice Matters* illustrates what can happen in a practical way in the absence of a theory of social justice. As this review has shown, the ideas and principles of justice take on many forms and operate in many ways throughout society. Justice is concerned with the distribution of public goods according to principles such as need, equity and equality, the operation of institutions, the application of laws and putting wrongs to right. How justice principles are coherently assembled, articulated and implemented is the work of a theory of justice. Barry (2005: 12) suggests that we need an 'independently derived idea of what a just distribution … would look like' before commenting on the fairness of a particular decision. According to Barry, institutions should be considered as a means to an end to deliver social justice. In order for institutions to be able to deliver justice there needs to be a theory of justice to articulate the principles by which resources are distributed. As Barry argues, facts drawn from an information base are inadequate in the absence of such a theory.

Another reason why a theory of justice is a necessity when considering how a distribution should be made, is the dilemma of competing interests in resource allocation. The legal philosopher, H.L.A Hart, presented this argument some 50 years ago:

> Very few social changes or laws are agreeable to or advance the welfare of all individuals alike. … When a choice has been made between … competing

> alternatives it may be defended as proper on the ground that it was for the 'public good'... It is ... clear that a choice, made without prior consideration of the interests of all sections of the community would be open to criticism as merely partisan and unjust. ... It would, however, be rescued from *this* imputation if the claims of all had been impartially considered ... even though in the result the claims of one section were subordinated to those of others.
>
> (Hart 1961: 166, 167, emphasis in original)

The important points in Hart's argument are that he recognises that there are competing interests as well as a general public interest and that not everyone will be satisfied with a decision. Nevertheless, a *just* decision can be made on the basis of an impartial consideration of these interests. Justice is then *seen* to be done.

Miller (1999) also articulates the need for a theory of justice and laments the lack of demonstrated commitment to social justice policies in contemporary politics. He proposes that a theory of justice should appear 'no longer as an external imposition conjured up by the philosopher, but as a clearer and more systematic statement of the principles that people already hold' (Miller 1999: 51). He argues for empirical evidence to play a role in formulating such theories to bring existing underlying societal values and beliefs into play in a structured way. In this way the different principles of justice that people use in everyday life can be revealed along with other motivations and values. Miller recognises that while people will protest if a situation is perceived as unjust, there is still a need to understand the basis for people's beliefs: 'a theory of justice brings out the deep structure of a set of everyday beliefs' and enables greater understanding of the distinctions between principles of justice (Miller 1999: 51). Understanding the basis for injustice is also a critical aspect of Simon's (1995) proposed theory of injustice. He suggests that a theory of injustice asks different questions than do theories of justice by examining the harm done to people through perceived injustices.

Summary: from theory to practice

This review of justice has covered a lot of ground, from abstract theories about how society should be organised, to the practical exploration of why and when people engage in justice. The challenge is to put these theories into practice in environmental decision making. There are several key considerations. First, this book takes an approach in which justice is seen from a normative or morally based perspective rather than a legal perspective, and where the notion of justice encompasses distributive, procedural and interactional elements (Figure 2.1). The interplay between these three elements is recognised, in that each one has some part to play in determining the overall acceptance of outcomes by those with an interest in the outcomes. Justice motives or reasons for people to seek justice are also acknowledged to be diverse, ranging from self-interest to justice as an end in itself.

A second key area is the separation of justice and injustice, and the recognition that injustice is not merely a lack of justice. A perceived injustice can be an event or outcome in a social context. The importance of context is also noted: individuals

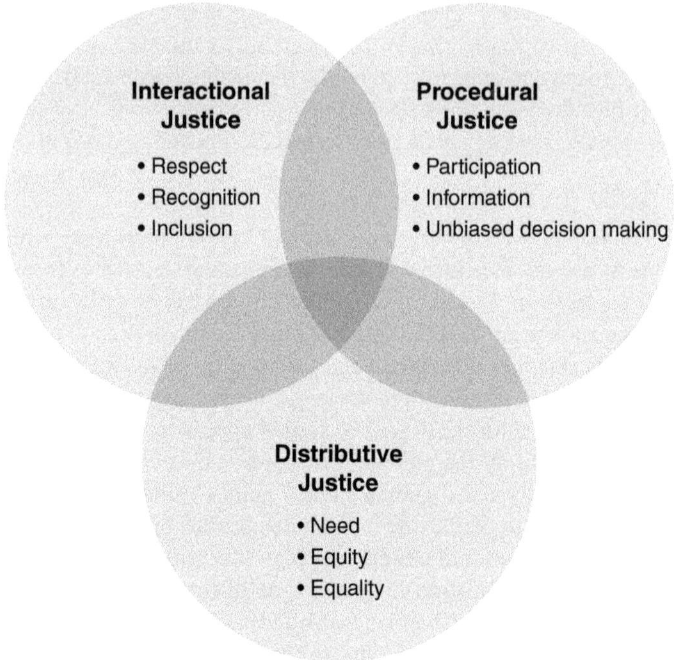

Figure 2.1 The three constructs of justice.

and communities can have a range of justice concerns, in any given societal context, and these concerns depend on their own situation and their interaction with others. Justice concerns can be tangible or intangible and can be invoked from a material, social or personal perspective. Thus the differing areas of justice concerns and the interplay with a variety of motives for seeking justice are recognised here.

A third key area to take forward is how people evaluate fairness and justice. This review shows that clarification is required in the way the terms fairness and justice are used. The review has also shown that there are many ways in which people evaluate justice and fairness: this can be in terms of specific aspects of a process or outcome, or as an overall general fairness assessment. By understanding reactions to decision-making processes and outcomes through fairness evaluations, greater understanding can be gained that can be used proactively to achieve greater perceptions of fairness in decision making.

3 Developing a justice-based research approach

Setting the scope of the research

The previous chapter has developed insights into an array of justice theories concerned with individuals, groups and the whole of society. The scope of this literature can be somewhat daunting to a practitioner setting policies or making decisions about resources. However, we saw in Chapter 1 that fairness is important in environmental decision making on renewable energy, and we discussed the importance of perceived injustice in Chapter 2. The challenge now is to devise an approach in which we can understand what is happening in a social conflict over resource allocation, and what we can learn from that to reduce conflict and bring about better outcomes for those involved. In other words, we need to devise a research approach in this middle ground between theory and the practical reality of conflict. At this point, those readers who wish to proceed directly to the two water case studies may continue on to Chapter 4.

An initial task is to acknowledge the scope in terms of who or what is included in the sharing of resources. An ultimate goal of environmental research must be to maintain the health and well-being of ecosystems as well as human societies. The theories of justice discussed so far have been human-centred. But what of the environment; should nature itself be included in considerations of justice? Researchers are well aware of the need to set boundaries around their research so that they can achieve their research aims within the limits of the time and resources available to them. However, it is worth acknowledging that these boundaries are not only artificial, but they are also porous because of the interconnections with other areas outside the research scope. This is where theoretical ideas of research can help frame a research project meaningfully within the bigger picture, and set it on course to achieve its aims. Extending the scope of justice from a purely anthropocentric view to include nature and the environment is part of this bigger picture. While the scope of justice *should* be extended beyond human societal boundaries to nature and the environment, it must also be acknowledged that research projects need to be limited to a specific area of enquiry. This enables a focus on local issues, and allows themes and implications to emerge that relate to the bigger picture. In this way much can be learnt about the application of justice ideas from within defined research boundaries.

A holistic and adaptive methodology

The next task is to consider a methodological approach in this middle ground between theory and practical reality. The term 'methodology' is used here to describe a set of theoretical ideas which together form the basis of the research approach, and from which appropriate research methods can be selected or devised (Midgley 2000: 105). The methodology adopted here derives from a philosophical position that recognises linkages between social systems (driven by human culture) and the biophysical environment. This perspective is holistic in that it acknowledges that there is a complex interplay of such linkages. Academic research approaches of a holistic kind include integrative research (Dovers 2005), human ecology (Berkes and Folke 1998; Boyden 2004) and transdisciplinary research (Ramadier 2004; Pohl 2005; Mobjörk 2010).

Justice research has been substantially enhanced by the emergence of transdisciplinary research that is not limited by academic boundaries. Pohl (2005: 1160) describes transdisciplinary research as searching 'for a viewpoint that lies between, or beyond, disciplines' and as 'knowledge which is produced and organised in accordance with a particular discipline and rearrange[s] it so as to make it useful and meaningful for socially relevant issues'. Brown *et al.* (2010) discuss the importance of imagination in transdisciplinary approaches for tackling complex environmental problems known as 'wicked problems'. They propose that imagination helps unleash the creativity required to explore possibilities and understand problems from a variety of viewpoints. Transdisciplinary research also recognises that knowledge must be drawn from a variety of sources, given the nature of the problem. For example, V.A. Brown (2008) identifies five sources of knowledge, including individual knowledge, local community knowledge, specialised knowledge, strategic knowledge and holistic knowledge. She argues that it is the interactions and syntheses between these sources that can contribute to a collective understanding of a complex issue. Brown suggests that each of these five knowledge platforms can develop its own separate mode of operation or thinking if it is isolated from the other areas. However, this separation can result in barriers that impede communication and cause problems in understanding and dealing with problems or conflicts. For example, community meetings set up to solve specific problems can become dominated by so-called experts and result in local knowledge being undervalued (V.A. Brown 2008).

Understanding which sources of knowledge are relevant to the research, including those inside, between and outside academic disciplines, and gaining access to them in a structured way, is a key challenge for the researcher. This is where organising frameworks that recognise diverse sources of knowledge and the linkages between them can be put to use.

Organising frameworks

By its very nature a complex social problem is a composite of a variety of positions of interests, perspectives, experiences, knowledge and contexts. Where social problems are concerned with natural resource management, there is an additional complexity: the varying nature of the resource itself. As Berkes and Folke (1998) point out, conventional resource management has typically failed, in part because resources have been exploited as commodities, and in part because of a lack of holistic resource management techniques. In particular they point to deficiencies in understanding the resource user, or the people side of resource management. Further, they suggest that understanding and reporting the linkages between social and biophysical aspects of resource management can mobilise 'a *wider range* of considerations and sources of information' than traditional approaches (Berkes and Folke 1998: 3, emphasis in original). A conceptual framework can help the researcher to 'think about phenomena, to order material, revealing patterns – and pattern recognition typically leads to models and theories' (Rapoport 1985: 256, cited in Berkes and Folke 1998: 15).

A human ecology framework, shown in Figure 3.1, which is adapted from an earlier version of Boyden's transition framework (Boyden, 2013), shows the relationships between cultural systems and the biophysical environment. This framework places emphasis on the impact of human activities and associated societal arrangements. Human activities are seen as biophysical *options* that have a direct influence on the biophysical environment, which in turn, affects the scope of options for future human activities. The point of this framework is that human societies are dependent on ecosystem health and must make choices that benefit both human and ecosystem health.

Organising frameworks have three main purposes. First, they recognise the links between human societies and their cultures, which strongly influence interactions with the living environment. Second, they encourage the researcher to consider a broad range of knowledge sources in the development of the analytical approach; and third, they can assist in the ordering of the empirical part of the research process.

A qualitative approach using semi-structured interviews

Having decided which organising framework to use, the next steps are to select appropriate research tools and identify the sources of knowledge to be explored. The research approach and tools must be appropriate to the context and capable of teasing out the core elements of the problem. However, there are still lingering disciplinary preferences for particular research methods, such as qualitative or quantitative approaches. Minichiello *et al.* (1995: 9) summarise qualitative research as being 'attempts to capture people's meanings, definitions and descriptions of events' whereas quantitative research 'aims to count and measure things'. However, this may be an over-simplification. Richards (2005: 36) provides a useful clarification on the difference between these two research method areas suggesting 'qualitative and quantitative data do not inhabit different worlds. They are different ways of recording observations of the same world'. The overall goal of the research design must be to address the research problem while recognising the perceived strengths and weaknesses of the methods chosen.

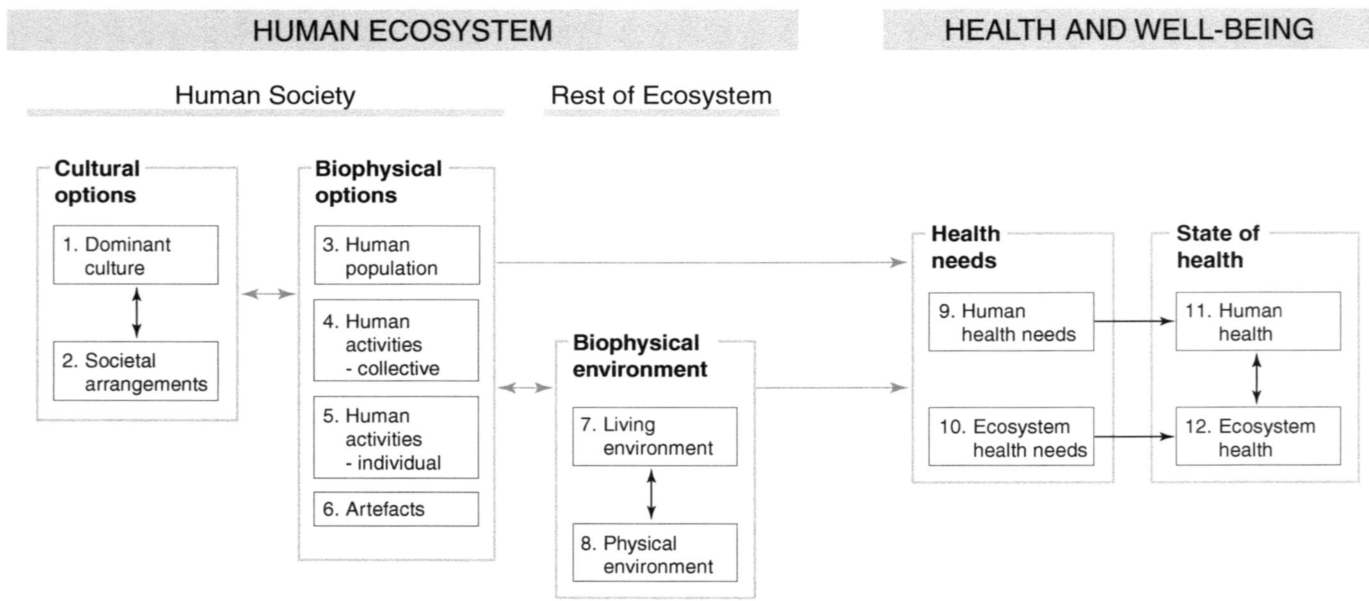

Figure 3.1 Human Ecology Framework.

A qualitative approach was chosen for the research informing this book, in order to explore from first principles what people thought about the conflict they were immersed in, and to seek their ideas of fairness and justice. A semi-structured interview approach allows questions to be asked such as: What do you think was at the heart of the protest? What motivated people to attend the protest? What were the perceived effects of the decision on the community? A semi-structured interview approach with key informant members of the community was therefore chosen as the method which would be most likely to draw out people's ideas about fairness and justice (Braud and Anderson 1998; Wengraf 2001) In a semi-structured interview, the researcher works from an interview guide or set of questions but these are used as a guide only: the researcher has the flexibility to ask questions in a different way or in a different order or use a different subset of questions. The semi-structured interview is akin to unstructured in-depth interviewing in that it allows an in-depth exploration of people's experience and perceptions while still addressing the main interests of the research (Minichiello *et al.* 1995, Wengraf 2001).

Adaptive theory: connecting theory and empirical data

The way in which the empirical part of the research process is connected to the theoretical aspects of the research and the continuing relationship between research practice and theory is the central feature of Layder's (1998: 37) 'adaptive theory'. At the heart of adaptive theory is the continuing engagement between theoretical aspects of the research and the empirical data. The actual process of the research is a continuous cycling between theories and the empirical findings, with each rotation cycle resulting in new explorations, and if needed, new theories. Adaptive theory can be visualised rather like the double helix of RNA and DNA which appears as two revolving strands as depicted in Figure 3.2.

In adaptive theory one of these strands represents theory and the other represents empirical data. Where they come close together, links and temporary or permanent connections can be made. Information can pass from one strand to another in either direction. New strands can emerge where theory and data combine to create new findings, constructs or theories. Some strands join up to become incorporated into a main theme, whereas others remain isolated or unconnected. As the researcher becomes involved with the data, there can be an almost automatic mental cycling between empirical data and theories as new thoughts, connections and discoveries are made. As Layder (1998: 133, 136) puts it: 'Adaptive theorising is an ever present feature of the research process' and 'in any particular research project … there will be a mutual interplay of influences rather than a single directional flow'.

The research underlying this book builds on the Taralga study, described in Chapter 1, in which adaptive theory was used (Gross 2007). The adaptive research outcome from that study became part of the starting point for this

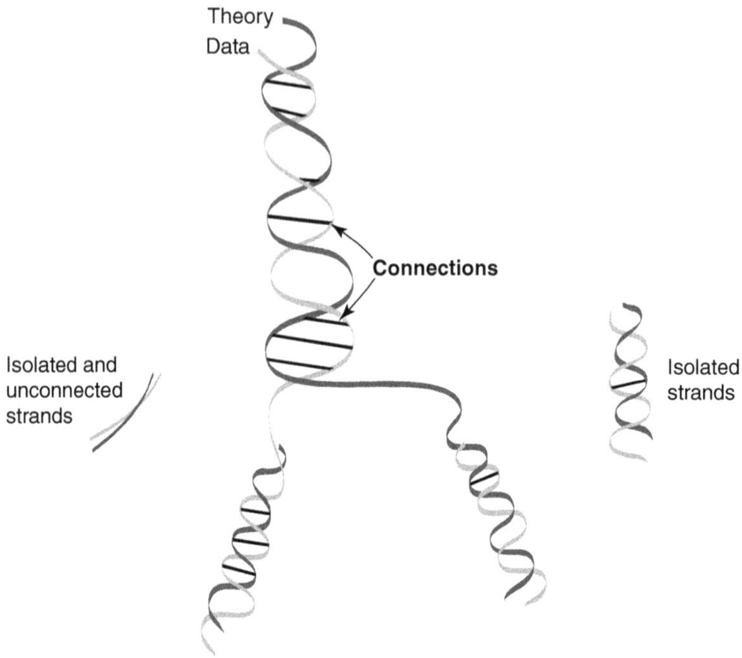

Figure 3.2 Adaptive theory: engagement between theories and empirical data.

research. In the Taralga study an investigative framework was used to explore social conflict. The theories and concepts from that study can be considered 'orienting concepts' (Layder 1998: 101) because they provide background and early direction for the next research project. The justice theories and concepts that are used in the investigative framework are selected from those early orienting concepts, but also include others that emerged in the course of the research.

The iterative cycle of adaptive theory allows the researcher to constantly think about and probe the empirical data in the light of background theories, such as those described in Chapter 2. This gives the researcher freedom to think from the ground up (the empirical data) or down from the more abstract theoretical level. Theories can be examined in the light of a specific social context, lived experience or interviewee perspective. The researcher can choose which theories are relevant to the research area and in turn the empirical data can resonate with and 'speak to' the theories. In summary, adaptive theory, while being a powerful research approach, is also one that naturally fits the exploration of complex social problems, and allows the researcher to work intuitively in the middle ground between theory and data. We now turn to the investigative justice framework which is where theory meets practice.

Table 3.1 The investigative framework

	Section	*Content*
1	*Case study context*	Includes information relevant to the case study drawn from a variety of sources including a historical perspective, biophysical factors, social context and institutional arrangements
2	*Interview questions*	
	Background information and context of interviewees	Occupation, connection with area, membership of groups and community or industry activities
	Concepts of fairness and justice	General understanding of the terms fairness and justice external to a context
	Understanding cause of issue and involvement	Awareness of the issue, attitude to the issue, what is at the heart of the issue, involvement in protests or opposition groups, personal opinions
	Area of interest in issue and reasons for interest (Adapted from Skitka's Accessible Identity Model, 2003)	Exploring how the issue affects the individual and community in terms of material, social and personal impacts
	Elements of process (Based on procedural justice principles described in Chapter 2)	Exploring experience and perceptions of events as the issue unfolded: notification, information, opportunity for participation and voice, opportunity for concerns and issues to be raised and responded to, respectful treatment and level of trust in decision-making authority
	Fairness and justice evaluation of process and outcome	Exploring perceptions of fairness related to how the process was managed, and relating concepts of fairness and justice to the overall issue at the heart of the conflict
	Interviewee suggestions	Exploring what could have been done differently to achieve a more acceptable or better outcome

The investigative framework

The investigative framework, shown in Table 3.1, consists of two sections: a contextual background and a set of semi-structured interview questions. This framework has three primary purposes: to consider a broad range of knowledge sources; to assist in the ordering and structuring of the empirical data collection, and to consider a range of linkages about humans and the environment they live in. The sources of knowledge are drawn from justice theory, the historical context, current institutional arrangements and findings from the local community. The framework also recognises that the context changes even as the research takes place.

The semi-structured interview questions draw on the theories and constructs of justice, particularly Skitka's (2003) Accessible Identity Model and the principles of procedural justice. The questions are designed to sequentially draw out interviewees' perceptions of the social conflict, starting with their general notions of justice and fairness and progressing through the individual elements of the decision-making process. The final questions are concerned with how individuals evaluate the overall process and outcome in terms of fairness and justice and their suggestions for how things could have been done differently. Skitka's Accessible Identity Model was chosen because it recognises that the situation can have a variety of different impacts on a person or group, and that these can be material, social or personal. The Accessible Identity Model also acknowledges that a person needs to have some level of engagement with the situation to think about it in terms of fairness and justice (Skitka 2003). The Accessible Identity Model is used here primarily as a way to explore the different impacts of an action or decision on people affected by that action or decision. It is used as a structured way to discuss impacts with interviewees. Giving interviewees the three categories (material, social and personal) to think about encourages them to think broadly about the impact rather than in terms of the most obvious category.

Fieldwork: establishing empathy and being adaptive

> An interview is both the most ordinary and the most extraordinary of ways you could use to explore someone else's experience – it is as ordinary as conversation, and as amazing as a brilliant film. It offers insights you never expected would come your way.
>
> (Richards 2005: 38)

As Richards describes in the quotation above, a research interview is multifaceted and the researcher must operate on many levels to gain insights, both from the interview experience itself and from what the interviewee is saying. This is important for the research process as well as the research content. How the researcher establishes rapport, how questions are asked and how the researcher adapts the interview process to interviewee responses are all important aspects of the interview (Wengraf 2001; Legard *et al.* 2003). The researcher must also consider maintaining continuity between interviews: for example, asking questions consistently yet recognising that some questions will not be relevant in all interviews. The ability to establish rapport and maintain empathy with the interviewee is vital in research that probes people's inner feelings about fairness and justice. Ideas about fairness tap into people's innermost feelings. It is therefore important to be adaptable when questioning and to think about the interviewee, rather than just about getting answers to questions. Thus the adaptive theory approach is not only applicable to connecting theoretical ideas about justice to practical situations; it is also about being adaptive within the research process itself. This adaptive approach carries forward when analysing the data, developing insights across the different social conflicts and identifying emerging themes.

Interviews were carried out on two case studies of social conflicts following which a third round of interviews was conducted with experts and key informants in the field of water management. As these interviews progressed, findings and emerging themes from one area built on a previous area, and were then also used as input to the next phase of the research. This process of analysis was iterative and in many ways unstructured. This findings interplay is depicted in Figure 3.3

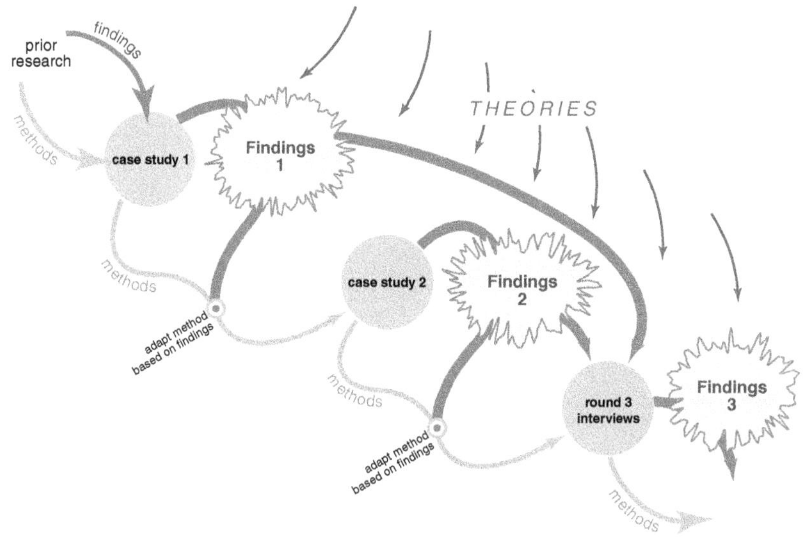

Figure 3.3 Adaptive research: findings interplay.

which shows adaptive research at work. At all times in the research process there was a constant cycling between theories of justice and the empirical data. The data revealed rich insights with a vast array of perspectives: associations with theories virtually leapt out of the data from all angles. The process of analysis was like mining a rich vein of raw materials containing nuggets and slivers of a whole range of different minerals: connections between the data and theories were identified often.

In summary, this chapter demonstrates the importance of developing a research approach that provides a structure for the exploration of complex social problems. It shows the benefits of a holistic and transdisciplinary research approach in which diverse sources of knowledge and linkages between social and ecological systems are organised in a research framework. Equally important is the adaptive nature of this type of approach whereby the researcher can take advantage of findings and new connections between theory and data as they arise. This approach has allowed the people involved in these resource use conflicts to be able to express their views of justice and fairness and how they interact with surrounding social and ecological systems. This approach has created an open conceptual space for the participants to fill, rather than academic theorists, giving us a much greater insight into what actually drives people to make the decisions they make.

4 Voices and stories

Two water conflicts in Australia

This chapter describes the stories of people involved in two water conflicts in Australia. These are the two carrier case studies in which themes of fairness and justice can be explored. This chapter works at the first and second levels of understanding (described in the Introduction and Chapter 1) by providing contextual facts and details of the resource sharing issue, followed by a range of perspectives held by those involved. The first part of the chapter sets the scene for the social conflicts, including the cultural significance of water and river systems, some biophysical features of water in Australia, and a brief outline of the development of water management in two states of Australia, Victoria and New South Wales (NSW). The next two sections tell the stories of the two water conflicts from the perspectives of those involved. These stories are from confidential interviews (see Chapter 3) with a range of people who were either affected by the water conflicts or who were observers. Each section starts with a general description of the circumstances of the conflict. The aim of the chapter is to give voice to the willing or unwilling participants in the conflicts and to show the progression of events through the eyes of those involved.

Water in a dry country

> I love a sunburnt country,
> A land of sweeping plains,
> Of ragged mountain ranges,
> Of droughts and flooding rains.
> I love her far horizons,
> I love her jewel-sea,
> Her beauty and her terror—
> The wide brown land for me!
> (Mackellar 1971: 4)

Australia is a vast continent of great natural beauty, variability and extremes. The second stanza of Dorothea Mackellar's poem *My Country*, published in 1908, with its famous phrase 'Of droughts and flooding rains', encapsulates the feelings of admiration, fear and devotion that water and this dramatic landscape bring to those within it.

In a land of climate extremes it is natural to expect that water conservation and management are important human activities. Indigenous communities developed innovative practical techniques to store and conserve water that lasted thousands of years. They used simple but effective means of permanent pools, traps and dams to catch food such as fish and eels (Lloyd 1988). However, with the arrival of white settlers in the late eighteenth century, water management became large-scale and much more intrusive on the landscape. Whole river systems were affected by the construction of large dams and the diversion of water to enable the development of inland irrigation areas. For indigenous communities and the European settlers who displaced them, water is symbolic and necessary in many aspects of culture, social well-being, traditions, values, mythology and spirituality.

Whole river systems have also become symbols of nationhood. The Snowy River and River Murray, both rising in the Snowy Mountains, are two river systems that have achieved national iconic status, and are a long-standing source of national pride, poetry and literature. But major developments, such as the Snowy Mountains Hydro-Electric Scheme, which in 1967 started diverting 99% of the headwaters of the Snowy River to the inland, have had a major impact, not only on the environment but also on those who live in the local communities (Snowy River Alliance 2013). The Snowy Mountains scheme had its origins in an era in which the primary drivers were population expansion and economic development, and in which society generally accepted the large-scale exploitation of natural resources as one way of achieving societal goals. The twin mantras of 'making the desert bloom' using waters that previously 'ran to waste to the sea' were widely used to justify these grand projects. But the cost was also to the rivers and landscapes. The fight over the diversion of the Snowy River has been long and hard-fought (Snowy River Alliance 2013). Differing perspectives and philosophies about water and how it is perceived, managed and used in different parts of the Australian landscape have left a bitter legacy. The institutional arrangements that have followed these myths and dreams have generally failed to deliver lasting social co-operation around water use. A variable climate makes matters worse when droughts or floods bring extreme hardship and push the limits for people and their ability to cope.

Water: a variable climate and biophysical constraints

Rainfall and water availability in Australia are highly variable across the continent. This variability includes seasonal differences as well as geographical differences: northern tropical areas typically receive the bulk of their rainfall in the summer whereas in the southern areas rainfall can be spread more uniformly across the seasons or can fall predominantly in the winter months (Letcher and Powell 2008). Rainfall is also subject to global climatic influences, such as the El Niño Southern Oscillation phenomenon which gives rise to patterns of extended dry periods, or droughts, that can span several years (Smith 1998). This rainfall variability is a major characteristic of the Murray–Darling Basin (Figure 4.1) in South Eastern Australia in which the two studies are located. The Murray–Darling Basin is a large catchment area, or river basin, that encompasses 14% of the total area of

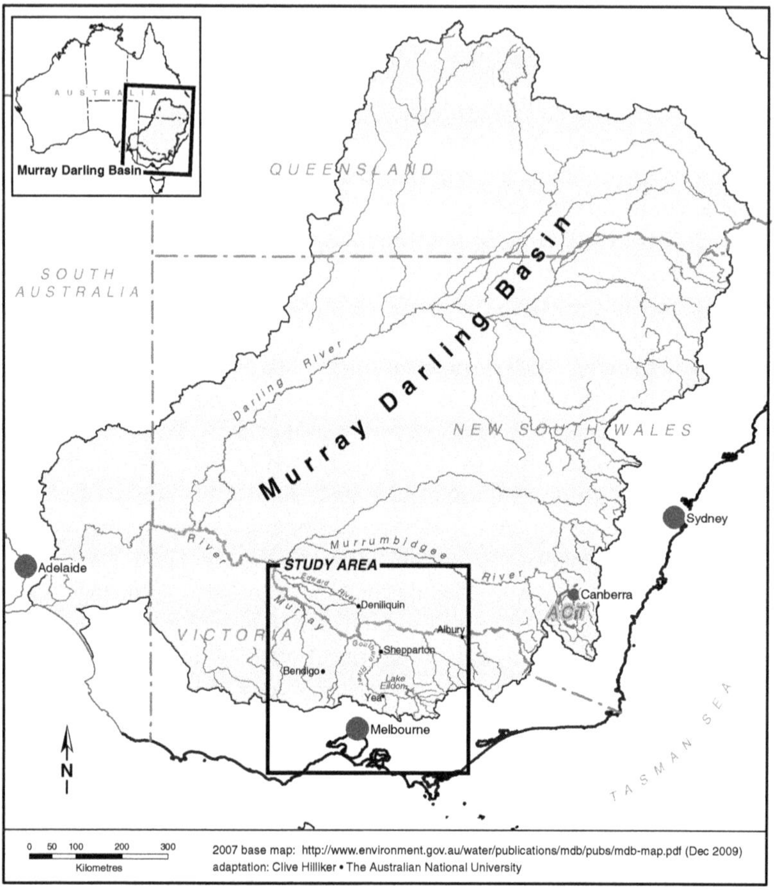

Figure 4.1 The Murray–Darling Basin showing the study area.

Australia and is just over a million square kilometres in size (Murray–Darling Basin Authority 2013).

The Murray–Darling Basin contains two major rivers, the Darling and the Murray (Figure 4.1). The River Darling drains the northern more arid area of the basin, flowing south-west from southern Queensland across the dry north-west of NSW. Its flow pattern matches the rainfall: it is highly variable and ranges from slow-moving floods spreading widely over the flood plain to a mere trickle linking waterholes in the bottom of the river channel. The River Darling joins the River Murray in south-western NSW. By contrast, the River Murray has a more reliable natural flow originating in the higher rainfall area of the Snowy Mountains in the south-east of the Murray–Darling Basin. The 2500 kilometre River Murray marks the border between NSW and Victoria and flows north-westwards into South Australia before turning south to reach the Southern Ocean.

The Great Dividing Range of Australia forms the eastern boundary of the Murray–Darling Basin. It consists of a connected series of mountain ranges and high areas starting in the far north of Queensland and then extending 3500 kilometres along the coastlines of NSW and Victoria until finally meeting the western Victorian plains. It is the south-eastern area of the Great Dividing Range that provides the most rainfall in the Murray–Darling Basin. This area, which includes the Australian Alps, is drained by the River Murray and its tributaries, such as the Murrumbidgee River in NSW and the Goulburn River in Victoria. The south-eastern area, comprising the Upper Murray, the Murrumbidgee and the Goulburn River catchments, accounts for 45% of water runoff despite being only 11% of the Murray–Darling Basin area (Murray–Darling Basin Authority 2013). The two studies are located in this south-eastern area of the Murray–Darling Basin (Figure 4.1), the first taking place in NSW to the north of the River Murray and the second taking place in the north-eastern area of Victoria south of the River Murray.

The Murray–Darling Basin is also well-known for its biodiversity and ecologically significant 'icon sites', such as the Barmah–Millewa Forest, a large 66,000 hectare river red gum forest located in the Murray River floodplain between Deniliquin, Tocumwal and Echuca. The Murray–Darling Basin includes some 30,000 wetlands, of which many are listed under the Ramsar Convention (Murray–Darling Basin Authority 2013). These provide important ecological functions for the area, for example, water filtering, refuges for wildlife and migratory bird breeding grounds. However, much of this natural ecological capital has been put under serious threat as a result of the exploitation of water resources in the last 200 years.

Water in Australia: development and myths

> To a large extent, the history of agriculture in Australia has been characterised by our efforts to turn this dry country with its poor, ancient soils into another Europe.
>
> (Botterill 2003: 199)

Three phases of water development

Since European settlers arrived in Australia in the late 1700s the availability of water for towns, agriculture and industry has been a continuing and predominant concern. Three main phases of water development are generally recognised (Smith 1998; Blackmore 2002), but the lines between these are blurred. In the first phase, pioneering European settlers set about finding and using water for domestic sanitation purposes and developing their livelihoods. A major drought from 1877 to 1881 in Victoria put water provision on the political agenda. Towards the end of this first phase, in the 1880s and 1890s, the first large water infrastructure projects had been launched and the first water legislation in Australia had been enacted (Smith 1998). In the second phase, economic development was the driver for large-scale public works such as storage dams and irrigation infrastructure.

However, tensions emerged between the three states sharing the water of the River Murray. South Australia viewed the river as an important navigation system for river trade. In NSW and Victoria irrigation industries were expanding (Clark 2002). Irrigation agencies responded to calls to increase the rural population by developing compact farming blocks based solely on irrigated agriculture (Smith 1998).

The second phase of infrastructure development continued until well into the second half of the twentieth century. The nineteenth century aspirations, now seen by many as myths, of 'making the desert bloom' by using 'waters which now run to waste' was a primary motivation for the most ambitious infrastructure project of all – the Snowy Mountains Scheme. Waters of the great Snowy River could be diverted west to the dry inland to be put to productive use by irrigators. How this could be achieved was debated from 1885 until 1949 when the final dual-purpose scheme was adopted. The water was to be used both for hydro-electric power generation and irrigation (Lloyd 1988). Whether the scheme's primary purpose was irrigation or hydro-electric power generation was an underlying issue then (Davidson 1969) and remains a discussion point to this day. The scheme was completed in 1974 and was an outstanding engineering success.

In the first and second phases of water use in Australia, people were driven by their need to develop their livelihoods, and governments were motivated by economic development. But agricultural problems such as erosion, rising water tables and salinity became serious issues. Political boundaries were recognised as a hindrance to effective natural resource management, and it became clear that a biophysically based catchment management approach for natural resource management was needed (Blackmore 2002).

The third phase, still current, can be regarded as a response to the problems created in the first two phases (Blackmore 2002) through the initiation of significant reform. The Murray–Darling Basin Commission, established in 1987, put a limit on water diversion in 1997. This is known as the Cap (Dole 2002). The 2004 National Water Initiative sets out a comprehensive national water reform process but also recognises that there are significant challenges and uncertainties in implementing the initiative (Stoeckel and Abrahams 2007).

The development of irrigation in New South Wales and Victoria

> Governments … aim was to use irrigation water to create communities of property-owning, independent, small farmers as a foundation for a democratic society. Large holdings were forbidden and water rights were tied to land titles to prevent the development of water market speculators … the formula worked fairly well for much of the following century.
>
> (Connell *et al.* 2005: 84)

Irrigation development in both NSW and Victoria has taken many twists and turns in response to a constantly shifting set of attitudes, political influences and economic and environmental constraints (Lloyd 1988; Powell 1989). The controversy and conflict that have doggedly pursued this development continue to this day.

According to Musgrave (2008: 36, 40) irrigation started with an 'ill-founded belief in the virtues of small-scale farming' and continued with a struggle between 'forces to retard it' and 'continued advocacy of irrigation … from a community which was reluctant to abandon its yearning to see the desert bloom'. This history has been well recorded by historians, industry experts and academics (for example, Lloyd 1988; Powell 1989; Martin 2005; Musgrave 2008).

The first major milestone was the passing of Victoria's Irrigation Act 1886, whose architect, Alfred Deakin, was convinced of the benefits of irrigation (Musgrave 2008). Deakin had investigated irrigation systems in the United States and he believed that irrigation could benefit Victorian agriculture. His vision included government support to establish the irrigation infrastructure of dams and distribution channels (Musgrave 2008). The Irrigation Act of 1886 transferred rights in natural water to the Crown, ending the so-called 'tyranny' of the riparian law inherited from English law but seen to be inappropriate in the Australian context (Lloyd 1988: 115). NSW followed suit with this transfer of rights although rather later, with the Irrigation Act 1912 (Lloyd 1988).

This transfer of rights allowed irrigation systems to be developed that included major infrastructure works, such as dams for water storage and channels for water distribution. State-controlled bureaucracies to manage this water development were created. Major storages in NSW and Victoria were constructed: in Victoria, Goulburn Weir on the Goulburn River was completed in 1889; Burrinjuck Dam in NSW was completed in 1912; and the first stage of Lake Eildon in Victoria in 1927 (Musgrave 2008).

In 1912, NSW formalised water rights for private irrigators and established the basis for joint water supply schemes and the development of government-owned irrigation districts and areas (Martin 2005). An important principle in the establishment of irrigation districts was that the water right held by an irrigator was to be tied to the land (Martin 2005). As the quotation at the start of this section indicates, this principle held until the water reform process initiated in the latter decades of the century specifically separated the water right from the parcel of land to enable water trading to take place.

The Murray Irrigation District, in which the town of Deniliquin is located, was developed over a 25 year period starting in 1933. Initially water for this irrigation district was to be used to drought-proof dryland pastoral farms and not for the intensive style of irrigation used in the closer settlement areas in other river valleys (Martin 2005). However, this changed as the irrigation industry developed in response to economic growth, and as new crops, such as rice, were introduced. In his summary of water resources development, Musgrave (2008) points out that the completion of the Snowy Mountains Scheme in 1974 and the profitability and expansion of rice cultivation were the two factors that maintained the momentum of the irrigation industry even as questions about its economic viability mounted. The collection and diversion of water by the Snowy Mountains Scheme makes available an average of 1210 gigalitres which is released into the River Murray annually (DNR 2006), with a similar amount being released into the Murrumbidgee River. The additional water from the scheme enabled an expansion of the irrigation areas in NSW, which many believed amounted to a significant subsidy of the irrigation industry because capital costs were not included in charges for irrigation water (Smith 1998).

Water reform and some consequences

> Indeed, the pace of change makes reporting on the current situation akin to hitting a fast-moving target.
>
> (Smith 1998: 273)

By the 1980s environmental and economic concerns over the use of water for irrigation brought a renewed focus on water reform at a state and national level. Langford *et al.* (1999: 1) summarise the problems that precipitated a period of extensive reform in Victoria between 1984 and 1994:

> Unfortunately the lack of financial discipline … left a legacy of irrigation enterprises of low profitability, small farms, financially unviable irrigation authorities, ageing irrigation infrastructure, a large public debt, and environmental degradation through salinity and water logging. Any reform of irrigation would have to overcome this inheritance.

While water development and management are primarily the domain of state governments – which is why different arrangements exist in each state – federal governments have also recognised the need for water reform that can transcend political and geographical boundaries. The 2004 National Water Initiative was put forward as a national framework for water reform that builds on earlier state and federal initiatives (Stoeckel and Abrahams 2007). Key elements of the National Water Initiative include identification of over-allocated water systems and restoring those systems to sustainable levels, modifications to water access entitlements to increase confidence in water property rights and expanding water trade to encourage water to be used for the highest economic return (National Water Commission 2013). This latter element – that water be used to its highest value – is at the heart of the National Water Initiative. Thus water markets with water entitlements that can be permanently traded form the centrepiece of this new national policy. While water trading had already been introduced within the states, for example, temporary trade was introduced in NSW in 1983 and in Victoria in 1987 (Langford *et al.* 1999; Martin 2005), the aim of the National Water Initiative is to introduce a nationally compatible water market.

Attitudes to reforms have varied within and between irrigation communities and government agencies, with some specific reform activities becoming significant points of concern and disagreement. Two areas in the reform process relevant to this study have generated significant discussion and disagreement. The first concerns the way in which 'sleeper and dozer' water licences are handled during the reform process. The second concerns the problem of 'stranded assets' that can occur when water is traded out of a district.

'SLEEPER AND DOZER' WATER LICENCES

The notion of sleeper and dozer water licences is concerned with the degree to which water is used under each water licence. Water users have different requirements for water extraction: some, such as irrigation farmers, use their water allocation to the full, whereas others, such as farmers with a mixed operation, use a partial allocation. In some cases no water is used at all. Sleeper licences fall into this latter category where there is no recorded water use against the licence and the licence is considered inactive. A dozer licence is one in which water is used from time to time but usually not up to the maximum (Martin 2005). In NSW the government reforms in 1995 recognised all of these licences as being a 'right' whereby a holder of a sleeper or dozer licence could sell his or her unused allocation on the market (Martin 2005: 88). Prior to this reform and the onset of trading, irrigators had generally benefited from the fact that some water licence holders did not use their water at all: there was more available in the overall allocation. However, when trading was introduced and sleeper and dozer licence holders were able to sell their water, the overall amount of water used within the system was perceived to have increased (Martin 2005). This was contrary to the overall objective of the reforms – to address the problem of over-allocated systems (Gardner and Bowmer 2007). Rights were now exercised over more water than was actually available.

'STRANDED ASSETS'

The second area of concern resulting from water reform and water trading involves the notion of stranded assets. Stranded assets are recognised as an 'inevitable' consequence of structural change in an industry (Roper *et al.* 2006: v). In an irrigation system the term 'stranded assets' refers to irrigation infrastructure assets that become less utilised and therefore less financially viable as a result of water being traded out of the system (Roper *et al.* 2006). Because irrigation systems were designed in an era when water was tied to the land, the cost of delivery of water and maintenance of the irrigation system were shared equally amongst all water users. With the onset of water trading and the separation of water entitlements from the land, water users could sell their water out of the system, resulting in the remaining costs of delivery and maintenance being shared amongst fewer users. This is the stranded assets problem. Those remaining water users would be financially disadvantaged unless a mechanism was introduced, such as exit fees, to offset the loss of water from the system (Martin 2005; Roper *et al.* 2006). The stranded asset problem is also perceived to have social impacts as well as financial impacts. For example, when water is sold out of a district there are structural and social changes within communities due to the loss of secondary business and trade, such as farm and irrigation supplies.

'MANAGED INVESTMENT SCHEMES'

Water trading has also facilitated the establishment of agricultural enterprises known as managed investment schemes. Managed investment schemes are organisations in which investors contribute to a common enterprise to produce financial gains. In the irrigated agricultural sector, managed investment schemes have developed new irrigation enterprises in areas that were not previously irrigated, in both NSW and Victoria. Managed investment schemes have been criticised for 'buying up farmers' water rights as a tax dodge' (Byrne *et al.* 2006: 1), in part because they are perceived to have received funding through investors seeking investment taxation benefits. Further, such schemes have led to over-investment in some industries, such as viticulture, which has distorted the market, and compounded the stranded asset problem (Byrne *et al.* 2006). Managed investment schemes have been heavily criticised for their impact on agricultural areas, particularly after the financial failure of many of these types of schemes (Locke 2012).

Summary

The water reform programme, including permanent water trading, has been met with a variety of responses, with some irrigation farmers seeing the benefit of water trading and others maintaining strong opposition. In some areas this opposition is deeply held. Byrne *et al.* (2006: 5) record their perspective in a book titled *High and Dry: How Free Trade in Water Will Cripple Australian Agriculture.* The following extract provides an example:

> What has changed to cause governments to unbundle 80 years of successful, scientific-based agricultural rules, property and water rights, neglecting enormous, accumulated institutional knowledge, to now allow the trade of water from farms to cities, and among irrigation regions?

The move away from long-standing administrative arrangements for water sharing to open water markets has resulted in a variety of consequences, some of which were anticipated and many of which were not. However, it is clear that water development in Australia is still clouded with disagreement and acrimony on many sides.

The New South Wales carry-over water study

The first case study is located in the state of NSW in south-eastern Australia. The study centres on the town of Deniliquin which is the hub of a rural community in the Murray Irrigation District that depends upon irrigation water for its social and economic well-being (Figure 4.2). In October 2006 the NSW government unexpectedly cut the water allocation during an extended period of drought. The irrigation community was taken by surprise. Irrigators had been led to believe that this water allocation was secure for two main reasons. First, this water allocation was part of a specifically developed and recognised risk management strategy; and second, because it was carried over from the water allocation of the previous year, so in theory the water should be available, held in the dams and water storages of the irrigation system. A further cut to the water allocation took place in November of the same year. Irrigators and members of the community voiced their protest

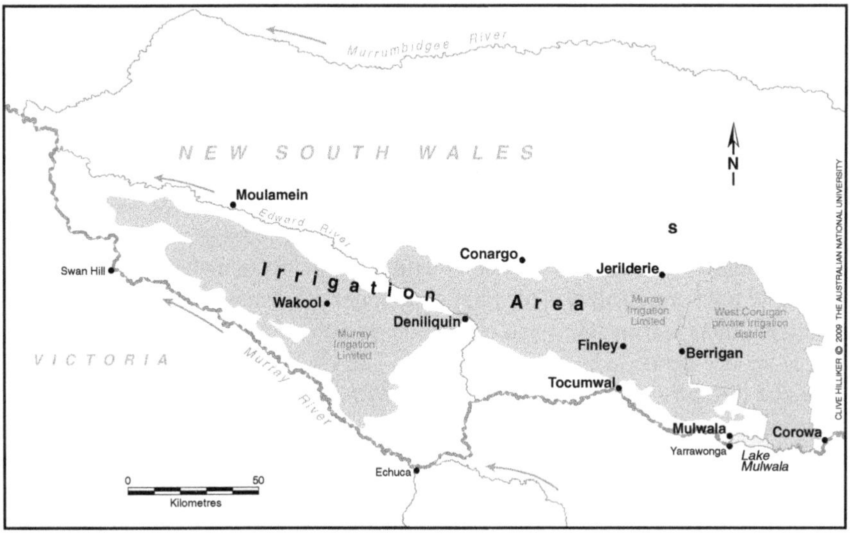

Figure 4.2 New South Wales study area.

over these cutbacks by attending a rally in the town of Deniliquin on 15 December 2006. It was clear from the relatively large number of protesters that this was a current and important issue to the local community: the protest had been reported in the *Sydney Morning Herald*, a metropolitan newspaper, with the catching headline 'Water thieves leave farmers parched' (Lewis 2006).

At the time of the study the responsible agency for water management in NSW was known as the Department of Natural Resources (DNR). The water allocation system in NSW recognises different water entitlements according to the level of security of the supply. The two main categories are high security water (for towns, stock and domestic supplies and irrigation of permanent plantings, such as horticulture and viticulture) and general security water (for annual crops and pasture). An annual allocation process determines how much water is available in each of these categories according to the volume of water calculated to be available in the River Murray system. A precise formula is used to calculate the 'announced allocation' which takes into account water in the system at the time and an estimation of future inflows for the year. In 2006 the NSW approach to water management was described in a document, *Background to Water Management in the NSW Murray and lower Murray–Darling River Systems* (DNR 2006). An objective of the allocation process was to give high reliability for high security users (with their permanent plantings) and an expectation for general security allocations to reach 70% of their allocation in 87% of years. In one year out of 100 general security would not rise above 10% of allocation (DNR 2006). This complex system of water management was designed to act as a buffer against variability in a region where widespread droughts occur with some regularity.

At the time of the study the allocation policy in NSW was to maximise the water available to irrigators each year, leaving minimum water reserves for the following year. This was in contrast to the allocation policy in Victoria, which took a more conservative approach by reserving water for the following year. The NSW approach was adopted in consultation with industry water user groups over many years. It was designed to put the decision making as to how much water is used at the individual water user level. Individuals therefore had the opportunity to use the water, trade the water, or carry some of the water over to the next season (DNR 2006). This ability to carry the water over to the next season was a risk management tool specifically developed to enable individual irrigators to manage their own risk regarding water availability. This carry-over water risk management tool was introduced in 1998 (Martin 2005) and enabled up to 50% of water allocated to an individual licence holder to be carried over from one year to the next. It is important to note that the carry-over water was not actually physically retained in the storages, but is accounted for as an entitlement.

The hierarchy for the allocation priority set out by the government determined that carry-over water from the previous year was higher up the ladder than high security entitlements that, in turn, were higher than general security entitlements. This was based on the rationale that carry-over water was an unused allocation from the previous year (DNR 2006). Irrigators were also able to purchase additional water from other irrigators through a trading scheme.

In the allocation year of 2006–07 the overall water allocation was announced according to procedure in July 2006. However, anticipated seasonal rainfall did not take place and the NSW state government found itself facing widespread severe drought and record low inflows into the water storages. On 15 October 2006 a government media release advised that cutbacks to the current water allocation would take place immediately. This was announced without prior warning to the irrigation community. A second cutback was announced on 10 November 2006, but this was preceded by discussions with irrigation industry groups. The first cutback reduced the allocation by 20% and the second by a further 32%. The cutbacks applied to any water held on water users' water accounts and included carry-over water and water that had been purchased through the water trading scheme. In November the NSW Government explained, in a published fact sheet, why the cuts had taken place. The primary reason was that the inflows into the water storages had been less than ever recorded, due to the low rainfall. Water availability for each season was calculated on a number of factors including an assumption on the minimum inflow that would occur each season. The inflows in this season were below the previously recorded minimum inflows. Thus the cuts took place because the water was not available in the system. The government advised irrigators that the water would be replaced when water became available.

The irrigation community protested on 15 December 2006. The government refused irrigation industry calls for targeted compensation regarding the water cutbacks, but did respond to irrigators' financial hardship. An Extraordinary Assistance Package worth A$20 million was announced by the NSW government in January 2007 in which irrigators had to demonstrate financial hardship to access up to A$50,000. This assistance package was subsequently amended in March 2007 to make the application process simpler for irrigators.

The heart of the protest

This section describes people's perspectives about what they thought was at the heart of the protest that took place in Deniliquin on 15 December 2006. With over 2000 people in attendance (from a region of approximately 8000 people), it was a significant event for the community.

Taking away an 'asset' with no compensation

A fundamental issue for many people was that the water held in people's water accounts (which included carry-over water and purchased water) had been taken away by the government with no prior warning and no compensation. This water had been considered to be the equivalent of a property right or asset, but, by its action, the government had shown no recognition of irrigator rights or ownership of this perceived asset. One irrigation company employee described it this way: 'The heart of it is that the government took this action, weeks went by and they did not do anything regarding compensation'. For many irrigators the loss of this water became a financial problem because they either had to buy more water or find alternative sources of feed for stock. This financial impact was a primary reason for the protest because the impacts of the two cutbacks were apparently not recognised by the government. The protest gave people the opportunity to express their frustration in public at this lack of recognition of either the property right or the negative impact on farming businesses. As one Deniliquin business professional described it: 'A third party had come into your territory and taken away your right, without any discussion or warning, so the heart of it is that it brings into question what it means to have a right'.

Impact of the loss of financial resources on irrigators

Many also thought the impact of the loss of financial resources on irrigators was a major reason for the protest. As one irrigator put it: 'There was frustration and a lot of it would have been desperation because people had put drought plans in place and these programmes were shattered on that day with little warning or no warning and no recompense'. Another reason for the protest was the perceived irony that the government action hit at the heart of what the carry-over water management tool was designed to do. The fact that the carry-over water was a risk management tool to use in times of drought, which some irrigators had come to rely on, was an additional frustration. As one irrigator commented: 'They have just basically hit at the whole reason that carry over is there for'. Another Deniliquin business owner said she disagreed with the government action because farmers had shown responsible farming practices and had been trying to work with the government and accept changes. Then action by the government was taken with 'no consultation and no real recognition of impact'.

The way people were treated

For many people the issue at the heart of the protest was the way the irrigators had been treated and the way the government had made the cuts without prior consultation or notification. One irrigation farmer was concerned with the process of how the decision had been made: 'I wanted the focus to be on the unfairness of how it happened, not on the fact that the department appears to have made a mistake'. Another thought that irrigators and the community 'were effectively treated with contempt'. Many members of the community who were not directly affected by the action were supportive of the protest because they disagreed with *the way* the government action had been undertaken, not why it was done. As one town business owner commented: 'If there is no water there is no water but don't take it away from us like they did and then ignore us … this could push people over the edge'.

For one community leader the 'lack of accountability' was the main issue at the heart of the protest because the government did not acknowledge either the problem or why the problem had occurred and 'did not want to take fiscal responsibility for their actions'. Therefore in his opinion the government was trying to push the burden on to the irrigation community, rather than accepting some degree of responsibility for the carry-over dilemma: 'We believed they were breaching many tenets of their water regime … they were expecting the irrigators to bear the full cost of their department's incompetence'. The main point was that, in his opinion, the government had been incompetent because they should have known *earlier* that not enough water would be available, in which case cutbacks could have been made differently, and people would have been able to make other arrangements.

Blame, lashing out or an ill-advised protest?

There were differing viewpoints about the heart of the protest. One person thought that the protest was 'ill-advised' because it seemed to be blaming the government for the lack of water, whereas the reality was that rainfall was insufficient and this was a time of severe drought. Another person thought the protest was to 'make a big song and dance about it and give people a reason to kick the government'. An irrigation company employee thought that in the context of drought it was 'understandable that people were going to lash out'. As he put it: 'The people are really hurting and they just saw this as an opportunity to kick back and they did'. He thought the irrigators needed to blame somebody and 'that is generally the people who control the water'. While he understood the reason for the protest, he also thought the irrigation leaders had been 'a bit unfair' in their reaction, by organising the protest. He explained this as being pressure from the members of the irrigation associations 'to *do* something'.

Impact of the cutbacks

Individuals and groups within the community were affected by the carry-over water cutbacks in different ways. People described how the cutbacks had impacted them in three main areas: material, social and personal (as outlined in the investigative framework in Chapter 3). Material interest was explained as affecting a person's livelihood or financial well-being; social as affecting the social structure of the community, such as relationships; and personal as affecting a person's core beliefs or values.

Material impacts on irrigation farmers

The carry-over water cutbacks did not affect all irrigation farmers uniformly. How each irrigation farmer was affected depended on how much water had been carried over from the season before, how much had been purchased or sold from last season's allocation, and how much water the farmer had used at the time the cutbacks were announced. Some had lost a great deal of water whereas others had lost a small amount. The people who had lost a smaller amount could be more distressed than those who had lost more and some were 'desperate to get some money back'.

In discussing the different types of impact, many irrigators talked about the impact on the whole farming community as much as the impact on their own business operation. Those who had experienced minimal impact typically expressed concerns for others who they knew were seriously affected by the cutbacks. Many talked about the combined effects of the material and social impacts, for example, by talking about a neighbour's predicament and then what they foresaw as a long-term consequence on the community in general. Irrigators who were minimally affected by the carry-over water cutbacks had either used the water prior to the cutbacks or had sold it on the market earlier. Others relied on the carry-over water much more. One farmer described the chain of events and escalating costs in losing the water and having to purchase feed for his livestock, which incurred extra debt that he had not planned for. Another described the 'mental pressure' of continually having to revise his decisions: 'It knocks you around with your thinking … and what you notice is you are just not doing anything and you're not being productive'.

Many rice farmers also suffered from significant losses as a result of the carry-over cutbacks. Rice farmers describe their decision-making window for planting their rice crop as being between 2nd October and 10th October, with many making a decision about how much to plant in the last week of September. Preparation includes cultivating the land and adding fertiliser, seed and water. One rice grower described how he had 400 acres of rice 'watered up' at the time of the first cutback on the 15 October. The impact of the cutback was that he stopped watering 150 acres of rice, which in effect let the crop and preparation go to waste.

Material impacts on other stakeholders in the community

In the words of one community leader 'there is nobody in Deniliquin that is not going to be impacted … because we are all totally dependent on water'. One business community leader explained how the local business community was dependent on the well-being of the irrigation farmers, who were the primary income generators for the area. Their expenditure on farm and domestic supplies and support services supported the local economy. While many people acknowledged that the drought was the primary reason for the downturn in the prosperity of the irrigation industry, many thought that the cutbacks to the carry-over water were also significant and similar to the 'straw that broke the camel's back'. A teacher described the indirect impact:

> Every community member will be affected in a material way. Water in our area is the absolute lifeblood to continued prosperity. It does not matter what occupation you follow, whether it is on the land or in business or as a public servant.

Social impacts: a community has to feel good

A community leader summed up the social issue by saying that 'a community has to feel good'. Many people talked about their concern for the well-being of the community in the face of the continuing drought and dependency on the viability of the irrigation industry. The carry-over cutbacks were seen as a significant blow to the community's overall confidence and 'faith in the region', as one community leader put it. Two people involved with the rural financial counselling service commented on the large numbers of irrigators seeking assistance, many for the first time. One described the extreme distress they witnessed in the counselling service: 'Men will just start crying'. The social worker in the area was described as being 'just absolutely flooded, inundated … cannot cope with it'. An irrigation company employee said: 'You cannot go anywhere without people talking about water and what the government has done and how terrible it is … it has undermined the confidence of the community … it undermines people's confidence in the water industry'. An accountant said of his clients: 'It has dented a lot of people's confidence and I have seen depression, and that has rocked me a bit, because it has surprised me who has got it and who is struggling'.

A retired dairy farmer commenting on the stress faced by many irrigators said that he 'could see it in their eyes as they walk around town' and was keeping an eye on people that he was worried about. He suggested that social breakdown would be inevitable, with people being unable to pay their bills and the resulting friction causing relationship breakdowns: 'That is when the family situations start to break down too, because they are under such enormous pressure … this is all an area that we do not know about yet. But it is scary stuff'. Some people commented on the friction and divisions within the community that had appeared since the carry over cutbacks. One irrigator talked about 'backstabbing comments' he had received because he was able to go out and buy more water. Water was available to purchase from other irrigators who would make more money by selling their water than using it themselves, due to higher water prices resulting from the drought. Another resident talked about his daughter at school being abused verbally because of her mother's occupation in a government agency, and her perceived role in the implementation of the cutbacks.

Personal impacts: reduced belief in the processes of government

Many people talked about the social and personal impacts as being combined or intertwined. Some became quite emotional, even close to tears, as they talked about the personal impact on themselves or on friends and neighbours. Some were willing to talk about these sensitive issues, whereas others touched briefly on the topic and then moved on quickly. Several avoided talking about their own personal experience preferring to talk in more general terms about the community. Some were philosophical about the issue. For example, one irrigation farmer described it as 'just another hurdle ... it's all part of farming really ... so you battle on'. Others talked about their anger. An irrigator who had been involved in discussions with the government said that 'personally, it did start to get to me ... the huge amount of uncertainty. Because of their incompetence I was indignant and I was outraged'.

Many people were disappointed and unhappy with the way they had been treated. Some described this as a severe disillusionment resulting in loss of confidence in the government and its ability to work with the community. Many felt that they had not been treated with respect and were not valued, either as irrigators or as producers of food. This went to the heart of their loss of belief in the overall system of government. One irrigator said that the episode had 'reduced my belief in the processes of good government'.

A common theme from irrigators was that this was yet another personal blow to them in the way that they are viewed by society. One vegetable grower suggested that 'we are held at the lowest level ... when it comes to water use'. He recounted how he found it ironic that it was reported in the news that 'Mr Howard is giving money to farmers to stop them wasting water' referring to the A$10 billion plan put forward at that time by the then Prime Minister, John Howard.

Another recurring theme from irrigators and business people was the erosion of community confidence as a result of this action. One business owner commented: 'I put confidence under a personal banner. We are struggling to keep the confidence level up with all these changes ... we need some sort of belief in the future'. He talked about his own personal endeavours to maintain community cohesion and help those in need. He had organised social events, offering free food and entertainment, to bring farmers and their families into town so that contact could be maintained. He described how committed he was to serving the community. His belief in a viable community was an important part of his value system. He talked about the impact of the 'intellect drain' when government and research organisations and staff had been relocated from country areas to cities. One impact was less 'debate at our local level' which affected decision making by government agencies who were less connected to the area and consequently had little understanding of local concerns. Actions such as the carry-over cutback widened the gap and 'devalues our confidence in the bureaucracy'.

Support for irrigators but some other perspectives

While there was overall community support for the irrigators affected by the water cutbacks, other related topics were raised in the discussions. These included how well people in irrigation communities understand specific water allocation arrangements; the bigger picture of water sharing in agricultural production; relations within the community; and relations between the community and government agencies.

One theme concerned how well people understood water allocation in general and to what degree they understood why the carry-over water cutbacks had taken place. Several people suggested that irrigators did not have a good knowledge of how the water allocation system worked. Some thought that irrigators lacked understanding and knowledge about water allocation, and that this adversely affected relationships between irrigators, irrigation companies and the government agencies responsible for water allocation.

An accountant described how the irrigation industry had undergone a lot of change and 'older people struggle with picking up the change'. Also, water had been 'cheap and plentiful' until the recent drought and water reform within the last 10 years, so people had not felt the need to develop a detailed understanding of water allocation policy. With the large number of organisations involved with water allocation, at the local, state and federal level, with multiple sources of information, it was difficult for irrigators to get a good understanding of this complex topic.

This lack of understanding was confirmed by an irrigation community leader: 'A lot of folks just don't get it'. He described efforts to explain to irrigators how the allocation system worked. These included the use of social functions and written material. The Southern Riverina Irrigators had also commissioned a book to describe the background of water policy on the Murray River. The book, *Water Policy History on the Murray River*, was published in 2005 (Martin, 2005).

The bigger picture of water allocation

A dryland farmer and conservationist, who was not directly affected by the water cutbacks, took a broader perspective of the problems facing the irrigation industry and environment. In his opinion the privatisation of water infrastructure, ostensibly in part to 'be free of inefficient government' had brought many problems to light: it was now the landholders who were responsible, not the government. He thought that they had been 'sold a pup' because the system had been more secure under government control while it was a 'socialised' system and the government had kept 'the whole thing propped up', but now the inefficiencies in the irrigation delivery system had become evident. He thought that an opportunity had been missed 15 or 20 years ago when the over-allocation of water was recognised. Stronger decisions could have been taken at that time to reduce water allocations. In his view the irrigation industry had not faced up to the fact that it was 'living a lie' due to over-allocation and not putting away for 'the bad times'. These concerns were echoed by an irrigation company employee who thought that the irrigation industry was 'fighting a battle of reducing resource'. Irrigators needed to understand water availability and risks. A future challenge would be for irrigators to take on their own risk with respect to water. He thought this would be difficult for the industry: 'Farmers want somebody else to take the risk because there are enough risks in their own business without adding the risk of that one [water allocation]'.

Relations between rural communities and government agencies

A community leader on rural issues described how government planning often seemed to be oriented around a desired outcome. Her experience of working with a government agency on floodplain management led her to believe that processes would be 'manipulated' to achieve a preordained outcome: 'We as community just feel that we are part of the process so they can tick off the box'. In her long experience of community consultation within natural resource management, she felt that there is little 'genuine' consultation and that governments repeatedly fail to engage people in communities and take 'the people with them'. In her opinion a key ingredient is to have 'community willingness' in a consultation rather than 'an imposed process'. Several people commented on problems that they had experienced working on natural resource management committees. A conservationist described a five year planning exercise in which he had taken part. He described his frustration when the same people repeatedly raised the same issues: 'I got sick of going to these meetings. I got sick of arguing about the same issues meeting after meeting and getting nowhere'. As a result he became 'burned out' and would not get involved in committees or community groups. In his opinion the biggest issue in natural resource management was the 'lack of ecological knowledge in the broader community on how systems work, whether they be rivers, native vegetation or wetlands'.

Relations within the community and community voice

While most of the criticism regarding the carry-over water issue was directed at government agencies, there were also problems with multiple voices representing different aspects of the community to the outside world.

That there were several different groups, such as the Southern Riverina Irrigators, the Drought Leaders Forum and the Murray Valley Community Action Group, was an indication that different groups felt the need to express their concerns in different ways. However, multiple voices also raised difficulties. A Deniliquin business leader pointed out the difficulties with 'getting the message across'. The need for 'one voice on water to government' was compounded with the privatisation of the irrigation infrastructure and the formation of Murray Irrigation Limited. With the privatisation, she felt the government response to community representation through Murray Irrigation Limited was 'you are just looking after your own backyard'. For this reason the Murray Valley Community Action Group became a voice in an effort to explain how government policies impacted the broader community. There were other interests besides self-interest. But one of the problems of multiple organisations was the danger of 'mixed messages' and confusion for the government because 'there are so many varying opinions as to what is the real issue'. Despite these initiatives, the community voice had not been heard and it seemed to this business leader that there was a 'lack of interaction between the decision-makers and even local government or business representative bodies'.

Summary: impact on the whole community

While the primary issue which sparked the protest was a government action that was widely perceived to be unjust, these narratives show that there were also indirect social and personal consequences. The broader community showed its support for those irrigators affected by the cutbacks, and there was recognition that the indirect effects of the cutbacks were important to the community as a whole. Although the cutbacks must be seen in the context of the drought, which was the main cause of the hardship facing many irrigators, the cutbacks were also important in the context of the relationship between the government and the irrigation community. The erosion of confidence in government as a result of the decision being taken with no prior warning or consultation had a serious impact on the community's perception of its own viability for the future.

The Victoria pipeline study

The second case study is located in the Australian state of Victoria. In 2007 that state government proposed a 75 kilometre pipeline, which became known as the North South Pipeline, to take water from the state's north to the south for use by people in the capital, Melbourne. The rationale was that Melbourne could run out of water by 2010 if drought conditions persisted. This water diversion was part of a larger government project that would fund major upgrades to reduce water losses in Victoria's ageing irrigation infrastructure in the northern area of the state. This was known as the Food Bowl Modernisation Project. In return a trade-off arrangement would share the saved water three ways: a third for Melbourne, a third for irrigators and a third for the environment. However, the project generated significant opposition. A grassroots protest movement, known as Plug the Pipe, raised objections, not only to the pipeline, but also to the rationale on which the whole project was based. Protest rallies were held in 2008 in rural towns and in Melbourne. A metropolitan newspaper article titled 'Pipeline opponents "quasi-terrorists"' described an episode in which insults were traded in a Victorian Parliamentary debate (Rood 2007).

The Victoria pipeline study centres around two locations: Shepparton and irrigation areas in the northern area of the state, and Yea in the central area (Figure 4.3). Shepparton is the regional hub for irrigation areas in the Goulburn–Murray Water Region of northern Victoria. It was established as a crossing point of the Goulburn River in the 1850s and has grown to a population of approximately 38,000. The township of Yea was settled close to the Goulburn River in the late 1850s as a farming and timber community. At the time of the case study the population was approximately 1000 and the Yea area was primarily a farming locality with some additional local tourism enterprises.

The Victoria pipeline study is concerned with two water infrastructure projects initiated by the Victorian government: the Food Bowl Modernisation Project and the North South Pipeline. The Food Bowl Modernisation Project was an initiative to upgrade irrigation infrastructure across the irrigation areas in the Goulburn–Murray

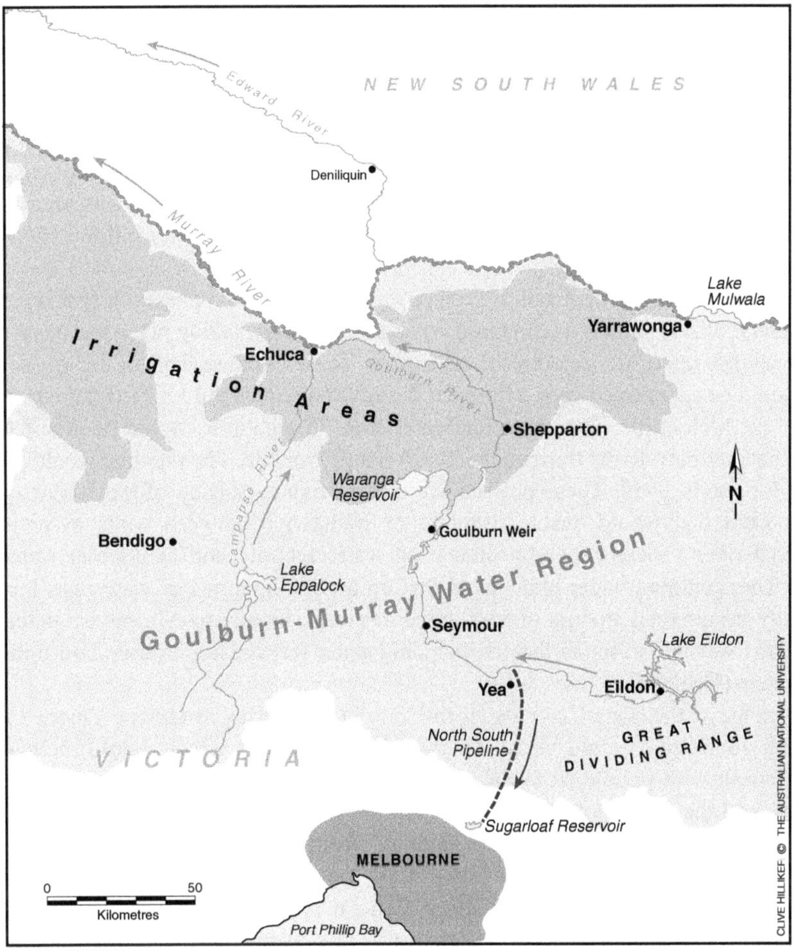

Figure 4.3 Victoria study area.

Water Region (Figure 4.3) in order to save water lost in transmission. The North South Pipeline is a 75 kilometre pipeline that takes a share of the water saved in the irrigation upgrade from the Goulburn River near Yea to the Sugarloaf Reservoir just north of Melbourne (Figure 4.3). Water that was saved would be held in Lake Eildon, upstream from the town of Yea. A pumping station on the Goulburn River would divert the water through the pipeline to Melbourne.

These two projects were developed by the Department of Sustainability and Environment (DSE), a Victorian government agency which carried out water planning for the state and provided advice to the Victorian government. In 2004 the Victorian government published its plan for water security in the state (DSE 2004), and in June 2007 published the next phase: *Our Water Our Future: The Next Stage of the Government's Water Plan* (DSE 2007). This plan outlined an investment of A$4.9 billion in water infrastructure projects and described the Food Bowl Modernisation Project and North South Pipeline. The context for this plan was the long-standing drought of over 10 years and the low levels of Victoria's water storages, which had resulted in widespread water restrictions. In addition the plan outlined the impact of climate change and the record low inflows to Melbourne's storages, which indicated that a 'step-change' in the region's climate may have already taken place (DSE 2007). This plan, published in June 2007, was seen as an emergency response to the lack of rainfall and record low water inflows (DSE 2007; Auditor-General 2008).

The Food Bowl Modernisation Project was planned in two phases: a first stage investment of A$1 billion would build on upgrades already taking place and enable water savings up to 225 gigalitres to take place. These initial savings of 225 gigalitres would be split three ways: a third for the environment, a third for irrigators and a third for Melbourne. The water for Melbourne, 75 gigalitres, would be diverted from the Goulburn River through the North South Pipeline. The pipeline would be ready for use in 2010. These projects were part of an expansion of the Victorian Water Grid that would enable water to be transferred between water systems (regional river valleys), thereby increasing water security and facilitating water trade. The Victorian water plan stated that up to 900 gigalitres of water was lost annually from a total amount of 3500 gigalitres in the Goulburn–Murray irrigation area. This was due to many factors including water leakage and evaporation from the system (DSE 2007).

To achieve the water savings in the Goulburn–Murray Irrigation District a steering committee would be set up to guide the project which would include consultation with people from the community including local councils, interest groups, and the Food Bowl Alliance. The plan also announced that work would begin immediately to develop the pipeline from the Goulburn River to the Sugarloaf Reservoir (DSE 2007).

In April 2008 the Victorian Auditor-General published a report which was critical of aspects of the Victorian government's water plan (Auditor-General 2008). The criticism centred on two areas: 'minimal stakeholder consultation' and 'inadequate levels of rigour applied to estimate the costs, benefits and risks of some of the key component projects' (Auditor-General 2008: 2). While the report acknowledged that the recent water plan was an emergency response to the lowest recorded inflows to water storages in 2006, it also concluded:

> It is incumbent on the government to provide full, accurate and timely information on its financial commitments and projects put before the community. The Victorian water plan did not provide this information. There were widely varying levels of rigour around the plan's costs and expected water savings benefits. The documentation did not explain this. This is essential information, especially when an emergency situation requires streamlined processes.
>
> (Auditor-General 2008: 2)

The report outlined 10 recommendations including one that a detailed analysis of the water savings estimates and costs of the Food Bowl Modernisation Project should be published.

The heart of the conflict: a realistic deal or an unjustified trade-off?

This section describes a range of affected people's perspectives of the North South Pipeline and Food Bowl Modernisation Project.

Yea district perspectives: pipeline construction and water diverted to the south

The most frequently cited reason for the opposition to the pipeline in the Yea district was that it was 'wrong to take water from a dry system to a wetter system'. This was because the water catchment area from which the water would be taken was perceived to be drier and generally receive less annual rainfall than the Melbourne area to which the water would be diverted. With Lake Eildon (Figure 4.3) at 23% of storage capacity, many people said it was a 'ridiculous idea' and 'there isn't any water to take!' One retired school teacher said she thought the pipeline 'will be seen as a huge folly', because, while she was not opposed to it in principle, she thought that in practice 'this one river is having to do an awful lot in that we are now providing water to Melbourne … and Bendigo'. Many thought that the water was needed by irrigators further downstream and by the Goulburn and Murray River systems themselves. This strong moral position about diverting water away from the natural river system, itself in the grip of a long drought, was a key part of the opposition in the Yea area. Also included was the question of where and to whom the water belonged. The pipeline was perceived to be taking water from one group of users, who needed the water, to benefit another group of users who had other options. Many thought that other these options for Melbourne had not been adequately considered, such as storm water harvesting, rainwater tanks to provide household drinking water, and additional recycling of waste water.

Environmental concerns were frequently raised as reasons for opposing the water diversion. A number of people referred to a recent report concerning the ecological condition of rivers in Victoria, in which the Goulburn River was listed as being in a seriously degraded condition. This was in addition to the critical state of the River Murray at the mouth of the Murray in South Australia and potential acidification of the lower lakes due to lack of water. Such environmental reasons were frequently expressed in relation to why water should not be diverted out of the Murray–Darling Basin.

All of the landholders who were advised that the pipeline would cross their land gave a variety of reasons for their opposition to the pipeline. None of them gave the construction of the pipeline on their land as the principal reason for their opposition. They were all opposed to taking water: first, because there was little water to take; second, because it was needed by irrigators and the river system itself; and third, because Melbourne had other viable options for water, such as storm water harvesting, whereas this area did not. They were extremely dissatisfied with the lack of consultation about the pipeline and how the authorities had dealt with them. All were concerned about the impact of the pipeline construction on their land and farming operations, and felt that the pipeline had been 'imposed' on them. As one landholder put it: 'The whole process I find mind-boggling and absolutely ridiculous'. For these landholders the lack of information and lack of response to their specific questions was a major issue.

A farmer associated with the opposition movement, Plug the Pipe, described how people had become increasingly angry at the way the government was going about the project. This included the pipeline construction process, the environmental assessment and an overall lack of 'due and proper process'. The heart of the issue had changed: at the outset it was a 'flawed project' but this had grown into a complete dissatisfaction with the way project was being conducted.

In the upper catchment of the Goulburn River people were concerned that sending water to Melbourne would reduce the security of water for businesses in the Goulburn Valley and Lake Eildon area. Tourism based on recreational activities such as fishing and boating on Lake Eildon was a major source of income for the area. One resident of the area was concerned that once the pipeline was built there would be little to stop large industrial organisations from the Melbourne area purchasing additional water rights, which would mean more than the currently proposed amount of 75 gigalitres per year being extracted. This presented a future threat to water availability in the region. A resident of the area with an engineering background was most concerned about the lack of discussion and planning around the construction of the pipeline. He thought it could have been designed as a two-way pipe which would have allowed water to move in both directions. He criticised the government for being in too much of a hurry: such large-scale infrastructure projects should be carefully planned, and include thorough technical, environmental and social aspects. His concern was that this was a big pipeline being rushed through to meet an 'artificial' timeline of 2010, which was more about politics than real needs. He contrasted this project with the Snowy Hydro Scheme, which had been meticulously planned and was generally perceived as extremely successful.

Two local government councillors commented on the Plug the Pipe opposition movement and its reasons for protesting. One councillor suggested, rather critically, that the opposition movement had 'lost sight' of the original central issue, and it was now 'the government they are against'. The other local government councillor suggested that the central issue for the opposition movement was in fact now a complex set of issues: taking the water; removing it from the catchment; taking the water before the savings have proven to be there; not knowing the precise details of Melbourne's entitlement to the water; the river health perspective; the irrigator dilemma of paying for the water but not receiving the water; issues of equity and fairness over who gets the water and for what purpose; the impact on tourism; and the impact on landowners whose land was being disturbed. For this councillor the central issue from her personal perspective was that it was bad water policy to take water over the dividing range and a lost opportunity for Melbourne to learn how to become a sustainable city.

While many people in the Yea area were opposed to the Food Bowl Modernisation Project and the North South Pipeline, there were others who described themselves as being 'neutral' or 'neutral to in favour' of the proposal. One academic with a background in environmental management thought that the community was 'a little bit hypocritical' in its approach to water. For example, he described how farmers had rushed to put in farm dams to beat state government restrictions in the late 1990s. He said 'we are all guilty of not using our water resources effectively', and further: 'it is hypocritical to be blaming our government, who we elected, to be taking action to improve the security of supply, for our state's most important economic centre: Melbourne'. A retired school teacher went further in his criticism of local opposition, describing the protesters as NIMBYs. He thought the local people were unrealistic and that one of the underlying reasons for the protest was that people did not want change in the area. Claiming the water as 'their water' he thought was wrong. He explained that the Eildon dam was not built for irrigation: in his view it was built for flood mitigation. The proposal to share water savings three ways seemed to be 'fair enough, that sounds reasonable to me', but he had some concerns that with climate change the rainfall may diminish substantially in the area, in which case the pipeline may not prove to be useful.

Two residents of the town of Yea said that they had a neutral attitude to the project. A retired schoolteacher, who had previously been an irrigator in the Murray irrigation area in the north of the state, said that she was originally against the idea, but now could see both sides, and saw herself as a 'fence sitter'. One of the reasons for her neutral attitude was that she did not like the way that Plug the Pipe had gone about the protest, although she thought that there should be other ways of supplying water to Melbourne. A Yea community leader and businessman said that he was 'probably neutral … I am ambivalent' about the proposal and 'I can see merit in the idea but I don't think the idea has been fully developed and it certainly hasn't been handled well'. For him, the main explanation for the opposition to the proposal was the way it had been 'handled and promoted'. At the outset he believed the opposition was linked to taking the water, but the argument had now shifted towards a community belief that the project would become a 'white elephant' and 'it is not going to work … because if Melbourne is in a dry period then we are going to be short of water too'.

Shepparton area perspectives: irrigation upgrade and an imposed trade-off

People in the Yea and Lake Eildon area had been inclined to focus mainly on one part of the combined proposal: the North South Pipeline and diversion of water to Melbourne. The government funding of the Food Bowl Modernisation Project in the Goulburn–Murray Irrigation District tended to be secondary and a minor topic. This was not the case in the Shepparton irrigation area. The Food Bowl Modernisation Project and proposed water savings were central to the overall issue. The combined proposal of the Food Bowl Modernisation Project and the North South Pipeline was the main focus. What was striking in the Shepparton area was the wide gap between proponents and opponents of the project. They appeared as two opposing groups. People in each group gave the impression of having absolute confidence in their fact base, knowledge and rationale, and that there could be no doubt that theirs was the correct perspective. Many of the people in these two groups had long experience in the area and were current or prior office bearers in agricultural industry groups or organisations.

A key concern expressed by people opposing the project was that the proposed savings had not been calculated correctly and were overstated and misleading. While there was general agreement that some savings could be achieved through the irrigation infrastructure upgrade, there was a great deal of scepticism about whether the savings that had been put forward were realistic and achievable. Some suggested that the way the water 'losses' were counted was misleading, and were not in fact actual water losses but only 'accounting' water losses. In reality the 'lost' water was being used by irrigators and the environment, and removing this water would 'permanently deprive' the water catchment area of 75 gigalitres of water. Since the rationale for the whole project rested on achieving savings of 210 gigalitres per year in order to share the savings three ways and thereby provide Melbourne with 75 gigalitres, this rendered the project 'flawed' and a 'concocted deal'. One retired agricultural scientist described it as 'a con' to estimate the savings in this way because the net effect was that less water would be in the system. On the other hand, to those in favour of the proposal, the savings were entirely realistic and would be achieved by reconfiguring the 'backbone' of the irrigation system, and by substantially reducing the number of channels delivering water to irrigators. By making these savings, more water could be held back in Lake Eildon and up to one third of this would be available to Melbourne via the pipeline.

While there was general agreement that the infrastructure upgrade would be good for the irrigation industry by increasing water security for the area, many thought that the government should already have been maintaining the infrastructure from the annual fees paid by irrigators for water delivery. A central issue was that the trade-off deal was wrong. In the first place the government had an obligation to maintain and upgrade the irrigation infrastructure; to base the upgrade investment on a deal to get extra water for Melbourne was seen as unfair. That the infrastructure had not been upgraded was seen as a failed obligation on the part of the government.

Many people were concerned about the transfer of water away from food production areas to urban areas. As one put it: 'We need our water to grow our own food … we need it for our own viability'. Concern about the pipeline opening up additional water trading was a constant recurring theme. The social impact of water that had already been traded out of the district was seen as evidence that water trading was a threat to the stability of the irrigation community. In contrast, those in favour of the combined project believed that the infrastructure upgrade would actually secure the future of the region, and that the trade-off to provide water for Melbourne was a small price to pay, although a regrettable one. The justification for this trade-off was based on need, as one irrigation farmer and former member of the Food Bowl Modernisation Steering Committee put it: 'Politically no government was ever going to fund this project or anything like this in a rural community if there wasn't something in it for the city dwellers. That is reality'. He suggested the upgrade was needed to stop water trading out of the area: upgrading the irrigation infrastructure would make the region 'attractive for people to want to invest in the region and farm here'. In his opinion 'if the region is to survive we need a huge revamp' to create 'critical mass'.

Those in favour of the combined proposal offered a number of reasons for the continued opposition to a project that appeared to be in all irrigators' best interests. One irrigator thought that underlying the opposition was 'the fear factor' with Melbourne taking 'something that people believe belongs to them … they still believe it is our water [in Lake Eildon]'. While he could sympathise with the notion that Melbourne had other options, he emphasised that Melbourne was actually paying substantially for this water through the upgrade. If Melbourne went elsewhere for additional water then 'nobody has come up with an answer for what happens here … what is our future?' Others emphasised the political nature of the conflict, with the current Labor Party being prepared to invest while, as one said, 'the conservative side of politics have never spent a bloody cent on the infrastructure here'.

Other perspectives: a fair trade-off in a time of need

A state government agency employee who was well informed about the project suggested that this was a practical solution based on real need: that it was foreseeable that Melbourne could run out of water by 2010 if dry conditions persisted. While other infrastructure solutions were available for Melbourne, each one had problems of implementation and would be likely to take longer than building a pipeline. Demand management – restricting urban water use – was seen as already pushed to the limit and further restrictions would be 'an infringement of rights', which could have a bearing on voter decisions at the election in 2010. A key part of the opposition was a fundamental misunderstanding of the project and the facts behind water losses and water savings. He also thought that landholders on the pipeline route had blown the issue out of proportion, and suggested that a pipeline was not nearly as bad as a freeway. The only doubts he had about the project concerned the calculations of the proposed savings: he thought they may be optimistic.

Another government agency employee from Melbourne, who was neutral about the project, while admitting that he knew little about the opposition or the project itself, suggested that the landholder opposition was about the pipeline itself, not the redirection of water. He believed that the interests of the majority needed to take precedence and the minority should not 'be allowed to drive the whole agenda'. NIMBYism was also the explanation used by a retired academic to explain part of the opposition. He thought that the opposition was an attempt by farmers to increase compensation and was also based on a misunderstanding of property rights. A retired engineer said that he 'did not believe we have a right to say the water is ours' and that it would be 'morally wrong and politically naive to say that governments are going to let towns run out of water'.

In summary, people perceived what was at the heart of the conflict in a variety of ways. These included beliefs about water use, sharing and movement of water;

Table 4.1 Perceptions of the heart of the issue in the Victoria pipeline study

Those against:

- Wrong to take water from a dry system in crisis to an area of higher rainfall
- There is not enough water in Lake Eildon to take
- Water is needed by the current users (e.g. irrigators) and river systems
- Melbourne has other options to gain more water
- Lack of 'due process' and consultation in the way the proposal was introduced
- Lack of consultation with landholders affected by the pipeline on their property
- Concern over potential for more water to be taken from the system through water trading
- Lack of detailed plans on the pipeline and the rush to construct it
- Deadline of 2010 to complete the pipeline seen as politically motivated and not genuine
- Lack of information on proposed savings: these need to be validated
- Potential impact on businesses that rely on Lake Eildon water levels

Those in favour:

- It is fair to share the water if Melbourne needs it
- It is a practical solution based on real need
- The three-way split of the savings (Melbourne, irrigators, environment) is a good solution
- The savings are achievable by reconfiguring the irrigation backbone
- The protesters are exhibiting NIMBYism and exaggerating the impact
- People don't understand how the savings will be achieved and don't like change

Those neutral or undecided:

- The pipeline may be a white elephant if it remains dry
- Can see merit but the idea has not been fully developed
- The way it has been handled and promoted was poor

practical concerns over technical and other issues with the pipeline; concerns about the way the project had been initiated and was proceeding; and explanations as to why people were protesting. These perspectives are summarised in Table 4.1.

Unfolding events in a shifting context: a ripple of reactions

A progression of events took place that influenced people's perspectives about the proposal. These events began when the proposal was initiated and include interactions between proponents and opponents as subsequent events unfolded. Sections of the community reacted differently to events: people described how their thinking and perspective had been influenced and shaped. Some changed their views about the proposal as they learned more about the project and as community interactions took place. This section is structured around the three main interest groups to show the origins of the proposal and how events and reactions played out.

Food Bowl Unlimited: the context and origins of the proposal

Several members of a Shepparton-based group Food Bowl Unlimited told their story about how the concept and original proposal behind the Food Bowl

Modernisation Project had originated. One member described how 'it all came back to water … water was the underlying factor that was going to change this area one way or another'. From his perspective as a dairy farmer who had invested heavily in infrastructure on his farm, 'it was a case of how do we connect everything together' to secure water for the future. One of the main problems facing the region was that the irrigation infrastructure was seen to be 'deteriorating markedly'. Another farmer outlined the complex interactions that he had been involved with over the years to address this issue. These were between irrigation industry associations, the Victorian state government, national farmer industry associations and the federal government. The irrigator groups could see that a massive investment was needed to upgrade the ageing irrigation infrastructure if there was to be a future for the region. But this was not on the scale that the irrigators could afford, and not covered by the maintenance fees that they paid. It needed government investment.

One person described the origins of the Food Bowl Modernisation Project as a 'convergence by chance of all sorts of things'. Melbourne needed water, which it could easily buy. Irrigators needed an investment in the irrigation infrastructure which they could not afford. Putting these two areas of need together, a group of Shepparton-based business leaders from Food Bowl Unlimited came up with a proposal which they put to the state government. The deal was worked out with a politician, John Brumby, who was responsible for regional development, and who later became Premier of the State. The state government would put up A$600 million, Melbourne Water (a state owned utility) would put up A$300 million, and the irrigators would put up A$100 million. The savings in water would be shared between Melbourne, the environment and the irrigators. Of significant benefit for the irrigators were the water savings that would be returned to become part of their entitlement, which they would be able to trade on the water market. However, a major difficulty that the group had not foreseen was getting people to understand the proposal. As one irrigation farmer who had been involved in this process described it: 'People are bamboozled … people can only assimilate two or three facets of an issue in their brain. This has six or seven facets. It has a time sequence associated with it'.

The Food Bowl Modernisation Project: reactions from the Shepparton community

Many people were angry that a small unelected group had made a deal with the government without involving the broader community. That the proposal was presented as a *fait accompli* was seen as 'completely wrong' by an irrigator who said 'they should have gone back to the irrigators to ask their opinion'. He was opposed to taking water out of the district through trading because this was undermining the irrigation system and people were 'losing belief in the irrigation system'. Another irrigator, a member of Plug the Pipe and an orchardist, suggested that the Food Bowl Unlimited group were aware that the proposal was likely to be unpopular, and were delaying the announcement until they had the details fully worked out. He suggested that many business people had originally been in favour but 'jumped ship when they realised what was really going on'.

Some had come out publicly, saying that they had been misled when they realised that the proposal was unpopular with members of the broader irrigation community. Another irrigator and transport operator said that the information received was mainly 'word of mouth … people did not know what was going on', and that there was no consultation at all.

An orchardist who originally supported the project changed his view as he learned more about it. He said that at first look 75 gigalitres seemed a cheap price to pay for the upgrade, considering that Lake Eildon holds 3000 gigalitres when it is full. But on closer examination he said, 'it is an expensive price to pay' because 'we don't lose that much water … much less can we save it'. His objection was that 'our government is being expedient drawing water from a system that doesn't have the water to spare to put into a system that, at the end of the day, with proper planning doesn't need the water'.

The lack of consultation and the presentation of a *fait accompli* were consistently raised as issues by those opposed to the project. Some referred to a meeting, held in Shepparton in July 2007, at which the then treasurer John Brumby explained the proposal to an invited gathering of irrigators and business people. What raised the ire of many was the suggestion that this was merely a proposal and the meeting was to seek feedback. Two attendees of this meeting told how John Brumby had assured the meeting that the proposal would not go ahead without public support.

The Food Bowl Steering Committee had been given responsibility to write a report with recommendations for the implementation of the project. This involved many community meetings throughout the Victoria. An irrigation farmer and member of Plug the Pipe, told how some of these meetings 'degenerated into a lot of angst, a lot of angry farmers, a lot of screaming matches'. The anger had been sparked because the report was merely a 'collection of ideas … what we might do … there is no technical report, no costing, no business case, nothing that you would normally expect when you spend A$1 billion'. Following the meetings there was a submission period of six weeks for public comment. This farmer was 'outraged' by the fact that after 140 submissions, and several public meetings, 'the final report came out and they had not changed one thing … so we had gone through all this angst and there were some serious concerns raised that were just completely ignored'.

Plug the Pipe: the grassroots opposition movement

The Plug the Pipe movement was formed in 2007 in opposition to the state government proposal to build the North South Pipeline. General membership, including several 'area leaders', came from across northern Victoria. According to one member of Plug the Pipe, none of the people who formed the movement 'have a high profile' and none of them wanted to be public figures, but 'somebody has to stand up and say hey this is stupid'. An original member of the group described how a group of irrigators talked about their concern and worry about the proposal, and how there had been no consultation or opportunity for input. He thought 'the mode of operation in this government is to make the decision and plant a consultation process on top of it'. He thought the A$1 billion expenditure on the project would mainly benefit Shepparton businesses but this would be at the expense of irrigators: 'Is it going to make your water cheaper? No it is not. Is it going to improve your water security? No it is not.' A prominent member of the Plug the Pipe group stated how the group had decided to be 'very vigorous … very vocal'. The group used several methods to voice their opposition to the pipeline. These included a media campaign, a website, regular newsletters, protest marches in Yea, Shepparton, Melbourne and Lake Eildon, and regular community meetings to provide information.

Plug the Pipe campaigners frequently attended meetings held by other organisations at which the Food Bowl Modernisation Project and pipeline were being discussed. Many people described how these meetings became contentious and were often rowdy, including one occasion when eggs were thrown and cars were 'keyed' or scratched. There was a good deal of criticism about some of the tactics of Plug the Pipe. Many thought that Plug the Pipe had become too politicised and that one of the organisers was using the movement as a political platform. One local government councillor in the Yea district thought that while some in the group were 'careful thinkers', others were 'hotheads' who were detracting from the movement. Another Yea district resident suggested that the group had become 'vigilantes' and that he was opposed the group, and would not go to group meetings because it had become 'either you are with us or you are against us'.

In the Yea community, Plug the Pipe had taken on a dual role: it was a protest group but it had also become a conveyor of information, through meetings and regular newsletters. This latter role was tacitly acknowledged by the local council, which had refunded Plug the Pipe expenses incurred in advertising public meetings. These meetings had filled a perceived gap: the lack of consultation process by the government. However, this created divisions within the community because only people who were members of Plug the Pipe or were sympathetic to them would attend the meetings. People who were neutral about the pipeline or were in favour of it did not attend. Three people said that this was because they did not want to be seen as Plug the Pipe supporters. As a result there was no real debate on the pros and cons of the pipeline and the voice of Plug the Pipe had, in effect drowned or muted other voices. This caused fractures in the community when people became afraid or reluctant to air their views in case of offending a neighbour, a customer, or a member of their social group. One teacher described how she had withdrawn from any discussions about the pipeline because she was afraid of potential repercussions at her job if her views became known. She described how 'the whole town is all of a sudden quite against everything, they don't want to hear' and that she had seen 'lots of ugliness'. She described an incident in which an indigenous member of a team surveying the area for heritage sites was 'spat on in the street by local people' which she described as 'just appalling'.

Summary

This section has shown that the origins of a proposal and how events then unfold are important in determining how people perceive the proposal and their attitude towards it. The lack of transparency in the origins of the Food Bowl Modernisation Project was a factor in shaping people's concerns about the project, as was the way in which it was subsequently handled by members of the community and the government. The formation of the opposition group, Plug the Pipe, and their activities also influenced people's perceptions and activities as the events unfolded. People altered their perspectives over time, with some becoming more involved and others becoming detached. There was a ripple of reactions throughout the communities involved.

Perspectives of fairness and justice: consultation and treatment

This section describes people's perspectives on aspects of fairness and justice for the process that they experienced, including how they felt they were treated during the process.

Due process? Heavy-handed and shabby

Many people were angry about the lack of consultation and lack of opportunities for communities to be able to openly discuss the project. People described the state government's failure to establish a consultation process as 'shabby', 'appalling' , 'atrociously handled', 'high-handed', 'it was sprung on us', 'heavy-handed', and 'we had no say'. Many thought that that not having a consultation process was unfair, because there was no input to the decision-making process, and there was little opportunity to engage with decision-makers after the project had been announced. This lack of 'due process' was exacerbated by the environmental assessment process in which the Food Bowl Modernisation Project was assessed separately to the North South Pipeline. That these two infrastructure projects were being presented together as a single project, with one dependent on the other, yet were not being assessed as such, was seen to be unfair and unjust. One person said that her main concern about this 'divide and conquer' approach was that there was 'no avenue ... to go to for justice to be done'.

Several people who were neutral or in favour of the project also thought that there was a lack of communication by the state government and by Food Bowl Unlimited. One person thought that this was justified because a decision needed to be made quickly, and a consultation process would only have delayed the project. A state government agency employee who was familiar with the project thought that 'it was not fair, but it had to be' because of the critical nature of Melbourne's water supply. He saw a difference between consultation and communication. With consultation there is the implication that the decision can be changed, whereas communication is about keeping people informed. He thought it would have been fairer to have 'an 18 month process ... before the final decision was made' but that 'time simply was not available'.

One of the original members of the Food Bowl Unlimited group acknowledged that some of the approaches the group had taken had not been fair, particularly the lack of communication and that 'people have been ridden roughshod over'.

This was because the group was keen to seize the opportunity presented, and if more time had been given to community consultation then perhaps the deal may have 'stalled'. He acknowledged that there had been 'a bit of injustice', justifying this with the statement that 'sometimes a large population don't really know what is good for them' and 'in 20 years time people will look back and say this is the best thing that ever happened in the Goulburn–Murray Valley'.

An orchardist irrigator on one of the Water Service Committees, an advisory body to Goulburn–Murray Water, explained how he had 'adopted a profile that is opposed to the pipeline and I have never been approached to this day by anybody in government authority to … see if we can fathom this out'. He found this 'frustrating' and 'they are not delivering justice, or not delivering fairness … because they are not listening to a substantial groundswell. The fact is they can walk down the street anywhere they like and they will find nine people out of ten that don't want the pipe'.

A resident of Yea who could see both sides of the pipeline issue explained how, in the absence of a formal consultation process, he had tried to work with both the government and the Plug the Pipe opposition group. However, he found that the government had been 'autocratic' and had underestimated the level of interest in the community. He thought that the Plug the Pipe group had an obligation to engage with the government which, in his opinion, they had failed to do. He was critical of both Plug the Pipe, which had become too 'emotive', and the government which had 'done an injustice' through its failure to communicate with and engage the community.

The big picture: where are the facts?

The lack of detailed information about the Food Bowl Modernisation Project and North South Pipeline had become a serious issue. One business owner in Yea said that one of the reasons he was ambivalent or neutral about the project was that 'I constantly have questions in my mind about trying to understand all the issues'. Another Yea resident who was opposed to the project, said 'I don't think we've been treated fairly because they don't tell you anything' about the pipeline and they are very 'mum' and 'keeping everything under their hat'. She complained that they had not been given an opportunity to have a discussion 'to know whether it was a good idea or not', which made her suspicious. A business owner in Lake Eildon described his numerous failed attempts to obtain detailed information from government departments about the proposed savings. He described how on many occasions he was told the data did not exist, only to later find out that there was a report in existence. He had come to the point where he believed 'government is misleading the public. I see injustice in this particular state … the government is encouraging dishonesty', referring to the reluctance of government departments to provide him with detailed information. He suggested that 'a project like this needs to be based on science and facts rather than political expediency'.

A Shepparton resident who was opposed to the pipeline had a similar concern about the validity of the water savings figures. He had carefully explained these in writing to the relevant government agency, but 'they did not want to know about that … this was a lack of justice and a lack of fairness because people were actively promoting a story that they knew was wrong'. He thought fairness was 'being open and honest. This is where this thing went off the rails at the start. It hasn't been fair … I don't think we have got to the justice stage yet … it will not be before the water is flowing to Melbourne … the justice aspect has yet to be seen'. A farmer in the Shepparton area pointed out the unfairness of not being able to discuss the bigger picture issues, such as the details of savings or where the water was coming from in the combined project assessment process. She said 'we were completely muzzled in that way … those were the only two formal consultation processes … they were completely unbalanced and completely unfair'.

The lack of information about other options to secure water for Melbourne and why the pipeline was needed was a recurring topic. Together with the unvalidated savings calculations, this lack of discussion about Melbourne's options had become a major source of unease. Many suggested that people in Melbourne, if they knew about the pipeline, would be against it, judging from conversations with their friends. A Shepparton district lawyer described how his Melbourne friends were uneasy about the pipeline and even against it, because they felt that they should be saving more water, including recycling stormwater. He was concerned that in other areas of the state the pipeline was not being debated, and it was only through the media campaign of Plug the Pipe that the pipeline had even received wider attention.

One of the consequences of a lack of public debate, suggested a Shepparton district dairy farmer, was that 'a great deal of injustice is going to be done to the people without their knowing, without them being fully aware of what is going to happen'. To another Yea resident the fact that there was no debate around the broader issues of the pipeline, such as the loss of water to that Murray–Darling Basin, was 'the crucial issue' but 'I don't think it's even seen as being important'.

Interpersonal treatment: with disdain

There was widespread condemnation of the way the government had treated people within the communities at Yea and Shepparton, particularly by those who opposed the project. Many felt that they had not been treated with respect and used phrases such as 'with absolute disdain'; 'very poorly … disdainfully really'; 'with contempt'; 'shabbily'; 'underhand and devious'; 'we were totally ignored'. One Yea farmer felt that she had been treated like 'a French peasant'. A Yea retiree who said that she was 'neutral to opposed' to the pipeline said she felt the government had treated the community as 'just a lot of country hicks' which 'engenders this feeling of disempowerment'. A local government councillor in the Shepparton district described how his local council, the planning authority for the area, had not been involved at all in the development of the Food Bowl Modernisation Project which he described as 'pretty shameful' treatment.

A local government councillor in the Yea district described a public information meeting at which a senior state government agency employee had addressed the gathering. She summarised the state government's overall message as being 'that Melbourne had a really bad summer and that they needed the water more than we did'. She described her reaction: 'It wasn't fair, but it was more than that, it was insulting. It sent a message that we really didn't matter in the bush, that our needs and our conditions, our lived experience, wasn't as worthy as those in Melbourne'.

Summary: a complex proposal and a complex set of perspectives

Although these two projects, the Food Bowl Modernisation Project and the North South Pipeline were initiated together and were inextricably linked from a political and funding perspective, they had little else in common. Yet two different regional communities comprising many social groups were deeply affected by the joint proposal. People in these social groups had to come to grips with what the project was about, why it had come about, how it affected them, how they could respond to it, and how their issues could be addressed. There was a different type of opposition in each regional area, but strongly connected by the Plug the Pipe movement, whose leadership came from both areas.

At the heart of the issue was a complex and interlinked set of beliefs, concerns, assumptions, arguments and viewpoints, and positions held by stakeholders concerned about this proposal. There was a diversity of perspectives throughout the two communities, with many viewpoints in complete opposition to each other. Evaluations of fairness and justice included matters of process, treatment of people and the availability and access to information about the proposal. The lack of consideration and engagement by the state government, particularly in the Yea area, was seen as unjust. Understanding the project rationale, getting details about different aspects of the project and being able to sort out whether and to what degree the project would have an impact on themselves or their community were critical factors in the formation of people's perspectives. These processes varied across the different social groupings involved in the Yea and Shepparton communities. A ripple effect of events and reactions was generated that resulted in disagreements, tensions and divisions between communities and the government and between different social groups within communities.

Photo 1 Turbines and a substation of the Capital Wind Farm, NSW, Australia, 2013.

Photo 2 Flood irrigation, Murray Irrigation Area, Deniliquin, NSW, Australia, 2007.

Photo 3 Protest sign, Shepparton, Victoria, Australia, 2008.

Photo 4 Protest sign, Victoria, Australia, 2008.

Photo 5 Paddock beside an irrigation channel, Victoria, Australia, 2008.

Photo 6 Trees beside an irrigation channel, Victoria, Australia, 2008.

Photo 7 Irrigation flow gate, Victoria, Australia, 2008.

Photo 8 Protest sign, Goulburn River, Yea, Victoria, Australia, 2008.

Photo 9 The North South Pipeline under construction, Victoria, Australia, 2008.

Photo 10 Lake Eildon, Victoria, Australia, 2008.

5 Finding injustice – seeking justice

This chapter steps further into the realm of justice and fairness through an analysis of how people in the two social conflicts described in Chapter 4 interpret and react to these two concepts. It moves the discussion into the third level of understanding discussed in this book (see the Introduction and Chapter 1), which is to seek out fairness and justice themes from people's perspectives about the social conflicts. The theme of injustice emerges strongly in both conflicts. The experience of injustice is explored more fully in the Victoria pipeline study and in discussions with key informants in the third round of interviews. The final section of this chapter investigates why people engage in issues of justice and their motives for seeking justice.

Conceptions of 'fairness' and 'justice'

Fairness

There was a wide range of conceptions of the word 'fairness' and several themes emerged which are categorised in Table 5.1. These categories show the diversity, richness and range of fairness conceptions that emerge from the two studies. Many responses could have fitted into more than one category because people often made more than one point about how they understood the term.

In the first category, fairness is considered to be the way in which people deal with or treat one another. Responses in this category were largely concerned with how individuals treat other individuals, or about interactions between individuals within a community. Examples include 'others treating you the way you would like to be treated'; 'treating people in a fair and even manner'; and being 'fair to everybody involved'. In the second category, fairness is concerned with being given the right level of consideration and respect in the big picture. Examples include 'fairness is where people are treated with consideration, listened to and treated with respect and then considered in an overall position' and 'in fairness you get both sides of the fence and look at the whole issue from all angles'. The fairness implication is concerned with interactions between an organisation and an individual, rather than between individuals: organisations and decision-makers have a responsibility to consider an individual's circumstances within the bigger

Table 5.1 Conceptions of fairness

1	Fairness as how people deal with one another 'Fairness is treating people in a fair and even manner.'
2	Fairness as consideration and respect in the big picture 'Fairness is where people are treated with consideration, listened to and treated with respect and then considered in an overall position.'
3	Fairness as everybody gets a fair-go 'Fairness is that everyone gets the same go, everyone gets an equal go.'
4	Fairness as basic morals and doing the right thing 'With fairness I think of basic morals … on a day-to-day basis with those around you.'
5	Fairness as dealing with an issue to achieve a reasonable outcome 'Fairness is where an issue has been handled to achieve the best community decision, bearing in mind that the impact of winners and losers has been considered.'
6	Fairness as equity 'Fairness is an equitable result to all concerned, to all stakeholders.'
7	Fairness as different from equity 'Fairness and equity are not the same thing. I see equity as treating everybody the same, but this is not necessarily fair because we do not all come together as being the same.'
8	Fairness as equality 'Fairness is about equality. Equality is about balanced decisions.'
9	Fairness as different from equality 'There is a difference between fairness and equality. Take farm succession planning: what is fair is that farm kids retain more than town kids, but what is equal is that they would all get an equal share of it, which would not necessarily be fair.'
10	Fairness as needs being met 'Fairness to everyone means taking into account their particular needs.'
11	Fairness as balanced 'Fairness is balanced, neither to the left nor to the right, neither zealot nor impassion.'
12	Fairness as a remedy for failed justice 'Fairness is when justice does not work … something might be just but it is not fair.'
13	Fairness as a personal viewpoint 'Fairness relates to more of a personal feeling, we all see fairness from our own point of view, which in fact is never fair because everyone has a different point of view.'

picture. In the third category, fairness is associated with the frequently used Australian notion of a 'fair-go' or equal opportunity. Examples of responses include 'you should treat everyone fairly, give them a fair-go'; 'fairness means equal opportunities for everybody' and 'everybody gets a fair-go'.

Responses in the fourth category involve morality, such as how individuals operate on a day-to-day basis where fairness is 'doing the right thing'. For example, 'to be fair to someone is what you would think the right thing to do, to be a fair person'. The next two categories involve responses that were concerned with outcomes: how an issue has been handled to achieve 'a reasonable outcome' and fairness as 'an equitable result'. For example, 'fairness means common sense, what is fair and reasonable and if there is a reasonable outcome'; 'fairness is just equity, sharing'; and 'fairness is what equity would dictate'. One person suggested that fairness was not the same as equity and another suggested that fairness was not the same as equality. Two people suggested that fairness was 'needs being met'. One person suggested that fairness was 'equality or a balanced decision', and another suggested that fairness was 'balanced, neither to the left nor to the right'. Another suggestion was that fairness was 'a remedy for failed justice' in which the justice system had not produced a fair outcome. One person thought that fairness was a personal viewpoint: 'We all see fairness from our own point of view, which in fact is never fair because everyone has a different point of view'.

This diversity and range of responses shows that 'fairness' holds different meanings for people across a broad spectrum including how people treat each other, how processes are conducted and outcomes are achieved, and according to morality and what is perceived to be right. Some responses about fairness alluded to justice principles such as need, equality and equity, as well as the notions of egalitarianism and the 'fair-go' and to the concept of justice itself. However, these references to justice principles were limited and fragmentary, some indicating confusion about the meaning of a justice principle: 'I see equity as treating everybody the same'. This suggests that people in these studies did not have a clear or definitive understanding of the meanings or range of justice principles, namely, need, equity and equality. On the other hand, responses that included examples drawn from current or past situations, for example where equity and equality were compared to fairness, did show that people think about these theoretical concepts in direct relation to their own lived experience.

Several people did not respond directly to the question about abstract notions of fairness or justice: their responses were related directly to the conflict and current context. Even people who were articulate about what these terms meant in the abstract also used examples from their lived experience. These findings show that in many cases the current context had a level of influence on these 'abstract' conceptions of fairness. This depends on the degree of involvement of the people in the conflict and their perspective on what has taken place.

Justice

The range of responses for the term 'justice' was narrower than for the term fairness (Table 5.2). As with the fairness categories in Table 5.1, the categories were selected to show the range and diversity of responses from the narratives. In the first category, justice is described as the legal system within society: 'justice conjures up views of the legal system and penalties for wrongdoing' and 'justice is the legal system and if fairness does not work then you have to use justice and quite often justice does not work'. In the second category, justice is considered to be the right outcome based on evidence: 'justice is about coming to an appropriate conclusion which is based on good facts and good analysis' and 'justice is a right and proper outcome'. In the third category, responses consider justice as a system to deal with a grievance, often to deal with a previous unjust outcome, such as 'where a wrong has been done and you expect to have the wrong righted'. Other examples include: 'the law appropriately dealing with something that is wrong' and 'justice means whether people had a grievance and had gone through a process where their perceived injustices were dealt with by the community'.

Table 5.2 Conceptions of justice

1. Justice as the legal system
   'When I think of justice I think of lawyers and the law. It is all the legal parts of society.'
2. Justice as a right outcome based on evidence
   'Justice is the right decision made on all the evidence available at the time.'
3. Justice is a system to deal with a grievance
   'Justice is where a wrong has been done and you expect to have the wrong righted and dealt with.'
4. Justice as what is within the law
   'Justice is about the law and we have to abide by the rules, not necessarily rules that fit everyone but that is how we make a civil society.'
5. Justice as a legal result
   'Justice is the outcome of being involved in the legal system.'
6. Justice as the political system and the legal system
   'Justice is legalistic and perhaps political.'
7. Justice as your right to have an opinion
   'Justice means everybody is entitled to have an opinion, to have their opinion respected and recognised.'

In the fourth category, justice is considered as people abiding by the law: 'justice is adhering to the codified laws of the land or the norms or the decrees that come from elsewhere'. The influence of context can also be seen, for example: 'Justice means that you have rules or laws that people are obliged to live by: it should apply to all people and not to selected people'. In the fifth category, justice is a legal result: 'Justice can be interpreted as a legal result which comes from fair dealing or non-fair dealing as the case may be'. One person perceived justice as the 'political system and the legal system' adding 'that is a joke, if you are very rich you can afford barristers, if you are very poor they get paid for by the government, and in between you cannot afford it so you cop it sweet'. Another suggested that justice is more about 'the right to have an opinion' and to 'have their opinion respected and recognised'.

As with conceptions of fairness described above, these conceptions of justice show a range and diversity of understandings and meanings across processes and outcomes. They also show that people think about justice not only in terms of a system or an outcome, but also in terms of the relationships between justice and the legal system, justice and fairness and justice and civil society. The influence of context can also be seen from some of the responses, and, as with conceptions of fairness, it is apparent that these 'abstract' conceptions of justice are also influenced by the current context and the lived experience.

Distinguishing between fairness and justice

People were asked whether they distinguished between fairness and justice. While not all responded, some became quite engaged and thoughtful in discussing the differences and relationship between justice and fairness. For many this distinction

Table 5.3 Conceptions of fairness and justice noting similarities and differences

1	Fairness and justice are similar 'Justice and fairness to me are both the same: they are synonymous. Justice is more of a formal term. Fairness is perhaps the layman's way of looking at it. Justice tends to be after the event. Fairness tends to be before the event.'
2	Justice should give fairness 'If someone commits a crime then justice is the punishment and the people who are affected by the crime would get compensation or recognition. If the two are working together you get fairness with the justice system, hopefully.'
3	Justice, legality and fairness: differing boundaries 'Justice is not always legal. I suppose there are a lot of ways you can look at justice, but justice is done if a wrong is righted. And that does not necessarily have to be legal.'
4	Differences between fairness and justice 'In my mind justice is a heavier word compared to fairness. You might be a bit waffly on the facts and I will be fair to you, but in justice I need to know the facts.'
5	Fairness and justice create the whole picture 'I think fairness and justice is the whole picture … if you do not get fairness in some action then it is unjust, or it is not justice in the legal sense … so it is something that goes hand in hand.'

was not something that they had thought about before. Some themes emerge (Table 5.3).

In the first category, fairness and justice are considered as similar or interchangeable. While some respondents started out by saying that they thought the terms were interchangeable or synonymous they then went on to say where they were actually different, for example:

> I think the terms are interchangeable with each other … Fairness feels like it is about a process … justice is about the outcome of that process and whether people feel like the outcome is what they expected and whether it impinges upon their rights.

In comparing these terms, this person saw areas that were interchangeable but also thought that fairness was more about process, and justice more about the outcome of that process. Another person who described the terms as 'the same, they are synonymous' then went on to describe justice as 'more of a formal term' whereas fairness is 'the layman's way of looking at it'. This respondent was quite specific in describing the terms as having the same meaning, but noted differences in *who* used each term and *when* it was used. The implication is that the terms have the same general meaning but the context determines when each one is used. Another person thought that fairness and justice were both 'about truth and openness' and stated: 'I don't distinguish between them'. Some defined the terms justice and fairness in relation to each other, for example 'Justice is whether people are treated fairly and fairness is whether justice is meted out'.

In the second category, the relationship between justice and fairness was that 'justice should give fairness', but that this did not always happen. For example 'if justice is properly applied it is fair and you get fairness if you are given justice'. Another suggestion was 'just and fair probably are along the same lines. Justice is that the law is there, but if you have a law that seems silly or unjust it may not always be fair'. Some contextual differences from the studies were referred to in these responses, such as 'a sector of the community can get justice but it may not be fairness to the total community'. In the third category, different boundaries between justice, legality and fairness were described: 'justice is not always legal' and 'fairness is what is equitable and fair but may not be legally correct'. One suggestion was that 'justice comes as a result of unfairness, because if everybody dealt fairly with one another, there would not be any need for justice'. One person compared the legal system with the justice system. In his view there was a legal system but not a justice system because 'a process may be legal, but not based on justice'. In the fourth category, there are differences between fairness and justice, for example, fairness being 'more intangible' than justice and justice requiring more 'facts' than fairness. Finally, in the fifth category fairness and justice together make up the bigger picture.

These conceptions of fairness and justice show that people do differentiate between fairness and justice but recognise that there are boundaries, areas of overlap, similarities and differences. People pointed out where they thought there were differences between these terms in the way the terms are used, formally or informally, the degree to which facts and evidence are required and in what type of situations each term would be used. It is not just the meaning of the two terms that people see differently, it is also the context in which the terms are used, such as in an everyday context or a formal, legal context.

Summary: fairness and justice

Some key findings emerge. First is that people described their conceptions of fairness and justice in terms of the way people are treated in processes, how processes are conducted, how outcomes are arrived at, and how the notions of equity, equality and need are considered. The second finding is that people do distinguish between fairness and justice. Fairness is generally seen to be about informal interactions on a day-to-day basis between individuals, incorporating what is seen to be reasonable to those concerned. Justice is largely viewed as the legal system in which more formal factually based deliberations occur to achieve a good or just outcome. A third finding is that the distinction between fairness and justice is not always clear-cut and people's conceptions show considerable complexity, interconnections between the two terms, overlapping areas and some confusion. There is richness and diversity within these conceptions where edges are blurred, where similarities and differences can be seen and where there are complex associations, connections and relationships. Fairness and justice are not simple concepts to understand or define.

A fourth finding is that the current context, or state of affairs, plays a part in how people think about fairness and justice. That some people were so caught up in their current situation that they found it difficult to express abstract notions of these terms is an indication that context plays an important part. People do think deeply about fairness and justice in their lives and many have deep moral beliefs about what is right in a given situation. Many have views of what they think justice and fairness should provide, and have developed thoughts and attitudes about what they perceive to be the justice system or legal system from their own lived experience. These findings reveal a continuum of contextual influence that ranges from a point where there is little to no influence, to a position where context is a substantial influence. In the former case this may be because the person is a minimally affected bystander who draws on earlier lived experiences to describe ideas about justice and fairness. A person at an early stage of a process may perceive justice or fairness to be concerned with involvement in the process itself, whereas at a later stage, when a decision has been made, they may be more concerned with fairness or justice aspects of the outcome, such as 'righting a wrong'.

The emergence of injustice

Injustice in the New South Wales carry-over water study

Injustice in process and outcome: the way it was done – the water was ours

While the original intention of the study was to explore perceptions of fairness and justice in a social conflict, it was clear that widespread perceptions of injustice and unfairness were at the core of the social conflict in the NSW study. People's perceptions of the issue at the heart of the protest varied but there was widespread concern across the community, and this was not restricted to material or financial concerns: it included social and personal aspects of what was happening within the community. While the core issue was a perceived violation of a property right – 'the heart of the protest is that the water was ours' – the way the irrigation community had been treated was perceived to be equally important by many, resulting in anger, dissatisfaction and strongly expressed emotions. Many community members saw the action by the government as both unfair and unjust, using terms such as 'grossly unfair'; 'unfair and poorly managed'; 'extremely unfair'; 'justice has not been done' and 'there is no fairness or any justice in what has happened'.

There was perceived injustice in the outcome of the decision, with nuances about how the cutbacks were unfairly allocated amongst different groups of irrigators; perceived injustice in the way irrigators had not been informed or included in the decision making process: 'it was the way it was done, not why it was done'; perceived injustice in the way the community had not been treated with respect: 'a complete contempt'; and perceived injustice in the way the government responded with its Extraordinary Assistance Package following the protest. There were several perceived injustices with this package. The first was that the government response was inadequate even though it was designed specifically to address the problem. It was seen as inadequate because it did not provide direct compensation for each megalitre of water taken from each irrigator. Instead the package offered general financial assistance to any farmer who could demonstrate financial hardship. Second, the amount was capped at A$50,000, perceived by many to be insufficient

Table 5.4 Perceptions of injustice in the New South Wales carry-over water study

Perception of injustice	*Type of justice violated*
Lack of notification, information and involvement	Procedural justice
Lack of respect in the way people were treated	Interactional justice
Perceived entitlement/property removed	Distributive justice
Burden of cutback inequitably distributed amongst irrigator groups	Distributive justice
Lack of recognition of actual harm done	Distributive justice
Equitable compensation not offered	Distributive justice
Inequity of Extraordinary Assistance Package	Distributive justice

in relation to their actual loss. Third, the administrative process to apply for this package was perceived to be unnecessarily complex.

These different perceptions of injustice amount to a series of separate injustices, all related to the original water cutback, but each taking on a separate identity. Connections between these perceived injustices and the different types of justice (procedural, interactional and distributive) are summarised in Table 5.4. While the injustice of inequitable burdens was central to the conflict, the importance of interactional justice and procedural justice was clearly portrayed by the calls for respectful treatment, recognition, information and inclusion.

No recognition of harm

The material, social and personal impacts of the carry-over water cutbacks were seen by many as being interwoven, and contributing to a sense of harm to the current and future well-being of the community. The impacts of the carry-over water cutbacks were felt across the community. While there was clearly an obvious direct material impact on those irrigators who had lost water in the cutbacks, there was also a range of social and personal impacts as the implications of the government decision became apparent throughout the community. The social and personal impacts had affected relationships, personal beliefs and people's confidence in the future in relation to the stability and structure of the community. Three business community leaders described the overall impact as a demoralisation, an erosion of confidence and a destabilisation of the community:

> The carry-over issue affects even the people not directly impacted, because there is an emotional impact – demoralisation – because of the process itself.

> I put confidence under a personal banner. We are struggling to keep the confidence level up with all these changes … we need some sort of belief in the future.

> It has hurt the community because it has destabilised the community. What underpins communities is partly the ability of people to be optimistic, to be positive about the future, therefore they are prepared to invest. Yet that action has destabilised those things.

A perceived injustice was that none of these impacts had been recognised as such by the government, nor was the actual harm that had been done recognised as harm, which in many cases could be irreversible. As one community leader put it: 'farmers have been crucified'. The failure to recognise the value of the water to the irrigator at the time of the cutbacks was seen as a clear and obvious example of this lack of recognition. That the government had offered to replace the water in a future year was described as unrealistic and further evidence of the lack of understanding of the actual impact of the cutbacks. However, the actual harm extended further than material harm. The actual harm was also experienced within the community as damage to the social structure of the community. The social structure of the community depended on the well-being and health of the community.

One aspect of social well-being is concerned with co-operation and a shared understanding of community life, including the relationship between the rural community and city-based government agencies. But there had been a gradual erosion in the common understanding of rural matters with the withdrawal of government agencies from the region. The loss of professional people who had contributed much to the social and intellectual life of the community was seen as detrimental to the overall well-being of the community. That this harm to the community's viability was not recognised by governments in their cost-cutting measures was described by some people. One community leader commented on the general lack of government willingness to recognise the social impacts of government decisions:

> In 10 years there has never been a true socio-economic impact study done along the Murray River on the changes to water management.

The carry-over water cutback was yet another decision made by a government that did not understand how their decisions impacted communities: 'these are things that bureaucrats don't understand'. Interestingly, while very clearly articulating her beliefs about the way governments treated rural communities – 'rural communities are rarely treated with respect: if there are no votes in it then we don't count' – this community leader also thought that the term 'fairness' was not applicable to the carry-over situation. She thought that a better way to describe it would be 'badly managed' because 'what is fair isn't always relevant when you get to a desperate situation and the drought has caused a desperate situation'. However, she felt that the government had demonstrated 'ignorance of the issue, which is not an excuse' and that 'there was certainly not fairness'.

This person's perspective on fairness shows the complexity of the context and the way in which some members of the community perceived the carry-over issue within the broader and long-term context of water management and rural-government relations. In contrast to others, this community leader did not use the term unfair to describe the handling of the specific carry-over water process: for her the unfairness was a long-standing lack of recognition, where the community was not considered within the overall picture and not treated with respect.

Injustice in the Victoria pipeline study

Following the emergence of injustice in the NSW study, people in the second case study were asked directly what they understood by the term 'injustice'.

Abstract conceptions of injustice

People generally had little hesitation in describing their thoughts on 'injustice'. Responses largely fall into four categories (Table 5.5).

In the first category, injustice is seen either as causing harm or some disadvantage to a person or group of people, or as a required action not being taken when such harm has been done. For example, one person described injustice as 'something that you start to react to, it provokes people to stand up and start fighting for their rights, when people perceive themselves as being victims of injustice it provokes a response'. Another described it as 'taking something away from someone that you are not supposed to'. One person compared injustice to bad luck: 'Injustice would have to be dependent on the context, it is formally delivered rather than just natural bad luck'. Another described it as 'where it affects somebody enormously, emotionally or financially, where they have no say or input'. These conceptions of injustice imply that there is an agent causing the injustice, which results in harm or disadvantage to those affected by it. Another suggestion was that injustice was 'where rules are imposed on people to suit the majority and the minority falls through the cracks' implying that injustice could occur through democratic processes.

In the second category, injustice is seen as a failure of the justice system, or where an action has been taken that is perceived to be not right or unfair. Responses suggest that injustice is: 'where the justice system has failed, for example with David Hicks' (referring to the case of David Hicks, the Australian held in Guantanamo Bay prison); 'outside the justice system and is similar to being unfair'; and 'when people have not been treated fairly'. One person suggested that injustice could occur within the legal system 'where laws are rigorously applied without taking into account the individual circumstances'. In the third category, people thought that injustice was related to how people were treated such as 'being lied to'; 'when somebody is not listened to'; and 'when the state pulls tricks on you without having a talk to you'. Another suggested that injustice took

Table 5.5 Conceptions of injustice in the Victoria pipeline study

1	Injustice as harm or disadvantage 'When one area is going to be disadvantaged to the benefit of another area'
2	Injustice as unfair, not right or where the justice system has failed 'When it is not fair, not right'; 'when something is morally indefensible'
3	Injustice as unfair treatment 'When somebody is not listened to or considered important enough to be listened to'
4	Injustice as power 'When a group of people think they are above the law and they can do what they like'

place 'when people close their minds, when they lose the ability to look sideways and see other people's points of view'. In the fourth category injustice is seen as power: 'when a group of people think that they are above the law and they can do what they like'. Another suggested that injustice is 'to do with misinformation, where the government is misleading the public'.

In summary, for many people injustice represented harm or disadvantage caused by an external agent, whether this was the government or another community group. For others it was more about something that was wrong or perceived unfairness in the way that someone had been dealt with. Several people thought that injustice was to do with the way people are treated, and some thought that it was when one group of people exerted power over another group of people. There were strong practical influences on the way people thought about injustice and what it meant to them. For example, the person who was concerned about 'misinformation' had been working – largely unsuccessfully – to obtain detailed information from various government agencies about the proposed water savings in the irrigation area. The person who described injustice as 'disadvantage' to the benefit of another area was strongly against taking water from the Goulburn River system to benefit people in the city of Melbourne.

Injustice in process and outcomes: shabby treatment, flawed policy

As in the NSW water study, there were widespread perceptions of unfairness and injustice in the Victoria pipeline study. And similar to the NSW study, perceptions of injustice in the Victorian study due to state government action spanned the way people were treated, the way the process was conducted, and the decisions and proposed outcomes. These perceptions of injustice and the associated type of justice violated are summarised in Table 5.6. There was a broad-based criticism of the way the government had approached the two combined projects and how the communities had been treated. Most people acknowledged that the government had not handled the project well, particularly in the way it was introduced. Many described some aspect of the process or outcome as unjust or unfair. Even people in favour of the combined project recognised that there were injustices in both the way people had been dealt with and in some areas of the final outcome.

Interactional injustice was perceived in the way individuals, communities and local government had been treated. Being excluded from planning processes was the most commonly perceived injustice in this area, but people were also unhappy with implications by state government spokespeople that their views and issues were less important than Melbourne's need for water. The way state government officials were perceived to have broken election promises and lied in meetings created injustices felt at the personal level by those who attended the meetings. Procedural injustice was perceived in the way the projects were conceived and turned into public policy, with decisions being made without full consultation with those affected. The lack of information and reluctance to provide details about the pipeline and water savings were perceived to be procedurally unjust. This procedural injustice was compounded by what people saw as the 'contrived'

Table 5.6 Perceptions of injustice in the Victoria pipeline study

Perception of injustice	*Type of justice violated*
Disdainful treatment of affected communities	Interactional justice
To break an election promise and lie in meetings	Interactional justice
Lack of consultation regarding initiation of pipeline and irrigation modernisation project	Procedural justice
Lack of information on pipeline and water savings	Procedural justice
To continue the process with inadequate consultation	Procedural justice
Lack of an environmental assessment which considers the pipeline and irrigation upgrade together	Procedural justice
Impact on the environment: removal of water from river system and loss of water flow	Distributive justice
Proposal based on unsatisfactory justification of 'need' by Melbourne, when other options for increasing Melbourne water supply have not been fully explored	Distributive justice
To remove water from irrigators who have paid for it through their annual fees and capital purchase	Distributive justice
To base the project on future water savings that are unvalidated and contested	Distributive justice

and 'unbalanced' approach to environmental assessment, in which there was no assessment of the overall movement of water.

Distributive injustice was perceived in many areas, ranging from the immediate outcome, to what people considered were hidden and future injustices. There was injustice to landholders affected by the pipeline who had already been subjected to the uncertainty of how the pipeline would affect their property. Irrigators perceived an injustice because water availability for irrigation would be reduced in spite of their entitlement and their payment of annual fees for the water. Many people perceived an injustice to the environment, such as through loss of water in the river system, through extra greenhouse gases generated by the pipeline pumping stations and through destruction of woodland habitat for the pipeline. The basis for the proposal was disputed and perceived to be unjust by those who believed that neither the 'need' for Melbourne had been established nor had the water savings been validated. Thus some perceived that the proposal would have hidden injustices that would manifest in the future when the impact of the unrealised savings became apparent. Ratepayers in Melbourne and rural areas would bear the cost of the infrastructure by paying more for water.

Ripples of injustice through the community

The state government of Victoria was heavily criticised for the action or inaction associated with these perceived injustices. However, blame for all instances of injustice did not rest with the government alone. The state government announcement of the pipeline and infrastructure upgrade was the start of a series of events that led to further perceptions of injustice as people reacted. While the formation of the opposition group Plug the Pipe was seen to be a justified response to the lack of government consultation processes, its subsequent activities set in train some further injustices that rippled out into the community.

Although Plug the Pipe received a good deal of support in the Yea and Shepparton communities, there were also people who disagreed strongly with their tactics and believed Plug the Pipe was responsible for exacerbating the situation and causing fractured relationships and divisions within the community. One person in Yea described how he had been 'publicly slandered' at a Plug the Pipe meeting and he felt he was often 'attacked' for his opinions. He thought that Plug the Pipe had 'intimidated and bullied people in the community who are trying to do the positive things'. On the other hand he thought that Plug the Pipe had been 'incorrectly and unfairly branded' as too political and that 'there are all sorts of little injustices throughout the whole thing'. He criticised Plug the Pipe for taking an 'emotive' stance and for not engaging the government with some alternative 'rational positions' regarding the pipeline. Another retired irrigator living in Yea who was largely against the pipeline would not support Plug the Pipe because she felt that their focus was too much on the local impact of the pipeline construction and not enough on the broader environmental issues of taking water, which is what she perceived to be the main injustice of the combined project.

The ripples of injustice extended to pipeline construction workers arriving in Yea to start work. A Yea business owner said that he had heard there was 'talk about a backlash against business that deals with the pipeline' resulting in some shops or businesses refusing to serve pipeline workers. These businesses were concerned that they would lose their local customers if they were seen to do business with the pipeline workers. Along similar lines in the Shepparton community, one dairy farmer in favour of the Food Bowl Modernisation Project and pipeline, and who was an original member of Food Bowl Unlimited, said that he had withdrawn his custom from businesses that actively supported Plug the Pipe. However, in the Shepparton community it was Food Bowl Unlimited that was seen to be a source of local injustice. As one irrigator described it, a small unelected group of businessmen had taken it upon themselves to do a deal with the state government without seeking the opinion of the local community first. An irrigator who opposed the pipeline suggested that Food Bowl Unlimited had instigated the deal to benefit themselves, not the community. She thought that the injustice occurred because there was no consultation by the state government with the larger community: the government only dealt with 'this handful of people … who see themselves as the intelligentsia of the region, they believe they know better and seem to have a perception that the rest of the community are uneducated rednecks, and that aggravates me enormously'. She elaborated, 'that has been the greatest injustice of all. The fact that this idea that will affect everyone has become concreted into policy, based on a few individuals'. However, an orchardist pointed out that members of Food Bowl Unlimited and their families had also suffered. As support for Plug the Pipe had grown in the Shepparton area there was a noticeable decrease in support for Food Bowl Unlimited. One social effect was that 'those that do support [Food Bowl Unlimited] have found that their children are not spoken to at school and that neighbours won't wave to them'.

Round three perspectives from key informants

Many key informants in the third round of interviews offered their perspective on events that had occurred within the two studies. These included explanations of what they thought had happened, as well as judgements as to whether they thought injustices had taken place.

One politician thought that people were angry in the NSW carry-over water conflict because they saw the responsible state government agency as being either 'lazy or inefficient', and that 'particularly on the land people want to have confidence in their decision-makers, they want to know that they have integrity and ability and they are working hard for them'. Her explanation for the government action was that 'they took a risk because no one knew that it was not going to rain'. A federal agency employee involved in natural resource management thought that the NSW government agency had 'stuffed up on their calculations' which was 'an information issue'. Irrespective of how it had happened, a Victorian government agency employee suggested that the NSW government was wrong to take back the water in the way that it did: 'I thought the clawing back of water was a shocker – it should never happen'. He suggested that the water should have been purchased back through the market mechanism which would have 'been consistent with the management regime in the National Water Initiative and how we are all trying to operate'.

Offering a different perspective on the NSW carry-over water issue, a NSW government agency employee said that he thought NSW irrigators lacked a thorough understanding of carry-over water and how it is delivered. He explained that carry-over water had always been specified as a product that could only be supplied if there was enough water to deliver it. In 2006 there was not enough water to deliver it because of low rainfall, which is why the cutbacks had to be made. As regards the outcome, he distinguished between irrigators who had purchased water and irrigators who had carried over water. He thought that there was an injustice to those who had purchased water, but not to those who had carried over water. He explained that the NSW department had not been able to administratively separate carry-over water from purchased water, which is why the cutbacks were applied to both groups.

Key informant perspectives on the Victoria pipeline study offered a variety of views on the deal and the way it was introduced. A Victorian irrigation company employee, who was also an irrigator, thought that the trade-off deal to give 75 gigalitres of water to Melbourne in return for the investment in the irrigation infrastructure upgrade was a good deal, but 'it was not done fairly'. He would have preferred to see a consultative approach from the grass roots level. He thought that people resented the way the deal was done, but that many agreed that the irrigation infrastructure need was real. In his opinion there was a 'huge group in the middle that don't want to be caught up in the debate because it does get ugly' and that many people were still 'weighing up the deal and seeing it unfold before them'. His explanation for the lack of consultation was that 'the heads of government, the bureaucrats said this is a good idea, we need to get on with this, we don't have time for mucking around' when the deal was proposed by Food Bowl Unlimited.

A senior state government agency employee from Victoria suggested that the main opposition to the pipeline came from an 'emotional state, driven out of a moral position rather than a technical position'. He suggested that the opposition was from a group of people who did not like sending water to Melbourne and who were using a range of technical arguments, such as the water savings, to support their position. He thought it came down to resistance based on 'rapid adjustment' in irrigated agriculture including, for example, the introduction of markets and the entry of managed investment schemes. In his opinion, many in the irrigation industry had been under pressure from these changes and wanted to maintain 'romantic notions of the past'. This squeeze on agriculture was happening independently of the pipeline, but the pipeline had become a conduit through which these emotions could be vented. With respect to 'procedural fairness' within the decision making process: 'The government basically made the decision because they couldn't afford not to. Because the risk may not have been that high, but the consequences were shocking'. He thought that a full consultation process would not have reduced the opposition significantly: 'with the pipe you would get nowhere'.

Two key informants talked about what they considered a pressing concern: the environment in the bigger picture. A senior NSW government agency employee said that he thought there was nothing wrong in principle with transferring water out of agricultural use to urban use. However, he thought that taking 75 gigalitres from the Murray–Darling Basin was an 'ad hoc fix up' that should not take place before a 'whole-of-basin process' had taken place to accommodate structural adjustments to water allocation in the Murray–Darling Basin. He thought that the 'higher level issues' had not been dealt with. These were twofold. The first was that 'it is in our own interest to maintain the functionality of a river in a healthy way so that the water is healthy'. The second was that environmental assets 'have a moral position that we should retain because they are valuable in their own right'. In discussing the complexities of the Victoria pipeline study this person proposed that:

> we have an economic system that is basically not reflecting equity and justice ... the environment and the farmer provide a subsidy for our cheap food ... I feel it is grossly unjust to expect farmers to get the blame for taking the water out of the river.

Although he did not use the term injustice to describe the lack of water for the environment, a second key informant from a NSW government agency suggested that the environment was a significant stakeholder 'whose voice has not been heard'. In NSW, water was being returned to the environment through water buy-backs in the water market. This informant was concerned that markets have been 'wasteful' with respect to the 'world of finite resources', and letting markets determine where water is used is a 'flawed policy' until 'the third leg' of environmental sustainability can be built in. As a result the NSW government purchases water in the market 'on behalf of the environment to gain some equity for the environment', but the problem 'begins with market failure in the first place'. That the environment is an important, albeit higher-order issue of justice came through strongly from these two people.

Summary: injustice, harm and understanding

These findings show that not only were there widespread perceptions of injustice throughout the study communities, but there are also was an *acknowledgement* of injustice by key informants who were connected in some way to the decisions or who had some special insight as a result of their work activities. The findings show that injustice can be experienced as a direct material impact or as an indirect impact at a social and personal level, and amounts to 'harm' in any of these areas. Injustice is not only to do with outcomes but is also concerned with processes and the way that people are treated. There can be a rippling effect of injustice within communities, which causes fractures and divisions within social groups and further harm to individuals. The inclusion of the environment in people's evaluations of harm and injustice is a further important finding.

This analysis shows the critical importance of *understanding* for the way in which people form their perceptions and views about an event. In the NSW study, a lack of understanding on the part of irrigators was used as an explanation for their opposition to the decision, with the implication being that if they had understood the rules around carry-over water, then there would have been little dissent in the community. On the other hand, irrigators felt that they had been misled: their understanding of the nature of carry-over water was at odds with the government agency's understanding of it. A common basis of understanding is important, because in its absence, opposition to a decision is likely to arise and persist. A common basis of understanding is an essential prerequisite for the acceptance of decisions. These findings – in which perceptions of injustice and harm have emerged as explanations for why people protest against decisions made by governments – demonstrate the importance of injustice in understanding opposition to decisions (Wolgast 1987; Shklar 1990; Simon 1995). Injustice – not justice – was the issue in these conflicts.

Motives for seeking justice

People affected by decisions have multiple reasons for engagement in matters of justice, which can vary according to their material, social and personal interests. People involved in the two conflicts offered many insights as to what should be done and why they were seeking justice. Insights from the NSW study are presented in a theoretical categorisation (Table 5.7) to show three areas: perceptions of an issue and the associated injustice; how that injustice could be remedied; and possible underlying motives for justice. Three social groupings are included: irrigators, the general community and individuals in the community with differing perspectives.

The community injustice framework (Table 5.7) shows that for each area of perceived injustice there are several possible measures to remedy the injustice and several possible motives for justice. For example, the perceived injustice of the water cutback being a violation of a property right, and the proposal that this injustice could be put right by compensation of a dollar per megalitre, could have several different motives for justice. To an irrigator the latter could include self-interest to

Table 5.7 Community injustice framework: themes from the New South Wales study

Community perceptions of the issues and associated injustice	*Measures to remedy the injustice*	*Motives for justice*
By irrigators:		
• Carry-over cutbacks as a violation of a property right • Lack of recognition of entitlement • Burden of cutback inequitably distributed • Inequitable Extraordinary Assistance Package • Lack of accountability • Disrespectful treatment	• Equitable compensation on the basis of a dollar per megalitre of water removed • Inclusion in the decision-making process • Transparency and accountability by government on 'rules' for water allocation	• Protection of livelihood • Self-interest • Mutual advantage • Justice as an end in itself • Justice as a remedy for injustice • Justice as structural stability • Irrigators to be valued as producers of food
By the general community:		
• Lack of recognition of impact • Lack of consultation • Lack of respect for local knowledge • Lack of recognition for contribution to society as an agricultural community	• Recognition of social impact • Consultation that respects local knowledge and local perspectives • Government agencies to recognise value of agricultural production	• Protection of interests of community: mutual advantage • Justice as an end in itself: to do the right thing • For their world to be just: structural stability and confidence in the future • Community to be valued for contribution to society
By individuals in the community with differing perspectives:		
• Delusion held by irrigation community that they had a 'right' to the carry-over water • Irrigators were unjust to blame the government for the lack of water • Delusion held by irrigators of the viability of the irrigation industry	• Government should clarify rules on carry-over water entitlements and property rights • Initiatives to address the large-scale problem of over-allocation • Irrigators should not blame the government for lack of rain	• Belief-in-a-just-world: derogation of irrigator victims because they lack understanding about water allocation and should have been aware of the below average rainfall • Justice as an end in itself to deal with issues on a larger scale including over-allocation of water and environmental degradation

gain maximum benefit; protection of livelihood (in some cases this could be vital to the survival of the farm), and justice to remedy a perceived wrong. To a general member of the community this same action of compensatory payment could also include motives for justice such as mutual advantage for the community, protection of livelihood (for example, a farm equipment supply business), and justice to remedy the perceived wrong. To a community leader an additional motive for justice could be that the compensation payment shows that the government values the contribution irrigation communities make to society, thus enhancing confidence in the structural stability of irrigation communities.

Table 5.7 also shows that people's different perspectives about the conflict reflect differing sets of motivations for justice. For example, there was some derogation of irrigators because of their lack of knowledge about water allocation and lack of foresight about carry-over water in the dry conditions: these could be manifestations of the justice motive Belief-in-a-Just-World, which holds that victims get what they deserve. These differing perceptions, restorative actions and motives for justice are likely to be mixed within these categories in the same way that individuals can have multiple ideas about fairness and justice and perceptions of injustice. This categorisation shows the deeper meaning underlying people's motives for justice, and provides a greater understanding of why people become engaged in issues of justice. This type of analysis is critical in understanding individual and community perceptions of injustice in situations of social conflict. This chapter clearly demonstrates that there are many motives for justice, with material self-interest being only one of several. Importantly, it shows that resource use conflicts cannot be simplistically and superficially dismissed as just being about NIMBYism or pure self-interest.

6 A sense of justice – processes and outcomes

The previous chapter focused on how people understand and react to fairness, or the lack of fairness, in environmental decision making. Up to this point the analysis has considered *individual* perceptions of fairness and justice. We now consider justice and fairness within the broader perspectives of process and outcome in decision making, although still drawing from individual perceptions. In addition, from this point on, the thread of injustice will be incorporated into the emerging justice picture. This chapter continues with an analysis of the findings from the two Australian water resource case studies. It deepens the consideration of the three major constructs of justice: interactional justice, procedural justice and distributive justice. An important aim of this book is to investigate how perceptions of fairness and justice from within a decision-making process contribute to people's *acceptance* of an outcome. These three constructs of justice are used as a way of organising the analysis in this chapter. These constructs can be envisioned as a set of three lenses, each focusing on different themes within the data that can highlight these areas. Insights are thus gathered and reflected back out through the lenses into the conceptual analysis. General implications can then be drawn from these insights.

Interactional justice and justice judgements

Interactional justice is concerned with the fairness of treatment that people receive (Chapter 2). This includes, for example, whether people are recognised as having an interest in a decision-making process, and whether they are treated with politeness, respect, dignity and honesty. In this section the water case studies are explored through the lens of interactional justice. There are two broad aims: first, to gain an understanding of the importance that people attach to issues of interactional justice; and second, to see how this fits into people's overall evaluation of fairness and justice within a social conflict.

Although the interviews were organised around a set of questions, people talked about how they were treated in many parts of the interview. Direct questions about respect and treatment were asked. In the NSW study the question was: do you feel you have been treated with respect? In the Victoria study the question was: how do you feel you have been treated? This was so that people were not restricted to discussing interpersonal treatment in the strict sense of the word, such as being treated politely in a meeting. The following three examples illustrate this point. A business professional in the NSW study was ambivalent and thoughtful about the question, commenting:

> I don't think we've been treated disrespectfully, well, we haven't been paid due respect, that's semantics but, I find this more and more frustrating … you find it increasingly obvious that you don't get listened to, that a bigger agenda is taking place.

This person at first interpreted the word respect in the formal sense – being concerned with direct interpersonal relations – but then elaborated further about respectful treatment in the bigger picture.

Only one person in the NSW study, a business community leader, said that he thought he had been treated with respect, again treating this in the formal sense of interpersonal relations, but then went on to complain about his correspondence going unanswered: 'I suppose because there is no communication, or very little, then how can you tell?' He was interpreting this question about respect in the strictest sense of the word. By contrast he summed up the overall management of the issue as 'totally unfair' because:

> Firstly they should have disclosed what caused the anomaly [regarding the water shortage] and secondly they should have compensated the people who owned that water at market rates without any question whatsoever.

Another person in the NSW study responded to the question (Have you been treated with respect?) as follows:

> No, to be honest … to say I am just going to take that [water] and you are on your own is just disrespectful. It could have been done in a respectful manner if they had said we will help you out, as opposed to 'it's been cut' and then walking away, turning your back. Yes I'm including myself as part of the community as a whole, because to disrespect the farmers in that regard is to disrespect all of us.

This person was not only referring to politeness between individuals: she was including the outcome in her evaluation. These three examples show that people incorporated other aspects of the process and outcome in their evaluation of whether they had been treated with respect. This included being listened to, being given information and being compensated as part of the outcome. In other words, people included respect in an *overall* evaluation of treatment, which was not limited to interpersonal relations. This evaluation included matters of process and outcome. The interview question to probe for interactional justice was broadened in the Victoria study, and similar findings emerged there. That is, people included aspects of the process and outcome in their evaluations of how they had been treated. People's evaluations blurred the lines between interactional justice, procedural justice and distributive justice.

These evaluations revealed that dissatisfaction with the way communities and individuals had been treated was a common theme in both studies. The way people were treated was perceived to be extremely important. Many were extremely critical of the state governments and government agencies of NSW and Victoria for the way they had treated people and communities affected by the decisions. In the NSW carry-over water study, some people talked about specific ways they had been treated, whereas others were more concerned about how the community was treated in general. Issues raised included that the state government had not been 'up-front', and that the community had been treated as though it did not exist. People were treated as 'second-class citizens', there was no explanation for the decision, and the government did not have 'the integrity to stand up in front of us and say: "look we didn't handle this particularly well"'. One irrigator, nearing retirement, said, with emotion, that he never felt he was treated with respect:

> We are the wreckers of the environment, the guzzlers of water, we are never seen as producers of food, no, we are not treated with respect at all. We weren't informed and we were told downright lies and that's not fair.

In the Victoria pipeline study, people characterised the government variously as: lacking honesty, being deceitful, treating people with contempt, and misleading people. As in the NSW study, many commented that the government did not value people or communities, was more concerned with its own self-interest than the welfare of people, and that an 'erosion of democracy' had occurred in the way people were treated over the pipeline.

There were marked differences in intensity of feelings about how people had been treated. Some merely commented on how they perceived the treatment, whereas others took it very personally, to the point of changing jobs or community involvement. Three people in the Victoria study changed their plans about their work or role on local government councils because they were so dissatisfied by the way they had been treated. One businessman was a member of a local council in the Shepparton region, this being the authority responsible for development application approvals in the area. He did not stand to gain or lose materially from either the pipeline or the infrastructure upgrade. He had been so deeply affected by the way the state government had treated the local council and himself, that he had become stressed to the point of a breakdown, and was resigning his position. He explained that he, with other local government council members, had been lied to by a senior state government official in a meeting prior to the announcement of the deal. He continued:

> As a conservative I intrinsically believe that the government is working in your best interests. My faith has been totally shattered. I am finding it hard as a human being to cope with that.

Another local government councillor in the Yea region said that she also could no longer continue her position on the council because of the way her council had been treated: 'We have been totally ignored'.

Several people in the Victoria pipeline study said that they would have preferred the state government to be honest about their plans, rather than implying that they had not made a decision and were seeking community views prior to making a decision. According to a Victorian irrigator: 'He [Premier Brumby] did not road-test it: he road-tested it with people who said what he wanted to hear and he is rejecting all viable alternatives that have been put up'. This person suggested that he would have preferred the government to be more honest and direct about taking water:

> Had they said to me I am going to take 150 gigalitres off you, we are going to spend a billion dollars, let's go out and effectively fix your system, I could possibly have accepted that. But because he dressed it up in this charade of everyone is a winner, we just felt cheated.

Another person in the Yea district, a state government employee who had worked with landholders for many years, was quite emphatic about why people were objecting to the pipeline:

> What their objection is, is the way it has been handled, which fits into the injustice. It's the way it's been handled and the methods used. No conversation, consultation or involvement. That is what has got their bristles up … it is not the physical pipeline … effectively they have just been walked over.

Two findings emerge. First, people attach great importance to the treatment they receive from authorities when a process is introduced. How people perceive that they are treated can have a serious impact on their personal well-being. Perceptions of poor treatment can be felt deeply and tap into a person's value system. Serious harm to a person's well-being, such as emotional distress, can result from perceived interactional injustice. Interactional justice is an important component of the overall sense of justice perceived by people within a decision-making process and is also important in the evaluation of an overall justice experience. A lack of interactional justice becomes a perceived injustice to those affected by the process or decision. Interactional injustice can directly result in social and personal harm.

Interactional justice is important because it is critical in the initial stages of a decision-making process or announcement. Identifying those people who have an interest in an area and setting up a communication with them indicates that they do have a legitimate and recognised interest and should be included in communications about that interest. It is the first step in a decision-making process. In this way, it can be seen that interactional justice comes first, and therefore has *priority* over procedural justice. This is similar to injustice coming before justice, as discussed in Chapter 5.

The second finding from this discussion is that the distinction between elements of interactional justice and elements of procedural justice and distributive justice is not sharp and clear from the perspective of the people involved: in their evaluations they were concerned with an *overall* evaluation of justice. These evaluations blended areas such as how they were treated, how they were affected by the outcome and whether they had received an explanation or not. That is, there was an intermingling of the elements of interactional justice, distributive justice and procedural justice. People responded to an overall experience of justice or injustice rather than focusing on specific aspects of justice in how they form their evaluation.

An important implication about outcome acceptance can be drawn in relation to the three justice constructs. In both of the water studies a decision was made without a recognised consultation process (procedural justice) taking place. In addition there was a perceived lack of interactional justice in both studies. The rationale for the lack of a consultation process was that the decisions needed to be made urgently, with the implication that there was not enough time for a consultation process. However, there was no rationale provided for the lack of interactional justice. As suggested by those involved, it would have been preferable for government agencies to take a more direct and honest approach, which could have improved interpersonal relations and could have had a direct influence on the acceptance of the proposal. The implication here is that if a decision has to be made, for example in a critically urgent situation, in the absence of a consultation process, then interactional justice becomes a *vital* dimension for the overall justice experience of those affected by the decision.

Summary: interactional justice contributes to acceptance of decisions

Interactional justice, or the way people are treated, is important for three reasons. The first reason is to avoid perceived injustice by recognising that there are people affected by the decision, and that they have a legitimate right to be recognised as having an interest in the process and outcome, together with an explanation or rationale for the decision. The second reason is that an approach that includes communication and honesty is more likely to lead to the acceptance of a proposal or decision, whereas an approach that is perceived to be lacking honesty and poorly handled, can lead to opposition. A third reason is that bystanders, or people who are neutral and people outside those communities, who are not affected by the decision can see that decision-makers are treating those affected with respect. While there still may be some core opposition to the decision within the community, for example by people severely affected by the decision or with a moral objection to it, there is likely to be less support for their position from the broader community if those affected have been treated with respect.

Procedural justice and a sense of injustice

In this section the lens of justice switches from interactional justice to procedural justice, which is concerned with the fairness of processes in which decisions or outcomes are made. As reviewed in Chapter 2, the principles of procedural justice include elements such as participation, voice, information, having issues responded to, timeliness, and trust in the decision-making authority to make an unbiased decision. Researchers have shown that procedural justice does lead to increased outcome acceptance, although exactly why this is the case is less clear

(Greenberg, 2001a). In this section the study data is explored with the aim of examining this important question.

From the two studies it is clear that people have quite different areas of concern within a decision-making process. These areas of concern, and the differing degrees of importance attached to them, vary according to the circumstances of those involved. The discussion below illustrates the way in which the different elements of decision-making processes were significant and how people reacted to perceived deficiencies. These procedural justice elements are italicised in the text.

The New South Wales study: information and consultation

Irrigators in the NSW carry-over water study were concerned about the material loss of water: it was important to know early in the season how much water they would have for the growing season in order to make decisions about planting crops, such as rice, or watering permanent pasture for dairy cattle. Therefore the *timing* of the announcement of the water cutbacks in October was critical: it came as a shock and many irrigators were angry that the state government had not given them warning earlier in the season that delivery of carry-over water and purchased water was under question. Had such a pre-warning been given farmers could have made alternative plans, such as collaborative arrangements with neighbours, which would have lessened the impact. As one irrigator said:

> Deals could have been done right across the district if the government had been upfront. But by leaving it so late with their decision-making process the opportunity for that sort of arrangement and ways of working around it had been lost … they told nobody and they were still hoping it would rain. Or they didn't have the guts to make a political decision.

Irrigators believed that the government should have known how much water was available, and believed that the government was either negligent or 'incompetent' in its failure to provide such an early warning, particularly because the government knew how important the timing was to the irrigators for their planning. In this way *timing* and *notification* were high on irrigators' list of important process events. For those irrigators who had executive responsibilities in organisations such as the Rice Growers Association and Southern Riverina Irrigators (which formed an official voice for irrigators in the area) the main issue at the outset was the complete *lack of consultation* associated with the first water cutback. One irrigator in such a position suggested that the government had 'not been truthful' by publicly implying that these organisations had been consulted. The government had also failed to provide any *information* to the irrigators about the rationale behind the cuts and explain why they had chosen to cut both carry-over water and water that was purchased through the water market. This angered many irrigators, as one described it:

> I would like to have had it explained how it came about instead of just being told you can't have your carry-over water. To put their hand up and say we

> have made a mistake in how we calculated it … or was it a computer. We were just told the carry-over water wasn't there. Well, that's not a good thing at all, it is very poor, it's not fair. If you tell people what the story is then you know what you've done wrong and you can usually get away with it. You don't just try and hide it.

This irrigator implied that people would have been more accepting of the issue if the state government had openly admitted a mistake or calculation error. It was clear from these sorts of comments that they believed the government had made a mistake. There was, however, general agreement by those involved in the second round of water cutbacks that the way these had been handled was much better, even though they were larger than the first cut. This was because of the involvement of the irrigation associations in the decision-making process and because their suggestions about how to make the cuts and who would be impacted were included in the final outcome. One industry association executive described how they had put it to the government:

> As stakeholders we need some involvement in this because otherwise you are going to do things and you will not have our support and we need to understand what is going on.

This difference in the way the two cutbacks were handled illustrates very well that a decision can be accepted even if 'it wasn't a nice outcome' as the same person described it, because there was full involvement of those involved.

The importance of *background information* in the NSW carry-over water study was also a key underlying concern that went to the heart of the dispute. Many irrigators believed that the carry-over water was physical water – 'water in the dam' – that was the equivalent of a real property right. According to an irrigation association executive the irrigation community had been told 'at countless meetings' that this water was a higher security even than the traditional high security water in NSW. This is what formed their belief about carry-over water, and was the foundation of their perception that their property rights had not been recognised when carry-over water was cut. However, this belief was not supported by explicit information provided by the government: this information deficiency was acknowledged by people in the NSW carry-over water study and a government employee interviewed in round three. This lack of specific information resulted in two different perspectives: some felt that irrigators had a poor understanding of carry-over water and should have known that carry-over water was only available if minimum inflows took place. The opposing perspective was that irrigators felt they were misled by the government when carry-over water was introduced as a risk management tool. All those who commented on this acknowledged that the information needed to be updated to clarify perceptions of either poor understandings or misunderstandings. However, at the time of the water cutbacks the beliefs that irrigator's property had been removed and that their rights had been violated formed a substantial part of their justice evaluations. As a result they demanded compensation for each megalitre of water that had been taken, as a way of putting right the injustice that had been done and reducing the material impact. This shows that *information in general* is a critical part of a decision-making process: it is not only information that is required to explain the actual decision, but also information that forms the basis of people's knowledge, understanding of a situation, and subsequent expectations in further interactions.

It was not only irrigators in the Deniliquin district who protested at the government action: many people in the general community expressed their support and empathy for the irrigators by attending the protest. One business professional said that his mother told him he had a 'strong sense of justice' but he rather thought he had a 'strong sense of *in*justice', saying that the biggest issue with the process for him was that the *community was not listened to*, either specifically or generally. For him the way the government made its decision, without recognising property rights, 'added to that element of uncertainty' and 'destabilised the community'. He said that 'if you want to take something from somebody you firstly must ask'. Further, he thought 'groups that need to be involved don't work collectively or collaboratively, so you get this mishmash of energies and I think that goes to the heart of justice and fairness'. His comments were not only on the specific issue, but were also more general, in that because the community was not to listened to, it was therefore not understood in the wider context. To try and remedy this he had been involved in the formation of a group of leaders, the Drought Leaders Forum, to give voice and leadership to general water issues in the area. Another Deniliquin business owner also suggested that the main concern for her was that the community lacked a *cohesive voice*: 'We have been striving to get one voice on water to government because mixed messages achieve nothing'. She described her feelings of being personally 'demoralised' when bureaucrats 'make radical decisions that can impact on you and you can do nothing about it'. For both these people their underlying concern was the viability of the local community. To this end state governments needed to be better informed about the social impacts of decisions, and be prepared to interact with communities during decision-making processes.

In summary, people in the NSW irrigation community expressed their dissatisfaction with many elements of the decision-making process culminating in the water cutbacks, but also indicated ways in which these could have been improved to make the outcome more acceptable. Of particular importance was the lack of timely information, lack of explanation for the cutbacks and the lack of involvement or participation of irrigation community leaders. Although the fundamental core problem was a lack of recognition of a property right, the way the irrigation community had been treated showed 'a lack of understanding and respect for people and their business of trying to get through this horrible drought'. It was also a major reason that the protest was held. People's support for the second round of cuts and acceptance of that decision was a direct result of their involvement in that decision-making process. However, this still left the issue of compensation for the water taken to be addressed. Others in the community, perhaps less directly affected materially, viewed this process as another manifestation of the community not being listened to as part of the bigger picture of water management. This posed a direct threat to the future viability of the community.

From this summary of the NSW study, findings about procedural justice begin to emerge. The first is that matters of process directly affect people's willingness to accept a decision. The second is that people have ideas about justice, or a sense of justice or injustice that is formed from their lived experience. They can bring this sense of justice or injustice to bear on their evaluations of justice in a particular situation, and it can also form a motivating force behind some of their activities in a community. Such activities include the formation of leadership groups to give voice to community concerns, involvement in protests when their sense of justice has been violated, and activities that contribute to a community's well-being.

The Victoria study: emotions running high and a sense of injustice

The Victoria pipeline study differed from the NSW carry-over water study in that the interviews took place much earlier in the process while the issue was being experienced: the communities were fighting a decision about the pipeline, which they thought could be overturned. In addition, the Victoria study was more complex because it involved two major projects taking place in two different areas of the state. People who were affected came from many different backgrounds and communities, with varying degrees of knowledge and concern about the combined project. Yet the Victoria study was also comparable to the NSW study in that those involved had similar concerns about aspects of the decision-making process. However, because the process was at an earlier stage, many people were focused on *what* was wrong with the process and proposal and *why* they thought it was wrong. They were angry with the way they had been treated, and the way the proposal had been presented, and this formed a major part of what they wanted to say. They were less ready to reflect dispassionately on matters of process. In comparison, much of the process in the NSW study had already run its course so people were more contemplative about the process and how they had reacted to it. This difference between the two studies proved useful for the analysis. In the Victoria study people tended to express their concerns about the *process* more emotionally than in NSW (where people were largely concerned about the impact) and to talk about why they were unhappy with it. This revealed insights about their sense of injustice, and their perceptions of fairness or unfairness, and contributed to the formation of their overall justice judgement.

A major complaint from people in the Victoria study was that the decision had been announced with what they perceived was *no consultation*. The way the state government announced the pipeline was the central issue for a Plug the Pipe spokesperson: 'The process all the way through has been unfair and unjust, in that right from the very start, the government told us in the very first meeting that this was a done deal'. She became involved, even though she did not stand to lose personally from the pipeline, because 'I could not stand by and let this happen … that an elected government can do this … I find that appalling and I cannot sit there and watch'. She talked about several areas in the decision-making process that she thought were 'wrong', as well as the central issue of taking the water. Her sense of justice had been violated in many areas – to the extent that she had spent a great deal of her time on the Plug the Pipe campaign. She thought that if the government had considered the project as a whole, and followed a 'correct process' of environmental evaluation, then 'it would have quickly become obvious that it wasn't a project that you should proceed with'. Other members of Plug the Pipe expressed extreme frustration with the government's approach and had also given up substantial amounts of their time to oppose the project. As another leading member of Plug the Pipe said: 'The public deserves better than this. People should have been presented with something concrete that would stand up to the highest scrutiny'.

Every person who was opposed to the pipeline had questions about the combined project and had not received a satisfactory answer. Many complained that there was *no avenue to discuss all the questions raised*, including, for example: alternatives to building the pipeline; alternative routes for the pipeline; when and how water would be taken from the Goulburn River; how the pumps, air valves and scour valves would operate on the pipeline; details of the estimated irrigation savings; who would be impacted in the irrigation district and where; and what would happen if the drought persisted and Lake Eildon remained at low levels. The fact that these questions were so important and yet remained unanswered was central to many people's overall opposition to the government's proposal and how the government had gone about it. One retired engineer said that his main opposition to the pipeline was the fact that it had been done 'without any planning'. He recounted a wide range of issues about the pipeline, from the technical specifications through to the route planning process that went against his engineering and planning principles gained from a lifetime's experience in the industry. In his opinion there was not one area which had been carried out well. This *lack of planning* was also raised by three people who were on local councils that had not been consulted prior to the announcement, or as part of the planning process. In their view there was a legitimate expectation that the state government would consult with local government about significant infrastructure projects in their areas. One local government councillor said, emotionally: 'I've been on the council five and a half years and I'm proud – we have consulted widely – and we try to do the right thing. We consult on just about everything, even the skate park. We do make hard decisions, but it is always done with consultation'. The state government action was completely against the principles and practice that had been implemented by his local council.

Finally, the *lack of information* issued by the state government, either proactively or in response to questions, was widely condemned, even by those who were mildly in favour of the proposal or neutral about it. The lack of debate, the lack of discussion of the rationale or of the options available, frequently came up in interviews. The complexity of the combined project and the difficulty in obtaining detailed information was a significant issue for those who were interested in and concerned about the project. As one Shepparton resident said: 'You have to sit down and think about it and understand how the system works to understand what is happening'. A resident of the upper Goulburn River area said that he was not opposed to the pipeline if the savings could be proven. But he had been prevented from getting documents by people in government departments. The latter he felt were told not to release detailed information or reports. In his examination of the data that were available, he believed the figures were flawed and 'the people that provided this information knew that it was flawed'. As a result he said 'the consultation process was a sham … the savings are mythical … it makes you lose confidence in the people who are governing and that is sad'.

Summary: unfair process leads to a sense of injustice

These findings show that people in the Victoria pipeline study had different experiences of the process, depending on how they were involved in it and the degree to which they became engaged in it. In many cases people felt that elements of the process were inadequate from their perspective, and violated principles, ways of operating, or beliefs that they held to be important. Some were excluded from the consultation process when they felt they should have been included as a person with an interest; some felt that they were ignored or that their questions were ignored, and therefore they were not valued. Many did not have their specific concerns addressed and were denied information requests.

What individuals and communities in NSW and Victoria had in common was a *sense of injustice* in the way they had been treated, and how elements of each decision-making process had failed to meet their needs or expectations. These needs and expectations tapped into some deeper sense of fairness or justice or understanding of what was right or fair under these circumstances. The absence of what were perceived to be essential elements of a decision-making process, such as honesty, transparency, information and opportunities for issues to be responded to, led directly to protests and disagreement with the outcome or decision. These perceived process deficiencies contributed to people's justice judgements and their unwillingness to accept outcomes while these deficiencies existed.

Distributive justice: packages, deals and trade-offs

Having established in the last section that the elements of a process are critical in how people formulate or re-evaluate their justice judgements, and are significant in their acceptance of outcomes, we now turn to the third justice construct, distributive justice, which is concerned with decisions and outcomes. There are three key principles of distributive justice: need, equity and equality. The narratives of people in the two studies are now considered through the lens of distributive justice, with these three components. The key aim is to explore how people evaluate a decision or outcome, and how their judgements about an outcome influence their reactions to the outcome. These reactions can include suggestions or demands for changes to the outcome and the way in which outcomes can be improved or made more acceptable.

The two case studies are similar in that many people were sufficiently motivated and engaged in the issue to organise public protests about the proposed or actual outcome. However, there are also some important differences between the two case studies. In the NSW carry-over water study, the water cutbacks (the decisions) had already been made and there was general community support for the irrigators and their demand for compensation. In contrast, in Victoria, although a decision had been made, implementation of the combined project was still in its early stages. There was also a variety of reactions to the decision within the communities affected. Although drought and a shortage of water were common factors in both case studies, the context surrounding each decision was quite different.

The New South Wales study: the rules keep changing

In analysing how people perceived and evaluated the outcome in the NSW study, four main areas stand out. First, the contextual basis or rules on which carry-over water as a risk management tool was based; second, how the water cutbacks were distributed amongst the irrigator groups; third, irrigators' suggestions for a more acceptable outcome and the state government's initial response; and finally the government's Extraordinary Assistance Package.

As described in Chapter 4, irrigators in the NSW study used carry-over water as a risk management tool that had been introduced for that purpose by the NSW government. Carry-over water could also be purchased by other irrigators. This tool had been developed specifically to be used by individual irrigators to make their own decisions about how they would spread their risk of potential water shortage from one year to the next in periods of low rainfall or drought. That this specific water was cut back just at the time it was most needed was seen as unfair, because those farmers who had 'done what the government had asked them to do for years' were precisely those worst affected. It was not only ironic it undermined the whole purpose of carry-over water. This irony and impact was not lost on the rest of the community, and was one of the reasons that the protest was supported by the community at large. Irrigators felt that they had been led to believe that carry-over water was more secure than high security water and would be allocated before high security water. Similarly their expectation that carry-over water was the equivalent of a property right was based on what they had been led to believe were the rules underpinning carry-over water. This belief was fundamental to the sense of injustice felt by irrigators. Irrigators now had the perception that the government had changed the rules midstream which had 'hit at the heart of the integrity of irrigation … and destroyed all the trust that we built up' according to one irrigator who had been involved in developing carry-over water as a tool. The outcome of the government action for the irrigation community was that the rules had suddenly changed, the integrity of the irrigation system had been undermined, and trust had been lost.

The second area in which the outcome was seen to be unfair was the way in which a small subset of irrigators in NSW was impacted by the water cutbacks. These were the irrigators with purchased water or carry-over water still in their accounts. As described earlier, irrigators used their water at different times of the season depending on the type of crop grown. Some irrigators had already used much of their carry-over or water that they had purchased at the time of the cutbacks whereas others had used very little. These latter irrigators therefore bore the brunt of the water cutbacks. The perceived unfairness was most keenly felt by those irrigators for two reasons: first they had taken more precaution than others by carrying over water until the next year, and second, because they typically used their water later in the season. They felt their burden of water cutbacks was greater than others, and that the burden was unfairly distributed. Irrigators were also angry that the cutbacks affected those who had general security water more than those who had high security water. That this was an unfair distribution was also pointed out by an irrigation company employee who suggested that 'what has happened has impacted on people very differently depending on their circumstances and that is what is unfair'. This person was very knowledgeable about water distribution within the Murray Irrigation District and was critical of the state government for not responding sooner, in which case 'a bigger group of people would have lost a smaller amount of water'. Thus the government was criticised for the unfair allocation of water cutbacks. Had the government warned the community earlier, and involved irrigation leaders in solving the dilemma, a better outcome could have been achieved in two areas. First, irrigators could have changed their water usage; and second, because the burden could have been spread across a greater number of irrigators.

The third area in which the outcome was perceived to be unfair was the government's initial response to the water cutbacks. Irrigators had called for compensation for the water that had been taken. They thought that the fairest and most equitable way to do this would be for the government to pay a dollar figure per megalitre that had been cut from each water account. This would be consistent with the water trading market that the government had introduced. In other words it would put the irrigators, as sellers, on equal terms with the government, as a purchaser, using the market mechanism. A precedent had already been set for this suggestion in a prior transaction with Snowy Hydro in a time of water shortage. In this case, irrigators were able to acquire water from the Snowy Hydro scheme allocation in return for a usage payment, and on the understanding that the water would be returned at a future time. This was referred to as the 'Snowy deal'. Irrigators thought that a 'reverse Snowy deal' was an appropriate response in which the government would purchase water from the irrigators to satisfy the current shortage. Irrigators felt this was a fair response, in part because they thought the government was responsible for a miscalculation of the carry-over water, and in part because of their belief that carry-over water was equivalent to a property right. However, the government did not accept this suggestion or accept responsibility for compensation. The irrigation community perceived this as an unsatisfactory outcome and organised the Deniliquin protest rally.

The state government responded with an Extraordinary Assistance Package (Chapter 4), the fourth area of this outcome analysis. The Extraordinary Assistance Package was deemed to be unfair because it was not directly related to the water cutbacks: any irrigator suffering hardship was eligible to apply. This meant that an irrigator who had not lost any water through the cutbacks could receive financial assistance up to a limit of A$50,000. Irrigators complained that this was unfair to those who had suffered a significant financial loss through the water cutbacks, and the package should be directly related to the cutbacks. Some irrigators who had suffered significantly from the water cutbacks might not be eligible for the package. Essentially, the government had based the package on a *needs* basis, and not on an *equity* basis, which is what the irrigators would have seen as a fair outcome. Some within the community felt that the package would create further inequities when people compared what they had received. In addition, the package was administratively complex and many perceived this as unfair because they thought it would be a deterrent to people applying for the package, and hence minimise the overall payouts.

In summary, the water cutback decision was largely perceived to be unfair for two main reasons. First because the burden of the cutbacks had fallen mainly on a small group of irrigators, and second because the government was perceived to have side-stepped its own rules concerning the allocation priority of the different types of water. The government's response to the irrigators' dissatisfaction with this was an Extraordinary Assistance Package which was perceived to fall far short of providing a fair or just outcome. The community was quite specific that an outcome based on a dollar per megalitre compensation would have been equitable and acceptable. A key finding here is that the irrigation community was very clear about what would be an appropriate measure of justice to restore the perceived injustice: an outcome based on equity, not on need.

The Victoria study: a 'trade-off' of needs

Analysing the outcome in the Victoria study is less straightforward than in the NSW study. In the Victoria study, the outcome was still being developed. It comprised a complicated set of plans, decisions and activities covering two major project areas, and, as discussed earlier, community reactions to it were mixed and information about it was scant. The analysis here comprises three areas. The first is the contextual basis including past political promises, and current procedures or rules underlying the proposed outcome; the second is the outcome in its incomplete form as a 'trade-off' or deal; and the third area is the future possible impacts after completion of the projects, when the proposed water allocation would be in effect.

Farming and irrigation communities in Victoria had experienced considerable change in recent years, as in the restructuring of institutional organisations, in water allocation, and the make-up of communities themselves. The background context had been in a state of flux for some time. This is why a later reiteration of an earlier promise made by the state Premier, Henry Bolte, in 1964, not to take water over the Great Dividing Range, by the then Premier Bracks was significant to rural voters. This promise underpinned the irrigation community's confidence in water security. The state government was perceived to have broken that promise with the introduction of the North South Pipeline. By failing to consult widely with communities about the proposed pipeline and irrigation infrastructure upgrade, the government had also undermined its own institutional practices in water management. This was ironic given its solid reputation in community consultation. By relying on a small group of business leaders in Shepparton to represent the broader community, the government had, in effect, inhibited a broad-based debate and had become party to a 'trade-off' which did not have widespread support. The combination of the broken promise, lack of consultation and lack of information left the proponents of the combined project open to criticism that the deal did not have a solid base. From the perspective of many in the broader community, the groundwork had not been laid. Promises, established procedures, and ways of working had been broken or bypassed. There was little in the way of rationale or explanatory framework for the outcome, which was perceived as a deal constructed primarily for the benefit of the state government and Food Bowl Unlimited, to the detriment of the broader communities. Although the pipeline had been presented on a 'needs' basis, this was widely thought to be spurious in the absence of a clear rationale.

The second area of analysis focuses on the nature of the outcome itself. At the time of the interviews the outcome was still a work in progress: it was not yet fully tangible and the resource allocation (water) had not yet been made. People assessed this work in progress from their particular vantage points with whatever information they had to hand, depending on their level of interest and on what information they had been able to obtain. Because many were involved in a process, to a greater or lesser degree, it was the process as well as the outcome that was the subject of fairness assessments, and these tended to be blended together and confined to an area that people were familiar with. However, fairness assessments of the outcome in its current shape were made. These were mainly in two areas: the trade-off of water between the irrigation infrastructure upgrade and Melbourne, and the pipeline itself. First, with respect to the trade-off, a widely held view amongst those opposing the trade-off was that the irrigation infrastructure upgrade should have been funded by the government in the same way that other public facilities, such as roads and hospitals were funded. So it was inequitable that a deal had to be entered into, to give away water in order to secure the funds for the upgrade. Those opposing the trade-off argued that there were already several irrigation infrastructure upgrades taking place, so it was false and misleading to suggest that the only way to get this upgrade was through a trade-off deal. In addition, the calculations for the proposed savings were held to be inaccurate, as was the fact that water could be 'saved'. The water was not lost: it was merely accounted for differently. In summary, there were three key reasons why people were opposed to this trade-off: namely, that the government should fund the upgrade; that several upgrades were already taking place; and the apparently erroneous logic behind the proposed savings that justified water to be sent to Melbourne.

In contrast, those in the community who believed the trade-off was reasonable under the circumstances, including members of the Food Bowl Steering Committee, firmly believed that the savings were real and could be achieved. On this basis the trade-off was justifiable and worthwhile: the outcome should be acceptable because the irrigation community stood to gain A$1 billion worth of irrigation infrastructure upgrades at a cost of 75 gigalitres of water leaving the river system. They believed that because this water was 'saved water' there was no actual loss of water to the irrigators, and therefore the trade-off represented a good deal to the irrigators. It can be seen that the 'saved water' was a critical element of the deal or outcome at that point in the process. The proposed water savings had been used to justify the trade-off and to convince the government to go ahead with the deal. However, at that point in the process the water savings took the form of calculations and plans. In other words, the savings were not yet tangible: they consisted of data and projections which in reality amounted to information.

Thus information had become a major component of the proposed outcome. From a justice analysis this is a critical distinction, because justice studies generally hold information to be part of the process, not of the outcome. The implication here is that as an outcome is being developed, as in the Victoria study, important components such as information and a rationale could be considered both part of the outcome and part of the process. In this study people on both sides of the issue concurred that detailed information about the trade-off, including the proposed water savings, was not made generally available for the community to discuss at the proposal stage (process) or when the decision had been made (outcome). Interestingly, this point was made very strongly by an observer of the process. During an interview which took place in the home of one of the irrigators who had taken a leading role in developing the proposal, the irrigator's wife interrupted the conversation to say to her husband:

> You could have done things differently but at the time you didn't want to push them … when you were talking to [a neighbour] the other night she wanted to understand it, but she had not been given the facts. Those facts had never been given to the community as you gave to her. Like the alternatives to the food modernisation scheme. I think that is where the big mistake was made.

The irrigator, however, brushed aside this point and talked about the public meetings that had been held across northern Victoria to explain the proposal. Providing detailed factual information was not, apparently, seen as a significant concern to the government or to the Food Bowl Steering Committee. However, to those opposed to the pipeline, a debate based on factual evidence would have shown up the pipeline as a 'flawed idea', thereby removing any public support, and possibly resulting in abandonment of the project. These findings show that a rationale and detailed information are critical components of both the process and the outcome.

The lack of information about compensation for landholders in the Yea community was also a source of concern. Those affected by the pipeline had not been provided with details about compensation for the use of their land. While this could be seen as part of the ongoing process, they were still concerned about two outcomes: how the pipeline would affect their land and how they would be compensated. Similarly, in the irrigation district, irrigators were generally unaware of exactly how the modernisation project would affect their own operation. It was known that that the irrigation backbone would be substantially reduced and that this would have a considerable impact across the irrigation district. However, the project had not reached the stage where individual discussions had taken place.

Turning now to the third area of the analysis, the future implications of the water redistribution: this was the most contested area of the three. For the government and irrigators in support of the project, the trade-off was seen to be fair. This was because the state government funding was thought to be generous, and the government could have taken an easier and significantly cheaper option of building the pipeline and purchasing the water in the water market. Thus the government believed that it was contributing substantially to the water security of the irrigation area, which was clearly needed. The trade-off outcome therefore would satisfy two needs: water security for Melbourne, and water security for the irrigation district. While irrigators and other community members universally supported the needs basis for the irrigation modernisation, they did not support the needs basis rationale for sending water to Melbourne. Thus the distribution rationale on which the whole project was based was heavily disputed. First, Melbourne had other options; and second, the river system had no other options and stood to lose 75 gigalitres of water per year. The notion put forward by the government that this was justifiable because it was 'saved water' was largely seen as a 'con'. An irrigator summarised: 'Melbourne is going to take its water, right or wrong, whether the savings are there or not'.

The loss of water to the environment and a river system that was known to be over-allocated and under stress from a prolonged drought was central to the broad-based opposition to the pipeline. This was a river system in need. To take water under these circumstances was seen by some as not only morally wrong but also as impractical because of the lack of actual water. Many pointed out that there was not currently enough water in Lake Eildon to send down the pipeline. A government response was to take water from an environmental reserve held in Lake Eildon, as an interim measure, until the water savings were available. But this was seen to be still a net loss to the river system. It was also a net loss to the irrigators because that water would have to be 'made up' in the next rainfall period which would mean irrigators would get less until the reserve had been restored. Proponents of the pipeline suggested that people generally did not understand that the savings would mean there would be extra water held in Lake Eildon. People opposing the project criticised the government for not being transparent and clear about the scenarios of how the water would actually be distributed under different rainfall conditions. This put future water security for the environment and the irrigators in doubt. With a river system that was already over-allocated, and already delivering water to the town of Bendigo, the pipeline to Melbourne would put another new demand on an already overstressed system. As one irrigator pointed out, in practical terms the pipeline would divert the majority of the water that was actually flowing down the Goulburn river, but the impact downstream of the loss of this water had not been assessed so 'of course it is not fair … it is blatant abuse of process'.

Fears for the future were at the heart of community concerns: once the pipeline was built then the risk of additional water being purchased by urban water authorities and industry could become reality. In terms of equity this created a problem for the irrigators, because they could not afford to compete for water on the same terms. Central to irrigator concerns were their existing investments in irrigation infrastructure on their properties, as well as their expectation for water to continue to be delivered under the current irrigation system arrangements. As one irrigator pointed out, he had consistently invested in infrastructure upgrades on his property, which had become a substantial part of his overall equity. This equity represented a lifetime's work and for many irrigators was their main source of superannuation.

To have the future put in doubt, first through water trading, and second through the pipeline, was seen to be unjust to those who had based their livelihoods and future security on a community-based irrigation system that had worked well until these – in their view unjustified – recent changes.

In summary, the unfolding outcome in the Victoria study consisted of a complex and contextually based set of issues in which the proponents had failed to present the big picture. There were strong convictions and deep divisions about the proposed distribution of water which was seen as fair by some and unfair by others. To those who saw it as fair it was an outcome based on needs and necessity brought on by drought. To those who saw it as unfair it was an outcome based on a dubious rationale which did not satisfy the needs of the environment or recognise irrigators' equity in the irrigation system. To this latter group and many in the broader community a needs-based outcome did not justify the abandonment of impact assessment within a consultation process and did not trump an alternative outcome which could have been the result of a fair decision-making process.

Summary: towards better and fairer outcomes

Some themes emerge from this outcomes analysis. People do make fairness assessments or justice judgements about outcomes which can be distilled down to the three distributive justice principles of need, equity and equality. In making these assessments people draw on a range of experiences, values, beliefs, judgements and factual analyses. As has been shown in these studies, there are similarities in the way people formulate their assessments, drawing on common values, shared lived and community experiences and shared expectations for the future. These similarities result in the formation of groups working to support proposals or groups in combined opposition. Where strong convictions are held, divisions occur which can result in divided communities. These findings also show that if an injustice is perceived to have taken place, then people have very clear ideas on what an appropriate response should be under those circumstances. In the NSW study a needs-based decision was not an acceptable response to a perceived equity based injustice. The findings from the Victoria study further showed that if a needs-based decision has been made that has a negative impact on a community, then a factual basis and clear rationale is required before the decision can be considered acceptable. In other words, the rationale needs to be part of the decision. In addition, the findings show that needs-based decisions can be hotly contested as to their validity, and this highlights the importance of sound information being available to support the proposal. Areas that are contested are not restricted to facts. Morals and what people consider right or wrong under the circumstances are also areas of disagreement, for example the needs of the environment, or people's current and future positions of equity. These findings show why fair decision-making processes are essential in gaining the acceptance of decisions, and why such processes are important in achieving *better* decisions and outcomes.

7 Muddying the waters

Worldviews, institutions and change

So far we have explored how people experience injustice, and how they are motivated to remedy injustices through opposition campaigns and calls for justice. We have seen how justice and fairness perceptions contribute to the acceptance of decisions and how better outcomes might be achieved. We have gained an understanding of individual and community perspectives of fairness and justice in resource sharing through the carrier case studies. The focus now broadens in scope to consider fairness and justice in resource sharing at a societal level, in addition to the individual and community level. Dilemmas of sharing between these three levels (society, community and individuals) create tension and conflict, such as when a decision is made for the overall benefit to society but is perceived at a local level as a burden and a harm to those individuals affected. A prominent example is the conflict over wind farms, described in Chapter 1, in which opposing positions have become entrenched and communities are split apart by the dispute. The difficulty in resolving these societal impasses demonstrates the importance of developing a thorough understanding of fairness and justice issues and their connections within and between these social levels.

This chapter shows that there are many inherent and obscure issues of fairness, justice and injustice in these levels, where resources are used and shared. The chapter reveals some embedded fairness and justice themes in water management and shows how these are generally applicable to resource sharing in a broader context. As in earlier chapters, water management in Australia is being used as a carrier study because it provides a good context in which societal fairness and justice issues can be understood. These water carrier studies are useful, not only in their own right as examples of global water-sharing concerns, but also because the issues and themes that emerge are common across a wide range of resource-using and resource-sharing scenarios. Many long-standing issues of fairness and justice came up in the carrier case studies in conversations about present-day disputes. A theme that emerged was how subtly shifting societal goals about sharing have a major impact on communities and individuals who have built a life-time of work and experience around a well-established set of arrangements for sharing.

Irrigated agriculture is particularly interesting as a carrier case study for a number of reasons: equity was built in as a feature of early irrigation schemes; irrigation in many countries became a deeply rooted culture and way of life; irrigation serves a public interest by producing food and fibre (e.g. cotton); and irrigation communities worldwide are now defending their role in society against accusations of wasting water and damaging the environment (see, for example, National Research Council (1996) for a discussion of the future of irrigation in the USA).

The aim is not to describe or expose *all* aspects of fairness and justice in water management in Australia, let alone globally. This would need volumes in itself. Rather, the aim is to show that fairness and justice issues arise over time and that these are not perceived or understood in the same way at different levels of society. This discussion involves an exploration of many 'muddy' areas of water management in which clarity is elusive and teasing apart the issues can be difficult. This chapter will show that such clarity can come with justice considerations.

Where people share scarce resources, such as land and water, there are inevitably differing perspectives about what these resources are used for and how to set up arrangements for the sharing of resources. In Chapter 1 we saw disagreement about how land should be used, how people value the landscape differently and why they oppose developments such as greenhouse clusters and wind farms. When water is scarce, questions are raised about what water should be used for, how much water should be allocated to different agricultural enterprises and industries, and how much should be reserved for river ecosystem health. A societal concern in Australia is the perception that the use of water for some types of irrigated agriculture, such as flood irrigated rice, is unjustifiable in a dry country. This goes to the heart of irrigation and the question of water use and sharing.

The first section of the chapter describes how those within an irrigation scheme perceive their community and way of life. While this is generally based on the heyday of irrigation, the purpose is to understand how irrigation schemes have worked and to explore how water as a resource has been shared. The second section explores the history and development of irrigated agriculture in relation to changing societal worldviews and goals. Fairness dilemmas resulting from tensions and divisions within these changing worldviews are discussed. The third section turns to more recent reforms in water management and explores fairness themes within the areas of markets, trading and public infrastructure funding. This includes a discussion on how to account for environmental issues in water sharing. The fourth section describes some experiences of specific water management initiatives and the way they were perceived as fair and acceptable by those involved. The chapter concludes with a summary of the implications for justice and fairness in natural resource management and environmental decision making.

Resource sharing as a way of life and a way to organise society

> At one level, irrigation is simply the application of water to grow plants. At another level, it is the basis for an economy and a way of life.
>
> (National Research Council 1996: 20)

What came out strikingly from the NSW and Victorian irrigation community stories is the strong sense of community, and recognition that the general health of the community was reliant on all parts working well together. This included relationships between businesses and irrigators, irrigators and government, and irrigation companies and irrigators. Irrigators benefited from having irrigation supply businesses within the township. Everyone benefited from local social services such as schools, health care, government and research agencies. Maintaining social cohesion was important: people talked about episodes of friction and how these had been satisfactorily addressed. Respect for other people's perspectives was an important aspect of negotiating processes. In such small communities, everybody knew everybody else and recognised the importance of getting along together. A NSW irrigator described how some years ago irrigators had been unfairly critical of a water-allocation decision by a regional government employee, who was well known to the community, and his regret about the incident. Many people underlined the importance of social cohesion to the future well-being of the community: if people felt good they would stay in the community. Sons and daughters would take over family farms and businesses. Knowledge about farming and local conditions would be passed from generation to generation. The community would thrive and there would be continuity for this way of life. Having community leaders and government agency employees demonstrate their commitment to the community by living within it, was also important for social well-being. That this had been in decline in NSW irrigation communities for several years was a serious cause for concern. Living in an irrigation community was more than just a past and current way of life – it was the future too.

An irrigation system as a decentralised societal structure

Taking the notion of an irrigation community as a way of life one step further, an irrigation system or community can also be seen as a way of organising society. This perspective was described by a retired scientist in Victoria who had lived and worked in an irrigation community for a good part of his professional life. He said that irrigation communities and irrigation districts were important because, of all the 'decentralisation schemes' tried in Australia, 'irrigation is the only one that has really succeeded'. He saw irrigation with its intensive farming practices as a means of organising society. This was for two reasons: to achieve a structurally balanced society of coastal cities and country towns, and to develop land as a resource. In his view irrigation was a way to generate wealth, support country towns and achieve diversity in society.

A NSW potato farmer talked about the 'socialisation' of water, and how that benefited communities that had developed within an irrigation system. The diversity of farming operations was important to the resilience of the community. Because this farmer had long-term contracts and could purchase additional water he was able to employ local people at harvest time which was important to the local economy during the drought. This 'socialisation' of water was fundamental to the structure of an irrigation community. People talked about their desires and expectations for their community, and the type of society they wanted to live in. These aspirations included stability, security for the future, being dealt with fairly, and being recognised and valued for their contribution to society. In this context many participants in this study lamented the fact that they did not feel they were valued as food producers, and that the nature of irrigation farming was frequently misunderstood.

A resource-use system based on the 'socialisation' of the resource

Irrigation communities in south-eastern Australia had been built in an era of nation-building. The so-called socialisation of water, in which water was supplied at low cost through publicly funded infrastructure, was a central arrangement that had persisted over the years. The original layout whereby water was tied to the land was an original design feature of the irrigation system. The irrigation system and community then developed in response to changing conditions, but the central feature of water supply remained intact until water reform in the late twentieth century. The success of this co-evolution in NSW with respect to the way water was allocated was articulated by a NSW government water professional:

> The different approaches have been worked through in each state based on their needs, based on their demographics, based on their soil types, based on their agricultural types … it would be really stupid to compromise that … it really has worked well for NSW.

He was referring to the different approaches in different Australian states; NSW, Victoria, and South Australia, in respect to water allocation, and the NSW distinction between general security and high security water. The point was that NSW had developed an equitable approach to the variable supply of water in NSW, which was different to the approach developed in other states. The two-tiered approach in NSW was highly successful because it enabled 10 to 15% of water to be classified as high security, so that in a drought year that water could still be supplied. This approach was valued by the irrigation community: the system that had evolved was seen to be fair and equitable under these water arrangements. The original allocation of water was based on equity, with the water entitlement being in proportion to the area of land. In seasonal terms, irrigators would share equally, or proportionally, in reductions or increases of water available to be allocated. Those irrigators with high value plantings, that were vulnerable permanent assets (such as vineyards and orchards) in comparison to annual crops, paid more for their higher security water, which was limited to 10 to 15% of the overall water allocated.

This allocation arrangement and the procedures by which the annual allocation were communicated by the government and delivered by the irrigation company were generally seen to be in balance. This provided a secure setting for farm and business planning for irrigators and the community alike, on an annual basis and into the future. However, the disadvantage of such a system is that people wishing to buy water permanently had to buy it with the land, and use it within the system. Ironically, despite water being tied to the land being an original design feature, this also became a reason for the reforms embodied in the National Water Initiative. What had changed was that water in the Murray–Darling Basin had become over-allocated, exacerbated by such actions as the sleeper and dozer activation (Chapter 4).

Summary: fairness characteristics of a 'model' resource-sharing system

An irrigation system can thus be seen as a 'model' community-based system of food production, in which resource sharing arrangements were part of the original design of the system and agreed as fair and equitable. The characteristics of the resource-sharing system were based on distributive justice principles of equity and equality. When the system was set up there was proportional allocation of the resource to the land acreage (equity) and subsequent adjustments when availability of the resource fluctuated were made equally to all resource users (equality). An important aspect of fairness in a resource-sharing system is that all individuals are bound by the same rules for the benefit of the community. This limits some individual freedom, for example, an individual cannot sell the resource entitlement unless the land is sold with it.

Another characteristic of fairness was that the system could be adapted in response to external changes and that there were agreed procedures and arrangements in place between irrigators and government agencies to accommodate these. The design and implementation of the water management tool to enable irrigators to carry over water from one year to the next is a good example of this adaptive management approach. This characteristic of fairness – collaboration in adapting to changing circumstances – is an important aspect of managing a fair and equitable system in a variable environment. It enables social cohesion between the parts of the system and allows for continual evolution of the resource system. The advantage for those living within this type of system is the relative stability of the arrangements for resource sharing, which provides security for the future.

Shifting worldviews in resource use: complexity and tensions

Divisions and perceptions of agriculture

> Most people just think the farmers continue to whinge and this time they are whingeing even harder … But Melbourne people are so far removed from farming that they have no concept of how food is produced.
>
> (Victorian dairy farmer and cheese producer)

The contribution to the nation's prosperity by irrigation communities in the NSW and Victorian 'Food Bowl' areas of the Murray–Darling Basin is considerable in food production but not in gross domestic product (GDP). A tangible rural–urban divide is keenly felt within irrigation communities. It may be due to the significant decline in the agricultural proportion of Australia's production in the latter part of the twentieth century, from 21% of GDP in 1948 to 3% in 1999 (Samuel 1999). Another major cause of city–country tension has been increasing environmental awareness by urban populations and concern about the impact of agriculture on river systems, native flora and fauna, and rural and coastal ecosystems.

There are widespread perceptions that irrigators are increasingly responsible for environmental degradation in those river systems suffering water shortage because of their use of water in pursuit of their own self-interest. Photographs of water-filled rice paddy fields surrounded by brown arid landscapes of the inland add to tensions and lead to the castigation of rice growers. Irrigation communities resent such accusations of 'wasting water' in the face of their efforts to achieve greater water efficiency and conform to good environmental practice. As a result many irrigators feel embattled and undervalued as food producers and contributors to the nation's economy. Irrigators defend their use of water and criticise these types of judgements as uninformed and lacking consideration of other farming criteria as to their use of water.

The gaps in urban knowledge about farming practices is recognised by governments and agricultural organisations worldwide (Filor 2007; Hopkins 2009). In Australia, national events such as the annual 'Farm Day' increase understanding of modern farming and how food is produced (The Land 2009). A similar education programme exists in the United States (Farm Futures 2009). Despite such well-intentioned initiatives, rural industries, particularly the irrigation industry, continue to face a continuing lack of understanding and engagement between rural and urban communities, and between rural communities and state and federal governments. This lack of engagement has resulted in strained relationships, a lack of understanding of potential and actual social impacts following implementation of government policies, and a lack of recognition of local knowledge in the development of plans and policies.

These divides are symptomatic of the differing worldviews held by groups or communities on either side about issues such as how natural resources should be allocated and used. Gaining an understanding of these views is a necessary step on the way to allocating or sharing resources in ways that achieves both fairness and social acceptance. A second step is maintaining a historical and holistic perspective on these worldviews in order to understand how embedded beliefs and values from different phases of development can persist through time, only to resurface in a different phase or place.

Development phases: old myths to new myths?

> To an important extent the approach to water management has been based on acceptance of a number of myths about the nature of the resource on the one hand and human behaviour on the other. To some degree the various myths are a result of ignorance, either of early settlers or of their successors, but they are also a reflection of various cultural and political factors.
>
> (Sewell *et al.* 1985: 231)

> The bitter irony of the current drought is that it has again called forth the same myths and false beliefs that got us into trouble in the first place.
>
> (Williams 2003: 40)

An appreciation of the historical context and how situations come about is important in developing an understanding of a current societal state of affairs, whether it is one of conflict or one that works well. As described in Chapter 4, each of the three phases of water development in Australia were driven by differing national objectives. Some well-known myths about the use of water in Australia were spawned in these phases. The second phase of nation-building and economic development was powered in part by two myths that still persist: that water runs to waste to the sea and that we can drought-proof Australia (Sewell *et al.* 1985; Edwards 2003; Williams 2003). Proposals to turn rivers inland and pipe water from one part of the country to another are presented regularly as solutions to water shortages in capital cities and specific country areas (Williams 2003; Watson 2007; Neales 2008). Examples of these water diversion proposals are the Bradfield scheme in north Queensland, the Ord River in the north of Western Australia, the Clarence River in northern New South Wales and the pipeline from Tasmania to Melbourne. These proposals lack detail, underestimate the complexity involved, and gloss over past experiences. In a response to a call for new dams to be built, the late Peter Cullen, a well-known water scientist, countered:

> You can't drought-proof Australia. We need to learn to live with the landscape, not trying to fight against it all the time. Reversing rivers is a simplistic reaction to a complex set of problems.
>
> (ABC Media Watch 2002: 1)

Fortunately, many of these types of large-scale infrastructure proposals are short-lived once details are worked out and the practical feasibility, costs and environmental impacts become apparent. However, the fact that these proposals do persist, despite being roundly criticised, suggests that these myths are not universally recognised as myths: they are still perceived as viable solutions to drought, water shortage and growing populations.

The importance of drought as a driver of change and as a catalyst for public investment is well known (Rutherford 1966; Lloyd 1988; Smith 1998). However, the urgency and threat posed by drought still remains a catalyst for large-scale infrastructure projects. The Victorian North South Pipeline is one example. Although the North South Pipeline was put forward and justified on a 'human needs' basis, its development brings to the fore many tensions. These revolve around the continued exploitation of natural resources to promote the prevailing economic paradigm (Mercer *et al.* 2007), and the need to find more balanced approaches, as described by Peter Cullen above. Peter Cullen's quotation aptly describes an emerging set of beliefs, many of which were put forward by people opposed to the North South Pipeline. For example, one Plug the Pipe campaigner suggested that the pipeline was a 'primitive' response to urban water shortage, and that 'micro-solutions' (such as recycling and household water tanks) were much more appropriate than large-scale public infrastructure solutions. Thus the notion of a large-scale infrastructure response to water shortage could in itself become a myth. Also, people concerned about the environment suggested that river systems should have rights over the water in that system irrespective of perceived human needs in another river system.

Nevertheless, a significant part of contemporary society, in Australia and many other countries, is based on earlier manifestations of myths. Australian examples of the latter include the River Murray irrigation schemes and the Snowy Hydro scheme, in which large volumes of water are diverted from one river system to another. In response to the suggestion that large-scale diversion of water is no longer acceptable, a NSW government agency employee suggested: 'We have lost the precedent for the argument about keeping water in catchments (river systems), even though it is a good one, and probably should apply'. Irrigators hold different viewpoints. Many believe that the Snowy Hydro scheme was built primarily for irrigation, and should be preserved for irrigation. One pointed out that without the dams and irrigation infrastructure the River Murray would not flow in severe droughts, so the social and environmental benefits of having water in the River Murray during a drought should be recognised as positive by-products of the irrigation schemes.

Maintaining a contextual perspective is important for a number of reasons. First, people hold subjective viewpoints and have individual life experiences. A lifetime of work based on the beliefs and values of a past era is unlikely to be cast aside unless there is good reason to do so. Second, the rationale and driving force that justified such schemes as Snowy Hydro, conceived in the earlier part of the twentieth century, were markedly different from the drivers of change today. People within and on the fringes of the schemes can be operating under a different set of beliefs without fully recognising – or admitting – the shift beneath them. Third, while the need for change may be broadly understood, the way in which change is introduced and the type of change required must take into account the starting position of the different participants. For some, a baseline and way of thinking comes from an earlier irrigation era, whereas for others, the starting position is environmental crisis caused by over-allocation of water.

Finally, a contextual perspective is necessary to understand the baseline from which issues of equity can be adjudicated. Recognising that drivers of change can be perceived simultaneously as old-fashioned myths and present-day solutions is a critical aspect of decision making. Governments responsible for policy changes must be aware of changing cultures and the metamorphic nature of their embedded myths: myths fade, they reappear and they are distorted or disputed. The question becomes: how can these different myths or perspectives be captured and understood together? The complexity of these challenges is not lost on governments. As a Victorian government agency employee commented on the North South Pipeline: 'It is a political game for the media and there are a lot of massive ignorances. These things are technically complex'. He went on: 'It is never a good idea to respond to media headlines which tap the emotional side with a whole lot of technical data which is actually complex and confusing'.

Summary: fairness in shifting worldviews and societal goals

The way societies use and share resources is a continually evolving process subject to a variety of societal goals such as nation-building, economic development, social prosperity, and environmental health. These shifting societal goals cause disconnections and tension in society about how resources should be used. When worldviews shift in emphasis the fairness implications of resource sharing are not explicitly considered. People can lose sight of an earlier rationale for decisions and arrangements. This causes a lag between the changing goals of society and the impact on the resource user at the individual and community level, where established arrangements and ways of working constrain change.

The point here is that fairness implications need to be more specifically considered in government thinking about drivers of change. Consideration must be given to the reason put forward to establish a 'need' for the resource and the consequences for current users as well as the environment. Those who use the resource have to be brought along with the changed thinking about the resource. Knowledge and understanding are critical elements of fairness when redistributing a resource. It is a government responsibility to maintain this knowledge and these perspectives across time, and to include these in the rationale for decisions about resource distributions.

Water reform: tensions and perspectives

While myths, ideas and disagreements persist about the problems of droughts, floods and resource sharing, there is no disagreement that south-eastern Australia has been in a long-standing water crisis. This section outlines some current perspectives and experience with recent policies and initiatives to address the crisis. The aim is to draw out the fairness implications from the local detail of this well-documented area of water management.

Water reform: introduction of water markets

The Australian National Water Initiative (see Chapter 4) is a national approach to water management in which environmentally sustainable water use is the primary objective (Connell and Dovers 2006). Essentially, this is to be achieved through the use of water markets in which the intention is for water to be used to its highest value. This objective makes the assumption that as a scarce resource, water will be more highly valued, with the market mechanism facilitating the transfer of water rights to achieve this highest value use. There is substantive agreement that as a reform programme, the National Water Initiative is ambitious and has many challenges, including differing legal and institutional state arrangements that are impediments to the national approach (Connell *et al.* 2005; Fisher 2007; Hussey and Dovers 2007b). However, there are also some fundamental concerns about the reform.

Water reform: water markets and water to the highest value

One fundamental concern is whether a free market approach to water use is an appropriate or fair way to deal with a scarce resource, particularly in countries such as Australia where the water supply is extremely variable. An orchardist irrigator in the NSW study suggested that there was a great deal of ignorance about the nature of irrigation. He was concerned about permanent trade increasing the amount of water allocated to high value crops. He suggested that only a small portion of the total water allocated should be made available for high value crops, because of the 'massive variation in rainfall and inflows'. This is why a range of industries had developed, which included high value crops such as fruit and some vegetables, and lower value opportunistic crops such as rice and cotton. He suggested that the current proportion of high security water, about 10 or 12% of the total water, was the right amount to be allocated to high value crops. This arrangement safeguards the amount of water available in a drought year for vulnerable crops (such as fruit trees) which take years to grow, and would die if no water was available. With respect to trading, the orchardist thought that temporary trading was a suitable mechanism to shift water where it is in excess to where it is needed. However, he was against permanent trading because it had facilitated new irrigation enterprises, such as managed investment schemes (Chapter 4), which had bought large parcels of land downstream from the major Victorian and NSW irrigation areas, and had transferred water to those areas.

The movement of water permanently out of an irrigation district has the potential to destabilise the operation of the irrigation system due to the 'stranded assets' problem (Chapter 4). This irrigator was concerned that 'massive changes' were being advocated within the National Water Initiative reforms without consideration of the potential impacts. He was also concerned about the possibility for 'today's high value industry becoming tomorrow's low value industry' owing to overproduction and oversupply, as had been seen with some varieties of wine grapes.

Another perspective was presented by a Victorian government agency water professional. He believed that water markets, which put decisions at an individual level, were the most equitable and efficient way of dealing with water resource management. In his view the market enabled willing sellers and willing buyers to trade. The markets worked 'in terms of equity brilliantly' from an individual perspective. However, from a local community perspective he believed that it was more important for individuals to make decisions for their families, and not to make 'sub-optimal decisions for the benefit of the local community'. While he recognised the stranded asset problem and the tension between individual decision making and the impact on regional communities when water is sold out of a region, he believed that the markets allowed individuals to make the difficult decisions rather than 'bureaucrats making decisions for individuals'. With respect to hardship and need, he believed that this should be managed through 'hardship provisions rather than mucking around with water management'. In terms of equity, equality and need he believed the best outcome would be for individuals to determine their own need: equality was achieved by people having the same choices available to them, and equity could be achieved by individuals working out how to meet their own need.

Water reform: complexity and lack of understanding

The complexity of Australian water reform is widely acknowledged, just as is the case with many resource reforms globally (Connell *et al.* 2007; Fisher 2007; Hussey and Dovers 2007a; Crase 2008). Connell *et al.* (2005: 93) suggest that water trading in the National Water Initiative will 'create a complex maze' in part because it promotes trading in entitlements with different levels of security. Gardner and Bowmer (2007: 54) also draw attention to the reform process whereby 'conversion of high-security licences to fully tradeable entitlements risks converting an insurance against need into a profit from other people's needs in times of scarcity'. In other words the original purpose of high security water – high reliability for high value plantings, such as orchards – will be transformed through the trading process into whatever the purchaser deems is a suitable purpose. The implication is that the water trading reform has the potential to disrupt a long-standing balance between the different types of water entitlements, including differing water security requirements for temporary and permanent horticultural and agricultural crops. The reform would also have an impact on an irrigation community's ability to adapt to these changes.

The significance and importance of maintaining a consistent balance between the proportion of water available for high value crops and opportunistic crops needs to be made clear. A lack of understanding of this point can lead to incorrect assumptions. This appears to be the case in a 2007 review of water policy in Australia by Mercer *et al.* (2007: 283) in which they state that 'the bulk of irrigation water is producing relatively small returns per megalitre' and compare the proportion of water used on high value crops (30%) versus low value crops (70%). By making the statement 'about 2/3 of the value of irrigated crops comes from about 1/3 of water used' (p. 283), the authors seem to imply that more water should be used for high-return products, in line with the market based objective. However, while it is possible that more water *could* be used for high value crops, it should also be recognised *why* the current proportion exists: to safeguard high value crops in times of drought. Opportunistic annual crops, such as rice and cotton, are only grown when the water is available and therefore also have value in irrigated agriculture. Equally, it should be recognised that water is but one of many decision-making points in an agricultural enterprise: investment in specialised machinery, irrigation technology, land suitability, access to markets, market demand, access to funding, and availability of staff are other important factors involved in farmers' decisions in determining what crops to grow.

As discussed earlier, in relation to maintaining a perspective about shifting societal goals, it is also important to maintain a clear *understanding* of the reasons that specific distributions of a resource or allocations are set in the first place. This issue of the proportional allocation between permanent plantings (high value crops) and opportunistic annual plantings (low value crops) is a fairness nuance understood and appreciated by those *within* the system. A resource distribution aims to achieve a fair balance, not only of fairness between the users of the resource, but also a fair balance of the end product. In relation to water use, people need a mix of different food types (grains, vegetables, fruits) and the water distribution in the irrigation system produces this.

Water reform: equity and the activation of sleepers and dozers

A number of irrigators in the NSW study expressed the view that the government reforms had actually *increased* the problem of over-allocation. This was because water trading enabled people to sell water held on 'sleeper' and 'dozer' licences (Chapter 4). People holding these licences either used none of the water (sleeper) or some of the water (dozer) available to them. The introduction of water trading essentially 'activated' these licences because holders could now sell their entitlement to an irrigator who would then put more of the water to use. This would *increase* the overall amount of water used for irrigation and potentially affect the security of supply for other water users (Smith 1998). It was estimated that up to 30% of water was held on sleeper and dozer licences (Bell and Quiggin 2008). That this problem was foreseen in the 1990s, but could have been avoided, raises questions about the way water reform has been implemented (Bell and Quiggin 2008).

The decision to honour sleeper and dozer licences rather than making a decision on whether the water had been put to use or not (history of use) was based on an assessment of equity for those licence holders (Gardner and Bowmer 2007). A NSW government agency employee justified this course of action by suggesting that it was the only option the state government could take to avoid future litigation. However, Gardner and Bowmer (2007: 50) suggest that an alternative 'use it or lose it' policy, such as used in the USA, could have merit in the context of transferability of water entitlements. This example, of the way people who hold an entitlement to a resource but have not used that resource are treated, is a dilemma in many resource-sharing scenarios. The fairness implication is this: people who have invested in infrastructure to use a resource are not treated as well in the redistribution of the resource as those who have *not* used the resource *or* invested in any infrastructure, but who are compensated for loss of the resource. This is the essence of a 'use it or lose it' policy which is arguably a fairer approach across a resource user base.

Equality and a voice for the environment?

Although concern for the degraded state of the Murray–Darling Basin was a principal driver for the water reform, it can still be argued that the environment does not yet have an effective voice. For example, some Plug the Pipe members in Victoria bemoaned the fact that Victorian environmental groups had not voiced any serious opposition to the pipeline, leaving the fight primarily to the Plug the Pipe group. The way national and state governments have responded to environmental needs for increased natural river flows in the Murray–Darling Basin has been to instigate water buy-back programmes.

A NSW government agency water professional suggested that the NSW government had effectively become the 'voice for the environment' through this buy-back mechanism. He characterised the government water buy-back programme as gaining equity for the environment and 'giving the environment some equality in water use'. While many criticised the government for 'pretending to be the environment', and thought that the government should not be in the market, in his opinion this was the only way to return water to the environment under the current market system. However, he thought that current policy was 'flawed' because environmental sustainability was not yet built in despite being talked about for decades. He was critical of the market approach – 'markets are quite wasteful, very wasteful' and can 'squander resources' – because rapid land use changes as a result of market forces have produced excessive waste when permanent plantings such as vineyards and orchards are 'ripped up'. In his opinion the federal government should focus on facilitating structural adjustment in some marginal irrigation areas, whereby environmentally problematic irrigation schemes would be closed down. Compensation would be used to purchase the water rights, shut down irrigation channels and return the area to dry land farming. This had been done successfully in some parts of Victoria. But the challenge for government to be able to facilitate such initiatives was in communicating the bigger picture and negotiating with people who may be unlikely to accept that as a fair solution.

A deep concern for the environment was also expressed by an executive-level professional involved in natural resource management in NSW. In his perspective there were some fundamental justice issues with the current government approach. First he described the economic model as 'unjust' because it does not take account of externalities such as environmental degradation. Externalities should be included in the product costing, and are currently incorrectly attributed to the farmer. Rather, he thought it is the consumer of the product who is 'taking the water out of the river' and not the farmer: the price of the product should reflect this. He thought it was unjust to expect the farmer to be responsible for the full cost of the irrigation system and for restoring river health. He strongly suggested that we cannot be 'just in our society' until 'we know about the footprint of our food choices and farming choices'. Regional structural adjustment was necessary 'to face up to the basic inequalities and injustice underneath this whole show'. The bigger picture and 'higher-level issues' of the environment were not being addressed. The scope of justice should be extended to the environment: the environment should be seen as valuable in its own right, not only because it is of advantage to our well-being to have a healthy environment. He also thought that the current '*ad hoc* fix-ups', such as water buy-backs and some infrastructure projects were part of culture of 'doing little bits and pieces' without a full appreciation of the 'bigger picture'. Thus he was critical of the North South Pipeline construction taking place before the overall Basin Plan for the Murray–Darling basin was complete.

In summary, these natural resource professionals were of the view that the water reforms do not go nearly far enough to address the structural changes required to put environmental or social concerns on an equal platform with economic considerations. In fact, to the contrary: in spite of the water buy-back programme, water trading has further muddied the waters, so to speak, with the rise and fall of some large corporate holdings of water entitlements. The failure of many agricultural managed investment schemes (Locke 2012) is another example of perverse consequences from an environmental and social perspective. The irony is that these were not 'unanticipated consequences' as such, but were foreshadowed in the 1980s before permanent trading commenced (Pigram 1993; Bell and Quiggin 2008).

As this record has shown, issues of justice and fairness are central to these sorts of reform strategies. These viewpoints clearly portray the need for the environment to be included in the scope of justice and given an official voice. Exactly how this is put into practice is yet to be determined. These perspectives provide evidence that markets in which resources are traded are not 'fair' to the environment when the market fails, involving the collapse of elements within the resource system, wasted environmental assets and harm to the environment.

Public funding and water savings: skeletons in the irrigation closet or more myths?

> Instead of a national symbol of progress and growth, some now see irrigated agriculture as a depleter and polluter of water, living off government subsidies.
>
> (National Research Council 1996: 24)

Much has been written about irrigation. But in spite of numerous detailed analyses by environmental historians, economists, agricultural scientists and academics from various disciplines, the *story* of irrigation is still confusing and controversial. Why is this? Is it due to a combination of complexity, a lack of broad perspective and entrenched viewpoints? It is useful to review briefly some past and current perspectives about irrigation schemes, bearing in mind, as we have seen earlier with the persistence of myths, that a past perspective is likely to still be operating in the present. These perspectives also bear on what people see as problems of fairness, justice and injustice in this general area of resource sharing.

Wasted public funding?

There are three fundamental reasons why publicly funded irrigation schemes in Australia receive so much scrutiny: first, they have benefited from substantial public investment to set them up, and second, they control and use significant amounts of water. A third reason is that irrigators are seen as part of a large and powerful rural lobby that is perceived to receive special treatment, for example, drought relief (Lloyd 1988; Crase 2007; Musgrave 2008). However, the twin focus of present-day disputes is the continued public funding of infrastructure upgrades and the degree to which water is used efficiently. While the last publicly funded irrigation scheme in NSW was introduced in the 1960s, it was in that same decade that criticism of irrigation from an economic perspective was voiced (Langford-Smith and Rutherford 1966; Lloyd 1988). The issue for economists was that public money could be better spent elsewhere: irrigation schemes could never be profitable. In 1969, Davidson, an agricultural economist, suggested that Australia would be better served as follows: 'If decentralisation is a desirable aim, it could have been achieved on a far larger scale by devoting a similar quantity of resources to settling new dry farming regions' (Davidson 1969: 4). Davidson was an important voice at this time because he boldly criticised the entrenched Australian belief in irrigation for the dual purpose of profitable agricultural production and drought-proofing. He suggested that accurate measurement of irrigation profitability would readily dismiss Australian support for irrigated agriculture as a cure for drought (Davidson 1969).

Although this period can be seen as a turning point in attitudes away from irrigation, the irrigation schemes were in place, the funds already spent, and communities were established. There was no turning back. But looking forward, state government policies shifted towards the 'user pays' principle whereby irrigators became responsible for maintenance of the infrastructure. Despite these government intentions and directives, the required level of investment from irrigators did not eventuate, and publicly owned irrigation infrastructure in Victoria was not maintained to the standard required. Water losses as part of the transport of water through the system increased. Eventually, in Victoria, the Food Bowl Modernisation Project was initiated. As we have seen, this has been a controversial project, and the irrigation infrastructure upgrade, even considered separately from the North South Pipeline, has triggered substantial critique. There are four key perspectives. First, from irrigators who are opposed to giving away water in return for upgrades; second, from economists or commentators who question using public funds for the upgrades; third, from the deal-makers consisting of the Victorian government and Food Bowl Unlimited; and fourth, the environmental concerns about the health of river systems.

A view described by many irrigators in the Victoria pipeline dispute is that the government should be responsible for funding improvements to publicly owned infrastructure. Their argument is two-fold: first, that they are price-takers, as they do not receive subsidies like some global competitors, and it would be uneconomic for irrigators to bear the full cost. Second, publicly owned infrastructure should be maintained by public funds, in the same way that roads and hospitals are funded. Unsurprisingly, economists take an opposing view. Watson (2008), an economist, acknowledges that while the public sector must deal with public investment legacies from the past, such legacies do not justify a current preoccupation with engineering solutions such as irrigation upgrades. He questions these investments in several ways. They are at odds with earlier government objectives of cost recovery; then, choosing between competing upgrade projects raises equity issues for those irrigators or irrigation organisations who have already invested in on-farm or off-farm improvements; and finally, he questions the validity of the water savings themselves.

Water savings under scrutiny: robbing Peter to pay Paul?

Also, raising concerns about water savings, Crase and O'Keefe (2009: 57) argue that 'the present enthusiasm for "modernising irrigation" stands to replicate and even exacerbate earlier mistakes'. Their contention is that the premise on which these upgrades are based is flawed. They suggest that there is confusion around the notions of water use efficiency, water savings and water losses and argue that return flows and recycling in an irrigation system have generally not been taken into account. They refer to the systems approach suggested by Gyles (2003), in which water flows within the river system or basin as a whole are considered.

Another economic perspective is that given by Crase and Dollery (2008), who suggest that reforms have actually benefited irrigators and irrigation organisations, at the expense of the state, because the establishment of markets has raised the value of water rights. This hidden potential benefit was not lost on several irrigators in the Victorian study who acknowledged that individually they stood to benefit by selling their water, but this would be at the overall cost to the community by exacerbating the stranded assets problem.

Another perspective concerns the Victorian government and members of Food Bowl Unlimited who constructed the deal. The deal whereby the government would fund A$1 billion worth of upgrades and in return receive up to 75 gigalitres of water from the savings was thought to be a good trade-off and a fair deal. As some people in the Victoria study pointed out, the government did have other cheaper options to gain this water: it could have built the pipeline and purchased the water through the water market. But by investing in the irrigation infrastructure the government was demonstrating that it *did* value the irrigation community and was willing to invest in it to provide future water security for the region. This approach, however, was questioned by some who thought there could be substantial water rate increases for Melbourne ratepayers, who perhaps, as yet, were oblivious to this future cost.

New myths?

What to make of these different perspectives? Embedded in these contested positions and perspectives is a range of difficult questions with roots permeating down through different layers of technical, economic, political and philosophical considerations and beliefs. Are the savings real or just a redistribution of water? Are irrigation farmers the 'meat in the sandwich' between consumers and markets or merely benefiting from the public purse? Can environmental externalities be costed into food prices? Should food production from established irrigation schemes be seen as in the public interest and therefore publicly supported? How can positions of equity be incorporated into decision making? These questions are all related to the sharing and allocation of natural resources, and therefore firmly within the domain of fairness and justice.

These and other questions are not unique to irrigation and water use in Australia or elsewhere in the world. In a broad review that takes a global perspective, Molle and Berkoff (2009) examine tensions that exist between cities and agriculture, including questions such as those above. They challenge many assumptions about the use of water including perceptions of an inefficient irrigation sector that impedes water being used to its highest value. They propose that irrigators are frequently *unfairly* branded as water-wasters, arguing that 'waste is often relative: if water has no other economic use and is not scarce, then "*wastage*" is of little concern other than for any impacts it has on the environment' (Molle and Berkoff 2009: 8 their emphasis). This type of analysis is important because it highlights trends in thinking about water use and challenges commonly held and often simplistic assumptions. As we have seen, myths from the past not only rise time and time again, but they can be wasteful in taking attention and resources away from new initiatives focused on gaining a better understanding of present-day issues.

Summary: fairness in resource sharing

This section has shown that resource use and sharing in irrigated agriculture and water management are deeply complex and frequently misunderstood. Embedded in this complexity are issues of fairness, justice and injustice. A fact-based approach is required to assess fairness issues, in which there is respect for the legitimacy of the differing positions of those people affected. Several fairness themes emerge:

- Fairness in distributing a natural resource is multilayered: there is fairness to the resource user who produces the product (e.g. food) and there is fairness to society at large in how the resource is deployed for the benefit of those who consume or purchase the end product.
- What is seen as equitable for an individual (e.g. individual choice) may not be equitable for the community as a whole (e.g. individuals opting out of established sharing arrangements).
- Distribution of a resource with the goal of seeking use to its highest monetary value does not necessarily result in a fair or wise distribution of the resource.
- Distribution of resources through markets can be wasteful of environmental resources when market failures occur, which can cause harm to the environment (e.g. wasted infrastructure and crops and diverted water).
- Reforms to long-standing sharing arrangements of a resource can be disruptive and result in unjust re-distributions if the complexity and unintended consequences of the reform are not fully considered.
- The costs and consequences of resource use at a societal and environmental level must be figured into resource distributions and infrastructure: the end-user of the product must be included in the bigger picture of natural resource sharing.
- The environment must be included in the scope of justice: consideration of resource use and reform must include how it will affect the natural environment and must minimise harm to the environment.

Fair and equitable solutions in water allocation

This chapter started with 'insider' perspectives of working irrigation schemes gained from the NSW and Victoria case studies. People within the schemes generally viewed the long-standing arrangements as being based on notions of equity and fairness: they *were* living within schemes which they perceived as fair and equitable. The schemes were based on a conception of water delivered as a public good whereby irrigators would add value by producing food to be used in the national interest for domestic consumption and export earnings.

We now examine the theme of fairness in water allocation more closely with some specific examples that were seen as fair and just in water allocation decision making. Challenges to effective water management decision making are also explored.

New South Wales: No magic pudding but a consideration of needs

'There's no magic pudding' is the term used by a government agency professional to describe the declining amount of water available to be shared by competing users in NSW. Nevertheless, some lessons in NSW had been learned. Starting with the first round of carry-over cuts in 2006, he suggested that tough decisions had to be made because this was a new situation, based on record low inflows, which had never before been encountered. In discussing the elements of procedural justice and the distributive justice principles of need, equality and equity, he recounted how, in 2007, in a similar situation of record low water availability, he was successful in gaining acceptance from a group of stakeholders to distribute water based on 'critical needs'. He described this in terms of distributive justice in which the needs of the various industries, such as permanent plantings, the paper mill, feedlots, winemakers and a munitions factory, were able to receive minimal amounts of water to keep operating. For this decision, taken outside the normal water distribution arrangements, NSW had been criticised by Victoria and South Australia for 'distorting the market'. However, this needs-based decision was necessary to ensure 'minimum damage to regional economies and regional communities as we could possibly get'. Importantly, participants from different stakeholder groups also agreed, albeit 'begrudgingly', with this emergency water distribution. As the professional described it, 'it worked exceptionally well' even though it was done on a 'preferential basis'.

In discussing overall water allocation policy in NSW, this government agency professional was comfortable with the two-tiered NSW water allocation arrangements and the government's ability to deal with new situations as they arose. He described how the NSW high security and general security water allocations had been worked out over time based on the characteristics of the irrigation industry, and these were based on the concepts of need, equity and equality. Although critical situations did arise, such as the carry-over water episode, these could eventually be worked out with a consultative approach based on the principles of procedural justice. The later 2007 water distribution, described above, was a case in point. The earlier carry-over water episode in 2006 was unusual in that it had many elements which failed together: failure of rain, a perceived underestimation of water by authorities, a lack of sophistication of administrative capability on the part of the government agency, a lack of understanding on the part of irrigators as to the constraints underlying carry over water, a lack of coordination between the institutions involved with water distribution in NSW, and a lack of preparedness of government agencies to sound a warning alarm sooner. Once the severity of the situation had been assessed, and stakeholder groups gathered together to discuss the situation, an acceptable outcome – the second cutback – could be achieved. This adaptive management style of decision making, made necessary by the record low inflows and requirement to satisfy critical human needs, had ultimately worked well, even though it was the first time the NSW government agency had faced this situation. It had little to do with market mechanisms.

New South Wales: procedural justice works

An executive-level professional involved in natural resource management in NSW was familiar with the theoretical notions of procedural and distributive justice, in large part from his knowledge of work carried out under the leadership of the Commonwealth Scientific and Industrial Research Organisation (CSIRO), Australia's national science agency. He described several areas in his experience where processes and procedures that included principles of procedural justice had been successful in obtaining outcomes that would otherwise have not been possible. In his opinion the value of a fair and transparent process in achieving acceptance of outcomes was proven 'absolutely' and he had incorporated this approach, as far as he could, into his work in natural resource management. He cited the work of the CSIRO in the Namoi Valley in northern NSW as being a good example of achieving success through the use of procedural justice principles. He suggested that a good process will often lead to a redistribution of resources that benefits the environment and that people are more likely to voluntarily give up natural resources, such as water, when these types of processes are employed. He said, 'I have lots of examples where people are willing to forego private good for public benefit' and suggested that this was particularly strong where people could see a connection to the outcome, for example, giving up water for wetlands to enable bird hatching to take place. Seeing an outcome such as a bird hatching event take place, gave people a sense of ownership. They could feel that they had made a contribution, and this added to their perceptions of how they were valued within the community.

Nevertheless, despite these positive experiences in natural resource management decision making in NSW, this professional believed that the principles of procedural justice and distributive justice and notions of need, equity and equality were generally not broadly discussed. To the contrary, he thought that the overall culture in NSW with respect to water allocation was: 'We will tell you what is going to happen'.

Victoria: consultation and infrastructure

According to a senior Victorian government agency professional, water legislation in Victoria 'is designed to enforce some procedural fairness'. In his perspective he was 'strict' in implementing strong consultative processes, which were significant for two key reasons. First, because they were important in enabling decisions to outlast changes of government; and second, to build 'understanding and support with communities who actually elect these people'. He made the point that water planning is not just based on empirical science – 'none of this stuff is empirical, it is all about values' – and since values were subject to political influence, the need for strong processes was paramount.

This water professional firmly believed that government action in Victoria to protect the environment should take the form of investment in infrastructure modernisation rather than through direct purchases of water on the water market. This demonstrated a government commitment to regional irrigation communities by showing that they are valued and that they have a future. He believed that governments buying water on the market only serves to 'exacerbate the problem' because it does not provide confidence for the future. He emphasised the need for good processes in infrastructure upgrades, including the principles of procedural justice, so that local groups could work out what irrigation structures to close down or modernise, and how incentives and decision making should be structured. He cited as a successful example the Pyramid Boort reconfiguration in the north-west of the Victorian irrigation area. This had taken two to three years of significant local engagement through a 'bottom-up' process involving the regional Water Service Committee working with local people to design an upgrade plan. A key factor in gaining acceptance of the proposed changes had been a substantial information base that detailed the infrastructure asset condition, the cost of delivering water to that asset, and a continuing expenditure profile for each asset. By placing the information in the public domain and allowing people who were affected to be participants in the process, the information could be scrutinised, and confidence in decisions based on that information could be gained.

The Pyramid Boort reconfiguration was described in some detail by an employee of the Northern Victorian Irrigation Renewal Project (the organisation responsible at the time for the infrastructure upgrades of the Food Bowl Modernisation Project). This water professional had long experience of working with people in the irrigation communities, initially as a water bailiff and later in operations working for Goulburn–Murray Water, a state government agency. He thought the Pyramid Boort reconfiguration had been successful for two main reasons. First, that people in the area recognised the need for change, and second there had been strong management by the Water Service Committee. The recognition of need only came about when the information had been gathered and people gained a real understanding of the implications for the area. However, while the majority accepted the proposed changes, strong management was still needed to 'push it through', because of the inherent 'conservative' nature of farmers and concerns of a minority of irrigators.

From this earlier experience and knowledge of the irrigation areas, he thought that a major challenge for the Food Bowl Modernisation Project would be in working out equity issues in the reconfiguration. These were in several areas. For example, the removal of channels from the irrigation backbone to individual farms would involve some irrigators being more adversely affected than others. Further, he believed that larger traditional irrigators had been cross-subsidising smaller farming operations, such as hobby farms, because large farms used larger volumes of water but all farms irrespective of size paid the same price per megalitre. Such equity issues would need to be addressed in the modernisation. Consultation and communication with individual irrigators and communities was critical to the success of the project. In his experience many lessons had been learned from successes and failures in earlier irrigation upgrades. He regarded farmers as generally conservative and unwilling to accept rapid change, and he recognised that people did need time and adequate consultation to explain how the change would affect their own operation.

However, he acknowledged that water allocations would change and 'convincing irrigators at the end of the day that we have not impacted on them is going to be very, very hard'. He also believed that water trading was 'fairly equitable' because everybody was able to trade their water. However, the impact of trading would be inequitable because the impacts on irrigators were different depending on the irrigation area. He believed that a new concept of targeted trading zones would be introduced whereby water would be allowed to be traded out of certain areas but not others. This would allow water to trade out of problematic areas, such as Pyramid Boort and Rochester, but would restrict trade out of the areas that had already been modernised.

Another government agency employee suggested that some irrigators would never get used to new ideas and change. He described the irrigation industry as being 20% 'movers and shakers', the next 40% being those 'who understand and follow' and 'there is 40% below that who have got no idea'. In tackling the challenge to communicate with this range of irrigation farmers, he suggested that a government agency's ability to provide information was limited by its staff numbers and expertise, but that even so, people still chose not to access information. This perspective was echoed by another government agency employee who thought that there was a skills shortage in government agencies of people who were able to engage with communities and communicate with them. He said unless people were directed to consult, they would not, because 'it is hard and tricky and they are likely to get shouted at'. Thus a consultation process that included communication as well as follow-up was vital, in addition to being able to convince people of the need for change.

Summary: fairness in decision-making processes

These examples of decision-making processes, in which scarcity of the resource forces difficult decisions, clearly demonstrate the importance of fair treatment and good processes. This includes having representatives of those affected by the decision involved in the decision-making process, effective information, and respect for long-standing arrangements that have stood the test of time. In times of crisis and unforeseen circumstances, these elements of fairness are essential in gaining acceptance of tough decisions. These examples also bring up the difficulties in working out the specific equity issues when distribution changes are required. Another general observation from these examples is the notion that acceptance of change varies within a community, with some being initiators and leaders, others being enthusiastic followers, and many being reluctant and grudging. However, society can often be too willing to embrace the new, heap praises on those who lead the charge, and denigrate those who advise caution. The point here is that respect for *all* perspectives is part of a fair approach in environmental decision making.

Understanding justice and fairness in natural resource sharing

The fairness, justice and injustice themes from this chapter highlight the difficulty that people have in understanding the fairness implications of decision making in natural resource management. The way fairness is to be achieved in sharing a resource, such as water, is not explicitly laid out in resource sharing arrangements. Rather, fairness and justice matters are expressed as individual opinions and viewpoints. The language of fairness and justice is ad hoc, delivered largely from an individual viewpoint, and languishes 'under the radar' of formal governance procedures. The fairness nuances of sharing a resource and the benefits and burdens that accrue to different levels of society need to be revealed in environmental decision making and become a routine part of discussions and decisions about resource sharing. This chapter has shown that there are multiple layers of interconnected fairness, justice and injustice considerations in resource sharing, many of which derive from arrangements made in an earlier era. These have implications relevant to a broad range of global resource sharing scenarios.

An important aspect of resource sharing is that what may appear to be fair at a societal level can have consequences that are perceived as deeply unfair at a community and individual level. This is particularly important where long-standing arrangements for sharing a resource are changed without due regard for fairness at the resource user level in the new arrangements. The implication is that governments must recognise the fairness issues at the root of tension and division between these areas, and develop a *deliberate* understanding of the fairness interactions between the three levels (society, community and individual). This chapter has shown that there are many cases where redistributing a resource has been successful, because fairness elements were included in the decision-making process. But these have been patchy in water management and, as we have seen, lessons learned in one area are not always applied in another area. This is why fairness principles must become part of the way of doing business in government agencies, rather than being ad hoc and dependent on the skills or interest of the person in charge at the time. Many decision-makers might argue that they do assess fairness and equity as a routine task, and so they may, but, as we have seen, many do not. Fairness considerations need to be explicit and made widely available for open discussion.

Agencies that make decisions about resource allocation must also recognise the importance of providing a rationale for decisions if acceptance by those most affected is to be gained. When societal 'needs' change and a new direction or mandate forces a redistribution of the resource, the impact on resource users must be identified during the decision-making process. This is where shifting worldviews cause tensions between the 'new' and the 'established'. Change that does not consider the established culture, livelihoods and investment in infrastructure at the resource user level is unjust. Decision-makers, as well as resource users, can lose sight of earlier reasoning about a resource, and may not appreciate the cumulative impact of many small changes over time.

The local detail of irrigated agriculture has been an excellent carrier case study for understanding fairness and justice in resource sharing for several reasons. Perhaps the most important reason is that 'model' resource sharing scheme characteristics can be identified. These include fairness in three main areas: in the resource distribution, in the way fluctuations of the resource are handled, and in the way adaptive arrangements are made. A key point here is that fairness is not only associated with the actual distribution of the resource (i.e. who gets what), it is also associated with how collaborative arrangements evolve around resource sharing (i.e. how to respond to changing conditions). The way people are treated in these arrangements and the processes by which changes are made are all aspects of fairness. These fairness characteristics have relevance and can be applied in many other resource sharing scenarios. Understanding these fairness characteristics is important in evaluating why some systems are successful, resulting in communities that are productive and cohesive, and why others are problematic. Lessons can be learned from those that are successful, as well as those that fail.

Another way in which irrigated agriculture and water reform are useful in understanding general themes of fairness and justice in resource sharing is the rich experience of those involved in the reforms. In water reform, markets have not achieved fairness from the perspective of all users. Markets can be disruptive and wasteful of human effort and environmental resources. However, these issues of fairness and injustice are embedded in people's experience, stories and knowledge and are difficult to tease out. Markets have the potential to disrupt carefully planned distribution arrangements, such as the balance of water between permanent and annual crops. Markets render discussions about how a resource is best used for society irrelevant: who bids the highest gets the resource. It is in this area that governments have a responsibility to think about how resources should best be used for society, and included in strategies such as food security and environmental health. Preventing harm to the environment should be included in these deliberations: the environment *should* be included in the scope of justice.

This chapter has shown the importance of *understanding* the nuances of fairness and justice in resource sharing. Understanding the fairness consequences of decisions is not limited to natural resources such as land and water: these apply equally to other societal resource dilemmas such as the use of lower cost overseas or imported labour in mining towns versus the employment of local people. Here there are two resources: the mineral being extracted and the opportunity to be part of the workforce. Denying access to jobs in the workforce for local people directly affects community well-being and creates divisions between local people and the temporary workers. Fairness in resource sharing is critical to the overall well-being of a community, which is an important fundamental societal goal. Structuring society around resource sharing – the socialisation of the resource – can be successful if fairness principles are designed in at the beginning.

8 Justice as a means and an end in environmental decision making

The focus throughout this book has been on gaining an understanding of individual and community perspectives of fairness and justice in natural resource sharing. The main purpose of this final chapter is now to show why justice is important in environmental decision making and to make the case for environmental decision making to be carried out within a theory of justice. As the previous chapter has shown, there are many practitioners in natural resource management who understand that a fair approach *can* achieve solutions that *are* perceived by those involved as fair and equitable. This chapter draws the findings from the earlier chapters together, with the aim of showing how concepts and the practical experience of justice can be put to use in the challenge to increase the social acceptance of decisions and enable better decisions to be made. Another aim is to show practitioners in resource sharing what fairness and justice in decision-making processes really *mean* to those involved and why they need to understand the importance of different aspects of justice in gaining social acceptance of decisions.

In practical terms we have considered social conflicts about water and wind energy and have reflected on the bigger picture of resource sharing, including the needs of the environment. Fairness, justice and injustice themes have been developed from the water resource case studies, by understanding the perspectives of those involved, in the context of the substantive issues of the resource sharing. Gaining an understanding of what happens in a *conflict* over resource sharing is a good first step in understanding how to apply fairness and justice principles that *avoid* or *resolve* conflict.

This chapter takes a step-by-step approach to describe the emerging justice and fairness themes. It shows the connections between perceived injustice and calls for justice, and how these relate to the twin goals of increasing outcome acceptance and achieving better outcomes. The chapter shows why decision-makers should develop a good understanding of the way fair treatment, fair processes, and fair outcomes contribute to decision acceptance. It builds the case for environmental decision making to be carried out within a theory of justice. A theory of justice incorporates a vision for how the resource is to be used and shared, using the justice principles from the three areas of justice: interactional justice, procedural justice and distributive justice. The chapter concludes with a reflection on the critical importance of fairness and justice in global environmental decision making.

Conceptions of justice and fairness: essential for decision making

People's conceptions of the terms 'fairness' and 'justice' include many aspects of decision-making processes and outcomes, including how people are treated, the processes by which decisions are made and how decisions and outcomes relate to what people perceive is right. While the lines between fairness and justice can be blurred, people do distinguish between them. Conceptions of fairness and justice include both process and outcome but this study has shown that fairness is considered to be more concerned with day-to-day interactions between individuals and organisations than justice, which is considered to be concerned with the legal system and more formally derived outcomes. Conceptions of fairness include a reflection on people's needs, fairness of opportunity and what is appropriate or right under the circumstances. Fairness is used to describe how people would like to be treated, as well as how they feel others should be treated. Conceptions of justice include justice as a legal outcome derived from laws, the righting of perceived wrongs through the legal system (or a grievance process) and emphasis on the use of evidence and facts in determining an outcome.

These conceptions confirm that people do relate and connect matters of fairness and justice directly to processes, outcomes and interpersonal treatment. Ideas and feelings about justice and fairness are central issues and are relevant in people's perceptions of decision-making processes. People strongly connect fairness and justice to processes and outcomes in the day-to-day interactions involved in resource sharing and environmental decision making.

People draw on earlier experiences and thoughts about fairness and justice when evaluating a present-day situation. How people use the two terms varies according to these earlier experiences and whether an issue of fairness or justice is a current concern. Their generalised concepts of fairness and justice include areas where the two terms are similar or overlapping as well as areas where they are distinct. In a social setting people use the terms 'unfair' and 'unjust' interchangeably in their evaluation of aspects of a social conflict. This shows that there is a difference between a conception of fairness or justice in the abstract external to a context, and a justice or fairness evaluation of a specific issue within a context. People's lived experience and current context do have some influence on the way they think about fairness and justice. For example, a person is likely to include the legal system in their conception of justice or fairness if they have had direct experience of a legal outcome.

Although the discussion about justice and fairness in this book has shown that people do distinguish between justice and fairness, these terms are frequently used interchangeably in social justice research (see, for example, Greenberg and Colquitt, who make this clear in their preface to the *Handbook of Organizational Justice,* 2005). While some empirical studies have explored different aspects of conceptions of fairness and unfairness (for example, Lupfer *et al.* 2000), the actual distinction between conceptions of justice and conceptions of fairness appears to have escaped scrutiny until, perhaps, Finkel (2001: 43) who pointed out the 'confusion and inconsistency' in social scientists' use of these two terms. The findings in this book are clear evidence that while the terms justice and fairness are close relations, with many overlapping areas, they also have areas that are distinct. The terms hold a variety of interrelated meanings for people involved in different stages of decision-making processes and outcomes.

Injustice as harm

The priority of injustice

Injustice emerged strongly in the social conflicts described in this book. In many cases a sense of urgency, anger and frustration came across, as did a sense of disbelief and, in some cases, despair. The protest in the small NSW town of Deniliquin was a call for justice from a community that had seen an injustice take place. Likewise, the opposition led by the grassroots organisation Plug the Pipe in regional Victoria was a response from communities that saw several injustices taking shape as government plans were implemented. People had different areas of concern, depending on their involvement and how each individual or community had been affected by elements of the process or the decision. Some were more concerned about how they had been treated whereas others were more concerned about the impact of the decision on their livelihood. There were widespread perceptions of unfairness and injustice in the way people were treated, the decision-making processes and the decisions or outcomes. Justice as an ideal state was not under consideration: injustice was the issue. These conflicts show that feelings of injustice come psychologically before any thoughts about justice or fairness. Injustice is not merely the absence of justice: it has immediacy and a separate existence. They show that injustice comes before justice, not the other way around.

Injustice as an event causing harm

These studies also demonstrate that injustice is an event in itself. People in the Victoria study described injustice as causing harm or disadvantage; they saw injustice as being where the justice system had failed to produce a right outcome and that injustice was concerned with unfair interpersonal treatment. Injustice resulted in perceived harm in many different ways, not only in material harm, such as financial loss, but also in social harm to communities, such as erosion of confidence and well-being, and personal harm to individuals such as emotional distress. It is injustice that comes first, and the call for justice is to remedy the perceived wrong. Injustice, as these conflicts have shown, results in harm that is experienced in different ways and that is both tangible and intangible.

Justice as an active process

Motivations for seeking justice: not just self-interest

People affected by a resource-sharing decision can have several concurrent reasons for engagement in matters of justice: these depend on the area of the injustice and their underlying motivation for justice. Injustices can arise in all three areas of justice: the way people are treated; the decision-making process and the decision itself. For any specific injustice people can propose a corresponding remedy for injustice and describe their reasons, or motives, for seeking justice. As seen in Chapter 5, perceived injustices can arise in many different areas, including social, personal and material areas. Being excluded from a decision-making process or denied information can be just as important as a material cutback to an actual resource. Thus, motivations for seeking justice are not restricted to the often-cited self-interest motive. While the direct motive of livelihood protection and indirect motive of protection of community interests were primary reasons for seeking justice in the two studies, there were also other less tangible motives far removed from self-interest. These included justice as doing the right thing or as an end in itself; justice for the environment in terms of its own resource needs; justice as structural stability for the future well-being of communities; and justice as recognition of the value of agricultural production as a contribution to society.

Individuals and communities can hold multiple motivations that interconnect. These motivations can seem to be in opposition to each other. For example, higher water prices as a result of the Victorian pipeline would be in the self-interest of an irrigator who wishes to sell his or her water entitlement, but would be against the interests of the whole community because it would make the irrigation system less viable. Thus social context and the differing levels at which resource sharing takes place, are important in understanding issues of injustice, remedies for injustice and why people are motivated to seek justice. As discussed in Chapter 7, decisions about resource sharing for the benefit of society must also incorporate fairness perspectives at the community and individual level. When a sense of injustice has been invoked at an individual or community level, this sets in train a series of activities that can exacerbate the resource sharing dilemma. This is why decision-makers need to understand that there are many reasons why people are interested in seeking justice: these can be on different levels (individual, community and societal) and there can be a complex interplay between these motivations and these levels. Motives for justice are not only complex but are deeply interrelated. The resolution of conflicts is therefore made difficult because an action intended to resolve one set of justice concerns can have consequences or side-effects that unintentionally harm or leave others dissatisfied, thereby creating new perceptions of injustice.

Justice as an active process to prevent or remedy perceived injustice

The perceived injustice of a proposal or event can result in a series of injustices rippling out through a community, affecting those who are not directly involved and even extending to children in the school playground, as seen in the Victoria study. The combined project of the Victorian North South Pipeline and Food Bowl Modernisation Project is an example where perceived injustices were observed and experienced throughout all the communities affected by the joint proposal. These studies have shown that it is not only government agencies or proponents of proposals that can do harm. The actions of those who oppose a decision can also invoke further injustices and set in train a series of events and corresponding reactions. This rippling action can make a situation much worse through people taking sides, refusing to listen or engage with others, which results in strained relationships, muted voices and stifled debate. Conflicts can be made more serious through the actions of strong opposition groups when two-way arguments become heavier and more aggressive, making the divisions deeper. Ultimately everyone in a community can be affected. The disagreement about renewable wind energy is a case in point, with proponents and opponents of wind farms engaging in a deeply antagonistic exchange (see, for example, Dingle 2013 and Delingpole 2013).

This is where the idea of justice as an *active* process to prevent or remedy perceived injustice (Cahn 1949) comes into its own. As we have seen, injustice comes first and calls for justice follow the harm of injustice. Justice is a responsibility for *everyone*, not just the decision-makers. While governments have a primary responsibility for designing and implementing fair decision-making processes, it is incumbent on all involved to respond with fairness. This includes recognition that differing perspectives about resource sharing are legitimate until evidence or information proves otherwise. All groups with an interest in a decision-making process and outcome need to respect each other's rights to hold a position, and that there are differing positions that are valid. Opposition groups and activist organisations can be particularly unjust in their attitudes and actions to those in the community who are neutral or who can see both sides of an issue. These types of organisation, which focus on one aspect of a debate, and have a major objective (such as an opposition group), need to think about their own role and the impact of their actions on those in the larger community. They need to consider those who may have distanced themselves, are neutral, or who make up the 'silent majority' and have doubts, lack information and would benefit from structured debate rather than confrontation. Perceived injustice can arise from any societal group: justice should be the responsibility of all involved, whether proponents, opponents or neutral bystanders.

The notion of justice as an active process to prevent or remedy injustice extends to all levels of society. Justice becomes the responsibility not only of decision-makers, policy analysts, resource users, and advocate groups, but also of consumers. Considering the example of food production, it is not only food producers that are responsible, but also retailers and consumers. These groups have choices in terms of how food is produced, what food is sold, purchased and what food people choose to eat. If the natural resources of the environment are really to be included in the scope of justice in their own right, then injustice to the environment in the form of environmental externalities caused by food production and other human activities must be taken into account. Each of these societal groups has a responsibility to become informed about the impact of their activities (such as food consumption), what choices are available to them and how they can reduce their impact on natural resources.

Towards decision acceptance

Interactional justice takes priority

As we saw in Chapter 1, gaining social acceptance of decisions where resources are scarce, or where one group is seen to benefit at the expense of another, is extremely challenging. It is here that fairness in the way people are treated and the way decision-making processes are conducted is crucial. Insights from the water and wind studies provide the local detail to show why fairness is essential if social acceptance is to be gained in the face of seemingly intractable problems of sharing. While people's assessment of how they were treated included elements of all three justice constructs – interactional justice, procedural justice and distributive justice (Table 8.1) – it was clear to many that what had really made people angry and invoked their sense of injustice was *disrespect* in way they had been treated. The type of harm that perceived interactional injustice can cause ranges from lack of recognition or exclusion in resource decision making, to being considered unimportant and not valued as a contributor to society. This causes emotional distress, anxiety and anger, and invokes a sense of injustice.

The case studies have shown that interactional justice, or the way people are included and respected as having an interest in a resource, is the first step for social acceptance. The important point for decision-makers to understand is that if people are treated badly at the outset of a process there is a domino effect of injustice. So getting it right at the outset is critical: this means actively including those involved in the process; treating people directly and honestly; listening to them and understanding their perspectives and needs; straight-talking about the options; and developing a decision-making process in which people are involved and respected.

The importance of interactional justice in gaining social acceptance for decisions is shown in Figure 8.1. This Decision Acceptance Framework shows the three constructs of justice (distributive justice, interactional justice and procedural justice) in a theoretical decision-making scenario. The left side is a scenario in which people generally agree with a decision or proposal on a distributive justice basis. The right side is the opposite scenario in which people disagree. For each of these options of 'agree' and 'disagree', there is a matrix of options in which interactional justice and procedural justice can be perceived as fair or not fair. For each set of options the result can be 'accept', 'reject' or 'reservations'.

Table 8.1 Three constructs of justice

Fair treatment	Interactional justice	Being treated with respect Recognition of interest in the resource being shared Inclusion in the process
Fair process	Procedural justice	Participation, information, time, answers to questions, unbiased decision making
Fair decision	Distributive justice	Clear rationale for the decision, based on need, equity and equality

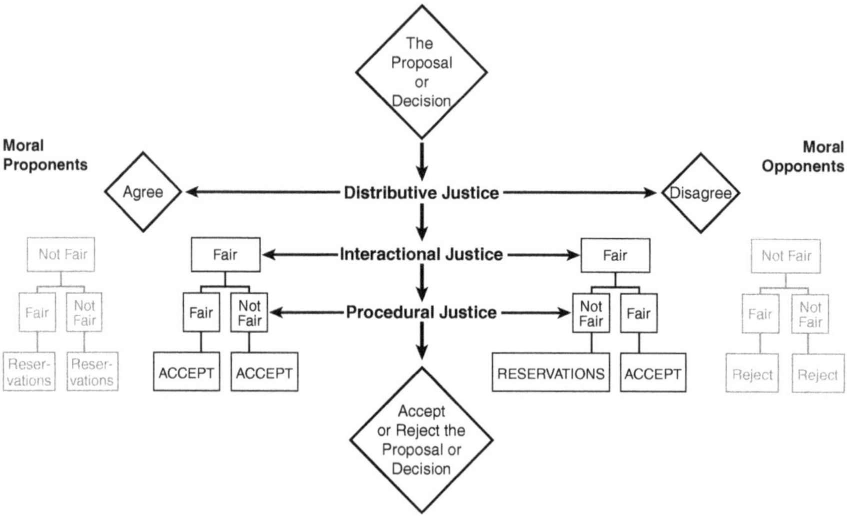

Figure 8.1 Decision Acceptance Framework.

What is meant by 'reservations' here is that people will go along with, or accept a proposal or decision, despite having some misgivings or reservations. These misgivings or reservations can be about the proposal or decision, treatment of those involved, the decision-making process, or the legitimacy of the decision-making authority.

The emphasis in this framework is the decision matrix where fair treatment – interactional justice – can result in *all* decisions being accepted to *some degree*, whether people agree or disagree with the decision or proposal. Specifically, if they *disagree* with the decision, and the process has been *unfair*, it is still possible for people to *accept* the decision, with reservations, if there has been interactional justice, or fair treatment. While this might seem counter-intuitive, consider the example of the pipeline in Victoria. Some people commented that even though they disagreed with the pipeline, thought the rationale for sending water to the state capital was dubious, and were angered by the lack of any consultation process, they believed that if the government had dealt honestly with the people involved, then there would have been greater acceptance of the decision.

This framework shows the importance of interactional justice and why it takes priority over, or trumps, procedural justice. In emergency situations, when difficult decisions need to be made urgently, social acceptance is more likely to be gained when people are treated openly and honestly and given as much information as is available. In the absence of procedural justice and distributive justice then interactional justice is *crucial*. Interactional justice is especially important in situations where a full consultation process is genuinely not feasible.

While there are clearly many nuances in these three areas of decisions, treatment and processes, and how they influence outcome acceptance, this framework is useful in drawing attention to different scenarios. Consider the case where people generally agree with a decision but feel that the process and treatment they have received is unfair (the far left of the matrix). This may be an immediate win for the decision-maker, but, as we have seen, an alerted sense of injustice leads to underlying resentment and opposition which may be the spark for opposition to a later decision. People have long memories about the way they are treated by authorities. These types of scenarios are common in many long-lasting environmental disputes that can smoulder in the background, such as the use of national parks for stock grazing and logging.

Thus, whether people agree, or disagree, with a decision on a distributive justice basis, acceptance can be won or lost based on how people perceive they are treated, and the processes of the decision making. Decision-makers may not have full control over the fairness of decisions, particularly in the case of scarce natural resources. But they *do* have control in the way they treat people, and to a greater or lesser degree, they can set up fair decision-making processes.

This Decision Acceptance Framework builds on the Community Fairness Framework described in Chapter 1 that was developed from a wind farm study. In that framework sections of the community were identified as being more concerned about the decision or outcome than about the decision-making process. This is because some people have an overriding belief in an outcome, such as the need for renewable wind energy as an overall societal benefit. Others are motivated by personal benefit or personal loss from the outcome. These groups can be identified as moral proponents, moral opponents, winners and losers. They are less interested in fairness of process or how people are treated because of their *primary* interest in the outcome. In the Decision Acceptance Framework (Figure 8.1) the two groups (moral opponents and moral proponents) are placed at the decision level on either side of the matrix, which reflects their lack of interest in either interactional justice or procedural justice (the statement 'the ends justifies the means' is an apt description here). There are two considerations here. The first is that the actions and behaviour of people within (and beyond) these two categories can deny others access to interactional justice or procedural justice. As we have seen the activities of protest groups and activist organisations in wind and water disputes have a polarising and muting effect on other voices. But this is due, in large part, to the absence of good decision-making processes. This brings us to the second consideration, that fair treatment and fair processes can act as a *balance* against the weight and influence of protest or support groups and their strong and often unyielding opinions. Fair treatment and fair decision-making processes not only lead to better outcomes, they also lead to broader acceptance within the general community. This broader acceptance within the community has the effect of reducing support for moral proponents or opponents. Well-structured debate within a fair decision-making process gives less 'air-time' to those with fixed opinions.

The purpose of the Decision Acceptance Framework is to provide a general graphical illustration of the importance of interactional justice in decision making. It is not intended to be prescriptive as a decision tree or to predict acceptance or rejection of decisions. It can be used in proactive planning for resource sharing as an aid to understand the different types of justice and how they work in gaining social acceptance of decisions. Clearly not every situation will follow this framework. But understanding the interdependencies between three constructs of justice (interactional, procedural and distributive) is critically important for government agencies if they are to devise and implement resource sharing plans and reforms that people will accept as fair.

Why interactional justice and procedural justice are important

Having established the importance of interactional justice in situations where consultation processes are unable to be carried out in full, the discussion turns to a broader review to explain why interactional justice and procedural justice are important in environmental decision making. As we have seen there are many elements of procedural justice (Chapter 2 and Table 8.1). Procedural justice is important because it *delivers* what participants *expect* in a decision-making process. This is one of the key findings of this book, because it explains *why* a decision-making process is important to people involved in the process. It delivers different things to different people depending on what they perceive as important to them. This can be as simple as a technical report or as complex as a thorough involvement in the whole decision-making process. For example, to a Plug the Pipe member, a fair decision-making process would have delivered a comprehensive environmental impact assessment of the combined North South Pipeline and irrigation infrastructure projects. To a local government councillor a fair decision-making process would have ensured their full involvement in the planning process.

A fair decision-making process would have delivered responses to the questions raised by those involved and would have provided a forum for debate. Had there been a full environmental impact assessment, genuine debate in the community and discussion of the technical concerns, then there would have been opportunities for people to understand and discuss the viability of the pipeline in comparison with more localised water-saving options in Melbourne. At the community level, a fair decision-making process would have given the opposition group an avenue to express their concerns: instead they had to create their own platform. At the individual level, a fair decision-making process would have provided local farmers with details about the impact of the pipeline construction on their land. A farmer wanted assurances that heavy trucks carting pipes and rock would not damage wet areas on his farm. He wanted to 'have a say' in the design of the replacement fences and gates. The point here is that decision-making processes deliver different things to different people, depending on their involvement and how they might be affected.

Procedural justice and interactional justice are active processes, delivering tangible elements such as information, an opportunity to speak, and answers to questions. When either type of justice is absent a prior perceived injustice can remain unremedied or a new perceived injustice can be done, causing harm. The harm becomes an event or outcome for that person, whether it is material, social or personal. This perceived harm can then become a motive for seeking justice. Procedural justice and interactional justice are important because they deliver things that people are entitled to, such as respect, information, and recognition of their right to be involved in a decision-making process. Involvement in a decision-making process indicates to those involved that their interests are recognised, and that their expectation to be involved is legitimate. As seen in the Victoria pipeline study, denying involvement results in a perceived injustice taking place, whereby people feel their needs and concerns are not recognised and are considered unimportant.

This explanation of why elements of a process are important – because they deliver what people feel they are entitled to – is also significant for justice research because it explains the 'fair process effect' through which people are more likely to accept outcomes following a fair decision-making process. Greenberg (2001a: 215) reflects on this point:

> [I]t remains unclear whether the effectiveness of procedural justice is based on one's hope that control over the processes is desired because it increases one's chances of receiving desired outcomes, or simply because it promotes one's acceptance of whatever outcomes result.

The narratives from the wind and water studies offer rich and detailed insights into *why* people care about processes, and answer this question above as to why procedural justice is effective. First, the insights show that it is not *control* over the process (as Greenberg suggests above) that is important, but whether *expectations* that people hold are *satisfied* by different elements of the process. Second, the findings show that this interest in process is not only concerned with 'desired outcomes' but is also concerned with what people feel they are entitled to from the process itself (such as voice, information) in order to achieve fair decisions. If these expectations are not met, then perceived *injustice* takes place, which directly affects people's acceptance of either the process or the resulting decision.

These narratives from the wind and water conflicts show tangible examples where people connected elements of a fair process with their willingness to accept the decision. Conversely, where they perceived that the process was not fair, or was unjust, they were less likely to accept the outcome. The narratives show a range of examples in which people described being involved with the process, receiving information, having needs understood and issues responded to, and being treated with respect, which resulted in their acceptance of a decision even if there was some negative impact on them from the outcome. Therefore, it is clear from these findings why procedural justice and interactional justice are both important: they are both key factors in gaining acceptance of decisions, irrespective of how the outcome is favoured.

The denial of interactional or procedural justice has implications for government agencies that can last long beyond the issue at stake. There are two areas. The first concerns legitimacy of the decision-maker as well as the decision. Where people feel that they are not generally valued or listened to, as felt by community leaders in the NSW study, then there is no working relationship or stock of trust to fall back on when difficult situations arise. A consistent denial of fair treatment not only casts doubt on the legitimacy of a particular decision, but also on the legitimacy of the agency itself. The agency develops a reputation for poor decision-making processes and the gap between decision-maker and those affected widens.

The second area concerns the power of the sense of injustice to sustain opposition to an unpopular decision. A person with a strong sense of injustice will carry out sustained actions to oppose an issue, even if they are not personally affected by it. For example, in the Victoria study people opposed to the pipeline took on strong moral positions – in effect becoming moral opponents – due to their absolute indignation at the way they had been treated. This moral outrage dominated their thoughts and lives for a period of time. Understanding these responses is important in implementing decisions. The concept of a sense of injustice is important because it helps explain why people respond vigorously, sometimes excessively, to a perceived injustice. These types of situation can be defused by fair treatment of those potentially affected by a decision. Over the long term it is the way governments treat constituents that either builds trust or undermines it. A gradual build-up of opposition is a direct result of a lack of fairness in the way people are treated.

Towards better outcomes

Having determined that the acceptance of decisions can be increased through interactional justice and procedural justice, we now explore how 'better' decisions and outcomes can be achieved. This need for 'better' outcomes is a direct response to the disputes that often accompany decision making about natural resources. Outcomes that are perceived as 'fair' are rarely controversial: therefore it is the outcomes that are disputed that require attention and resolution. An important goal in environmental decision making is to achieve outcomes that can be perceived as fair and equitable by those concerned, or be accepted even if they are perceived as unfair in some way. However, as we have seen, a fair outcome delivered through treatment or processes that are perceived to be *unfair* may be accepted, but will not be well-received overall. In other words, the end does not justify the means.

Justice as a means and an end

As we have seen, people place a different emphasis on the treatment, processes and decisions they experience in a decision-making process. We have established that the three constructs of justice can be seen as active processes important in preventing or remedying injustice. Interactional justice and procedural justice are important in delivering the essential components of a decision-making process. Thus the idea and nature of justice as an active process and as a *means* to an *end* can be established: the means is the decision-making process and the end is the decision or outcome.

Fair and equitable outcomes: achievable but challenges exist

The discussion has shown that people actively involved in decision making are aware of many of the concepts that underpin procedural and distributive justice.

They relate these to their own experiences of fair and equitable outcomes. Study participants with experience of such initiatives could describe how and why outcomes that were seen as fair could be achieved, and relate them to their current situation in the resource sharing dilemma (Chapter 7). Two main characteristics included having an overall plan, or vision, and implementing it within a thorough consultation process that allowed people to develop an understanding of the initiative. But there were also considerable challenges that had to be overcome. Government agencies frequently lacked staff with the skills to engage with those concerned, and effective communication in which people could be convinced of the need for change was difficult. The different types of resource user made the communication task much harder, with many being unwilling either to see the need for change or to engage in the process. As community leaders in the water studies pointed out, the gap between government and resource users is widening. There is a need for people on both sides who can effectively communicate and work together collaboratively within a decision-making process. This is a continuing major challenge that governments and communities involved in any resource sharing scenario must address: having people available with the right skills to enable fair decision making. Good communicators, who understand both the resource and the principles of justice, are essential if the 'means' of justice is to be enabled – fair decision-making processes – to achieve the 'end', a fair outcome that is broadly accepted.

Fair and equitable outcomes: the principles of need, equity and equality

There are three key principles of distributive justice: need, equity and equality. Many people in the studies discussed these notions of need or equity or equality in relation to their perceptions of decisions and outcomes that they had experienced. Although they were not familiar with these being three key principles of distributive justice, many showed a basic understanding of one or more of these, either through past experience or the current resource conflict. While in some cases people were not entirely clear about the formal meanings, they nevertheless thought about sharing resources in ways that included these notions. Many people in the NSW water carry-over study were specific in their view that a fair or just compensation for the water that had been taken away should be based on dollars per megalitre removed, in other words, on equity. Their views of why an action was perceived to be unjust were related to all three notions, for example, the burden of cutbacks being spread inequitably across irrigators. Similarly, in Victoria, people on both sides of the debate discussed issues of equity and need in relation to water being reallocated to the large urban centre of Melbourne, as a result of savings in the irrigation area. The complexity of the problem was not lost on those who struggled to understand the overall trade-off and the underlying logic. Many questioned the apparent 'need' and lack of factual explanation or rationale.

People may think in fragmented terms of the three principles of distributive justice, but lack a complete understanding of the three principles and how they differ and relate to each other. However, where there are facts on which discussions can be based, people do develop justice-based arguments to show how better outcomes can be developed, such as in the NSW study. Conversely, where facts are perceived to be absent, as in the Victoria study, then people have greater difficulty in formulating views about better outcomes, but are clear about the specific fairness and justice deficiencies that they perceive within decision-making processes. People know there are issues of fairness underlying the issues, but lack a full grasp of the constructs and language of justice. These findings show that the three principles of need, equity and equality are useful and practical in helping people understand how different outcomes affect those who have an interest in the resource. Therefore, through debate, they are useful in achieving better outcomes. These three principles of distributive justice need to be included in the day-to-day language of resource sharing. Discussions about need, equity and equality should be routine in decision-making processes, first in developing solutions and then in understanding the basis for the distribution, once the decision or resource allocation has been made.

Fair and equitable outcomes: towards a theory of justice

Achieving fair and equitable outcomes also involves the nature of the resource itself and societal arrangements to manage the resource. Returning to the example of water resource sharing, we have seen that people have concerns with the way water in Australia is seen solely as an 'economic good' and the impact of that policy on the future of irrigation farming. Water reforms that separated water entitlements from the land, and the introduction of permanent water trading, were seen to have had serious consequences for irrigation communities, putting their future in jeopardy. These reforms have eroded a largely stable set of arrangements that had evolved over many years as a result of state governments, irrigation industry associations and communities working together. Many described the water reforms as flawed policies that created the stranded-assets problem when water was sold out of an irrigation area. In other words, the *vision* of an established irrigation system operating in the public interest using water to grow food had been displaced by the new economic paradigm in which water should be used to its 'highest value', whatever that might be. Water had been considered more like a public good in a traditional irrigation system and the water reforms changed this to treating water as an economic good. While many people recognised the need to return water to the environment – a key objective of the water reforms – they thought the shift to economic goals was already having a detrimental effect not only on communities, but also on the environment. In addition, this impact on farmers and the environment was seen as an injustice: both farmers and the environment took the brunt of environmental externalities that should actually be attributed to the ultimate water user, the consumer.

These viewpoints tap into the core of distributive justice, concerned with the distribution of resources (and burdens). While a particular piece of Australian public policy acknowledges that water is part of the country's natural capital it does not provide a specific vision that guides how the resource is to be used other than an overall objective 'that optimises economic, social and environmental outcomes'

(National Water Commission 2004: 3). A later 'vision statement' from the National Water Commission does not provide a vision other than the 'unifying national objective' of 'cost-effective water use efficiency … throughout Australia' (National Water Commission 2006: 1). Syme and Nancarrow (2008: 243) point out the general lack of social vision concerning water use in Australia and argue for a 'national debate' on societal values to be used in determining water management criteria. In other words, there is recognition that, in the case of water, government policy lacks a comprehensive vision that is underpinned by societal values about how water – a critical and scarce resource – should be used.

A vision for how a resource is to be used and shared is required for distributive justice to be achieved. As discussed in Chapter 2, theories of justice are important because they set out the principles and rationale for how resources (and burdens) are to be distributed and shared at a general societal level. In the case of water, a debate would bring up important questions such as whether water is a public good, a private good, or an economic good (or, as one person suggested, a mixed good). A vision for how any resource should be used can be developed within a theory of justice. Where there are competing interests for a resource, a vision can determine where resources are best used in the public interest. An *impartial* consideration of competing interests can be made in a vision, thus enabling fairness to be built in at the outset. This is why a theory of justice is required in which decisions about the distribution of resources are made for the benefit of society as a whole.

As we have seen in Chapter 7, the environment must also be included within the scope of justice. Environmental health is necessary for human health. Within a theory of justice in which environmental needs as well as human needs are included in the scope of justice a vision can be developed that guides decision making using the principles of need, equity and equality. A vision for resource use, such as water, is particularly important where conditions are constantly changing, requiring ongoing adaptation and management. Every decision that is made – particularly under extreme or changing conditions – requires a rationale and explanation, with sufficient information for those affected by the decision to understand the basis for the decision and to have their issues and concerns addressed. The theory of justice proposed here recognises that justice is not only about how resources (and burdens) are distributed but includes procedural justice and interactional justice: in other words, justice consists of all three justice constructs (Table 8.2). Decision making within a theory of justice requires a vision and a rationale for why a proposed resource distribution is a *just* distribution under that vision.

Table 8.2 Decision making within a theory of justice

Distributive justice	Requires impartial decisions under a vision/social rationale
Procedural justice	Requires open and fair decision-making processes
Interactional justice	Requires that people are treated with respect and their interests are recognised

Reflections: justice must be done and must be seen to be done

The idea of justice is both concrete and slippery; sharp and vague; clear and opaque. It is a universal concept but also contextual. Justice is hard to define but we surely know when an injustice has taken place. This book has traversed the conceptual and empirical ground between fairness, justice and injustice and has provided insights into how these ideas are perceived in environmental decision-making processes by both observers and participants. A final summary task is to answer the questions: why is justice important and why is a theory of justice important? Answering these two questions shows how seemingly intractable resource use disputes can be resolved.

Why is justice important?

Justice is important because it prevents injustice and remedies injustice. As an active process justice delivers tangible things that people expect: information, understanding, respect, and avenues for engagement and information flow. As this book has shown, decision making in natural resource management affects not only those individuals with a direct interest in the resource but also individuals and entire communities with direct and indirect interests. We have also seen the complex interplay of a range of material, social and personal impacts of social conflict. In these conflicts perceived injustice takes place, and subsequent activities create ripples of injustice throughout communities. Justice is important in preventing these ripples of injustice as well as remedying those that do take place. Injustice can be instigated by decision-makers if they do not implement just procedures; it can be dealt by opposition groups through actions that divide communities; and it can be invoked by observers through their lack of understanding, lack of involvement in helping people understand different perspectives, and derisory comments about participants. Interactional justice and procedural justice are important because they confer legitimacy – seen by all – on the process, on those affected by decisions, and on the decision-makers. They not only confer legitimacy: they render the decision-making process a *just* process.

Where interactional justice is absent, and there is no respect or recognition of people's right to be involved in a process, then a perceived injustice is done to those directly affected. This is where the latter part of the phrase 'justice must be done and must be seen to be done' becomes important. Observers may generally take one of three positions in relation to those to whom the perceived injustice has been done: they can have empathy and show support; be neutral about it; or take a derogatory stance on the issue in which they think self-interest is the primary motivation. It is here that the NIMBY label is often applied. Where interactional and procedural justice is present and those with an interest are shown respect and included in a decision-making process, then perceptions of injustice are reduced. As we have seen, communities are not homogenous: they consist of groups of people with different opinions and perspectives. Some groups may still be opposed to a decision, even if it results from a fair process. However, if there has been a fair process, then the broader community is less likely to show empathy and support to those who still oppose the decision. The broader community can have more confidence in the decision-making process. Reasons for broad-brush derogatory explanations, such as NIMBYism, are reduced. The main reason is that the details of *why* people are opposed to a proposal can be explored through debate in the community, and their questions can be answered. Thus, there is a more widespread understanding of the reasons that people are opposed to a proposal. Under these circumstances those with a legitimate interest in the resource are seen to be treated respectfully by decision-makers. Justice is *seen* to be done. Justice becomes the responsibility of everyone involved, including decision-makers, participants and observers. Even people who think that they are not involved have a responsibility: to inform themselves about the issue, to discuss it with friends and neighbours, and to play their part in making sure that justice is done and injustice is prevented.

Why is a theory of justice important?

This book has made the case that decision making in natural resource management is best carried out within an overall theory of justice in which a social vision for the resource is developed, and in which all three justice constructs are adhered to. We have seen in Chapter 7 how a shifting set of worldviews, delivered through government policies of the time, has damaged and degraded not only the natural resource base but has also frequently impeded the development of good working relationships between communities and institutions. This is not just a modern phenomenon. For instance, since the beginning of irrigation in Australia policies have been developed under a single dominant imperative: at first this was to populate the inland and now the dominant paradigm is that water is to be used to the highest value. With a theory of justice a lasting resource vision can be developed that is not dominated by a single narrow economic paradigm, but includes environmental and social implications of resource sharing. With a theory of justice all three components of justice (interactional, procedural and distributive) are invoked in decision-making processes: this becomes part of the decision-making routine. The three key principles of distributive justice – need, equity and equality – are broadly understood and considered in resource sharing.

A theory of justice is important because decision making within a theory of justice can help resolve seemingly intractable resource disputes. At the heart of these types of dispute lie different perspectives and interests as to how the resource should be used and shared. Consider the case of wind energy and a proposed wind farm (discussed in Chapter 1). If there is no long-term vision for how the land and the landscape are to be used and shared, then the conflict centres on the more immediate dispute around the perspectives of local winners and local losers. The bigger picture of resource sharing and how wind energy contributes to society overall is not part of the decision-making process. Supporters of wind energy see those opposing the wind farm as nothing more than NIMBYs complaining about various potential health and environmental impacts. But, as we have seen in Chapter 1, the NIMBY explanation is overused and discredited. There are many more issues that need to be understood before decisions can be made. In a scenario where the big picture is considered, the role of renewable wind energy and how communities use the resource of land and landscape would be debated as part of a vision for the resource. Communities could work out what the development of a wind farm would mean locally. They would consider local benefits and burdens as well as the interests of society at large. Developing a vision is not a simple process. It requires investment in time and debate to work through information and different perspectives. But it is necessary if communities are not to feel that they are being ridden over roughshod in the pursuit of a single overriding paradigm.

The type of social co-operation that is required to develop a vision for a resource is enabled within a theory of justice. As discussed in Chapter 1, fairness and justice is a societal aspiration, not only for resource sharing, but also in the way society is structured. People want to live in a society in which fairness is a cherished value, because with fairness comes peace, security and confidence in the future. This notion came out clearly from irrigation communities: fair decision making has a direct connection with people's belief in their future well-being and confidence in the future of their community. What is needed is a general recognition of this connection between fairness and security: fairness in society is essential for future security and well-being. We have seen in Chapter 7 how irrigation communities can be considered resource sharing models, underpinned by fairness characteristics. They can also be considered ways of organising society around a resource. But, in reality, *all* of society is structured in some way around the sharing of differing types of resources: fresh air, clean water, land for food production, access to health services, freedom from crime, and the ability to work and be valued as a contributor to society. So resource sharing is a basis for structuring society with fairness and justice essential elements. This is why a theory of justice is required; to provide the rationale (vision) and guidelines (principles of justice) for decision making to take place that recognises the interests of those involved, but which also *arrives* at decisions, even if not accepted by all. The difference between many types of present-day natural resource decision-making processes and what is proposed here, is that a vision is usually lacking and the bigger picture is not taken into account. This is one reason that there has been so much acrimony over renewable wind energy and similar resource use disagreements, and why there are many intractable disputes.

The implication for decision-makers is quite simple. People want confidence in the future. To have confidence in the future they need decision-makers who treat them with respect and make fair decisions using fair processes. Politicians, policy-analysts and decision-makers would like their decisions to be accepted by their constituents and voters, as well as being seen to be a good or right decision. To achieve this they need to adopt fairness in developing resource decisions and implementing them. This is best accomplished within a comprehensive theory of justice. Those politicians and bureaucrats who think they have the answer and it is the people that 'don't get it', should consider the strong connections between confidence in the future, fair treatment and decision acceptance, described in this book.

Water under the bridge

The phrase 'water under the bridge' implies that a one-time troubling issue is now in the past, is no longer important or relevant and can be let go and forgotten. But just as water that has flowed under the bridge returns at some point in the hydrological cycle, so do some of the myths that go with it. An ever-present and frequently unrecognised challenge for governments and societies is to learn from these lessons of the past, recall them in debates and activities, and maintain a clear perspective on the value that past worldviews, perspectives, approaches and mistakes can bring to solving intractable long-lasting problems. Human culture has the capacity to learn from the past: so why doesn't it appear to have absorbed these lessons? For example, why are large-scale infrastructure developments still proposed when less environmentally harmful alternatives exist? One explanation is that people lose the *capability* to appreciate other perspectives when the *language* of fairness and justice is missing. As the case studies have shown, fairness requires an explicit understanding of differing perspectives, past and present. These are lost when governments focus on an overriding policy, as we have seen from the irrigated agriculture narratives.

This book has shown why natural resource management should be carried out within a theory of justice, in which these perspectives about resource sharing can be maintained. Justice is not an obscure abstraction or an intangible theoretical idea. If governments are serious about achieving fair and equitable outcomes in natural resource management, they need to operate within a theory of justice. They need to provide the capacity and environment for fair decision making processes and the people to carry them out. Using the language of fairness and justice people can work collaboratively to solve intractable and difficult resource sharing problems. That justice can be a means as well as an end offers people a way for their voices to be heard and their futures to be considered within the bigger picture of sharing natural resources.

What does this mean for global environmental decision making?

The central concern of environmental decision making in every institution worldwide *should* be about deciding on the best use of resources and then how to share them fairly amongst competing users. But the outlook is bleak. Competition for natural resources across the globe involves widespread community conflict as well as outright war between nations. The growing human population is putting alarming pressure on the natural resources of the planet. The foreshadowed effect of climate change is a dark cloud over every horizon. Water conflicts are endemic in some parts of the world: even peaceful countries with well-established water management often get decisions wrong. Also on the rise are disputes about landscape use, mineral extraction, and mining for gas deposits across large tracts of the landscape. Animal welfare has become an international battleground as meat for food production becomes more industrialised and the well-being of animals takes second place.

In this context of overuse and misuse, the wise and sustainable use of natural resources must become the primary consideration of all societies. Fairness is at the heart of sharing: to the resource itself, to those who make their livelihood from the resource, and to consumers and society as a whole. The domain of sharing and the responsibility for sharing must include all those with an interest in the resource if sustainability of the resource is to be achieved. But fairness is still an ideal that must be *actively* and deliberately sought: politics, power, dominant ways of thinking and financial self-interest are real obstacles. It is here that the principles of justice are important in guiding society to make sharing decisions that can be seen as *just* decisions, even if not all agree. A carefully considered vision for a resource sets the scope and boundaries to guide decision making. A vision can evolve and adapt as conditions change, by using principles of justice. Lessons can be learned *if* mistakes from past experience are turned into knowledge that is maintained within a long-term cultural perspective. Respect for contextual knowledge and the interests of those who are closest to the resource is crucial in gaining acceptance of outcomes. Sharing a resource under a long-term vision where decision making is guided by justice principles can outlast political manoeuvring. These principles are based on the three justice constructs of interactional justice, procedural justice and distributive justice, with all three working together.

If human society is not to descend into a world of perpetual and ruthless resource conflict we must act to prevent it. Fairness is at the heart of a co-operative society. It is intrinsic to human nature. One could say it is a basic human need. But it is not automatic: fairness needs work to bring it about. Without fairness some other paradigm prevails that is not based on fairness or justice. Justice theorists have been coming up with ideas about social justice for centuries. Ideas about environmental justice, ecological justice, global justice and climate justice have broadened the scope of justice as a basis for ordering society. The discussion in this book has added depth and local detail to this justice discourse to reveal the realities of injustice and justice. It has shown the power of injustice at the individual and community level in generating opposition to resource sharing decisions that are perceived as not fair. It has shown how one injustice invokes a deeper sense of injustice in people, whose actions then add to a compounding effect of injustice that divides and harms communities. An appreciation of how injustice can take hold has led to a fresh understanding of how the three constructs of justice – interactional, procedural and distributive – work together. This book has shown how constructs of justice can be used to achieve greater social acceptance of difficult decisions where there is disagreement and conflict. It has provided decision-makers with the *means* – justice principles and an *understanding* of why they work – that they can use to achieve the *ends*: decisions that *can* be accepted as fair and just. Faced with choices of fairness or fighting, human societies must choose fairness and justice.

References

ABC Media Watch, 2002. *Media Watch: Jones' Pipe Dream*, ABC. Available at: http://www.abc.net.au/mediawatch/transcripts/141002_s2.htm (accessed June 20, 2013).

Adams, J. S., 1965. Inequity in social exchange, In *Advances in Experimental Social Psychology*, **Vol. 2** (Ed., Berkowitz, L.) Academic Press, New York, pp. 267–99.

Ambrose, M. L., 2002. Contemporary justice research: a new look at familiar questions, *Organisational Behavior and Human Decision Processes*, **89**: 803–12.

Ambrose, M. L. and Arnaud, A., 2005. Are procedural justice and distributive justice conceptually distinct?, In *Handbook of Organizational Justice* (Eds, Greenberg, J. and Colquitt, J.) Lawrence Erlbaum Associates, Mahwah, N.J., pp. 59–84.

Aristotle, 1959. *Ethica Nicomachea*, Clarendon Press, Oxford.

Auditor-General, 2008. *Planning for Water Infrastructure in Victoria*, Victorian Auditor-General, Melbourne.

Barnett, J., Burningham, K., Walker, G. and Cass, N., 2012. Imagined publics and engagement around renewable energy technologies in the UK, *Public Understanding of Science*, **21**(1): 36–50.

Barry, B., 2005. *Why Social Justice Matters*, Polity Press, Cambridge.

Bell, S. and Quiggin, J., 2008. The limits of markets: the politics of water management in rural Australia, *Environmental Politics*, **17**(5): 712–29.

Bergek, A., 2010. Levelling the playing field? The influence of national wind power planning instruments on conflicts of interests in a Swedish county, *Energy Policy*, **38**(5): 2357–69.

Berkes, F. and Folke, C., 1998. Linking social and ecological systems for resilience and sustainability, In *Linking Social and Ecological Systems: Management Practices and Social Mechanisms for Building Resilience* (Eds, Berkes, F. and Folke, C.) Cambridge University Press, Cambridge.

Berry, R. and Higgs, G., 2012. Gauging levels of public acceptance of the use of visualisation tools in promoting public participation; a case study of wind farm planning in South Wales, UK, *Journal of Environmental Planning and Management*, **55**(2): 229–51.

Bies, R. J., 2001. Interactional (in)justice: The sacred and the profane, In *Advances in Organizational Justice* (Eds, Greenberg, J. and Cropanzano, R.) Stanford University Press, Stanford, CA, pp. 89–118.

Bies, R. J., 2005. Are procedural justice and interactional justice conceptually distinct?, In *Handbook of Organizational Justice* (Eds, Greenberg, J. and Colquitt, J.) Lawrence Erlbaum Associates, Mahwah, NJ, pp. 85–112.

Blackmore, D., 2002. Protecting the future, In *Uncharted Waters* (Ed., Connell, D.) Murray–Darling Basin Commission, Canberra, pp. 1–8.

Bosselmann, K., 2008. *The Principle of Sustainability: Transforming Law and Governance*, Ashgate Publishing Limited, Aldershot.

Botterill, L. C., 2003. Beyond drought in Australia: The way forward, In *Beyond Drought: People, Policy and Perspectives* (Eds, Botterill, L. C. and Fisher, M.) CSIRO Publishing, Collingwood, Victoria, pp. 197–207.

Boyden, S., 2004. *The Biology of Civilisation: Understanding Human Culture as a Force in Nature*, UNSW Press, Sydney.

Boyden, S., 2013. *A Transition Framework*, Nature and Society Forum. Available at: http://www.biosensitivefutures.org.au/biosensitivefutures/part-3-our-place-in-nature/7.-a-transition-framework (accessed 21 June 2013).

Braud, W. and Anderson, R., 1998. *Transpersonal Research Methods for the Social Sciences: Honoring Human Experience*, Sage Publications, Thousand Oaks, CA.

Brockner, J., Fishman, A. Y., Goldman, B., Reb, J., Spiegel, S. and Garden, C., 2007. Procedural fairness, outcome favourability, and judgments of an authority's responsibility, *Journal of Applied Psychology*, **92**(6): 1657–71.

Brockner, J. and Wiesenfeld, B. M., 1996. An integrative framework for explaining reactions to decisions: interactive effects of outcomes and procedures, *Psychological Bulletin*, **120**(2): 189–208.

Brown, D. A., 2008. *The Ethics of Allocating Public Research Funds for Carbon Capture and Storage*, Available at: http://rockblogs.psu.edu/climate/2008/10/the-ethics-of-allocating-public-research-funds-for-carbon-capture-and-storage.html (accessed 30 April 2013).

Brown, D. A., 2013. *Climate Change Ethics: Navigating the Perfect Moral Storm*, Routledge, Abingdon.

Brown, V. A., 2008. *Leonardo's Vision: A Guide to Collective Thinking and Action*, Sense Publishers, Rotterdam.

Brown, V. A., Deane, P. M., Harris, J. A. and Russell, J. Y., 2010. Towards a just and sustainable future, In *Tackling Wicked Problems: Through the Transdisciplinary Imagination* (Eds, Brown, V., Harris, J. A. and Russell, J. Y.) Earthscan, London, pp. 3–15.

Byrne, P. J., Eagle, N., O'Brien, J. and McDonald, D., 2006. *High and Dry: How Free Trade in Water Will Cripple Australian Agriculture*, Freedom Publishing, North Melbourne, Victoria.

Cahn, E. N., 1949. *The Sense of Injustice: An Anthropocentric View of Law*, New York University Press, New York.

Cahn, E., 1964. *The Sense of Injustice*, with a personal epilogue by the author, A Midland Book, Indiana University Press, Bloomington & London.

Cahn, L. L. (Ed.) 1967. *Confronting Injustice*, Victor Gollancz, London.

Cain, N. L. and Nelson, H. T., 2013. What drives opposition to high-voltage transmission lines?, *Land Use Policy*, **33**: 204–13.

Cass, N. and Walker, G., 2009. Emotion and rationality: The characterisation and evaluation of opposition to renewable energy projects, *Emotion, Space and Society*, **2**(1): 62–9.

Cass, N., Walker, G. and Devine-Wright, P., 2010. Good neighbours, public relations and bribes: the politics and perceptions of community benefit provision in renewable energy development in the UK, *Journal of Environmental Policy & Planning*, **12**(3): 255–75.

Clark, S. D., 2002. Divided power, co-operative solutions?, In *Uncharted Waters* (Ed, Connell, D.) Murray–Darling Basin Commission, Canberra, pp. 9–21.

Clayton, S., 1992. The experience of injustice: some characteristics and correlates, *Social Justice Research*, **5**(1): 71–91.

Colquitt, J. A., 2001. On the dimensionality of organizational justice: a construct validation of a measure, *Journal of Applied Psychology*, **86**(3): 386–400.

Colquitt, J. A., Conlon, D. E., Wesson, M. J., Porter, C. O. L. H. and Ng, K. Y., 2001. Justice at the millennium: a meta-analytic review of 25 years of organizational justice research, *Journal of Applied Psychology*, **86**(3): 425–45.

Connell, D. and Dovers, S., 2006. Tail wags dog – water markets and the national water initiative, *Public Administration Today*, vol Jul-Sept: 17–23.
Connell, D. and Grafton, R. Q. (Eds), 2011. *Basin Futures: Water Reform in the Murray–Darling Basin*, ANU E Press, Canberra.
Connell, D., Dovers, S. and Grafton, R. Q., 2005. A critical analysis of the national water initiative, *The Australasian Journal of Natural Resources Law and Policy*, **10**(1): 81–107.
Connell, D., Robins, L. and Dovers, S., 2007. Delivering the national water initiative, In *Managing Water for Australia: the Social and Institutional Challenges* (Eds, Hussey, K. and Dovers, S.) CSIRO Publishing, Collingwood, Victoria, pp. 127–40.
Cowell, R., Bristow, G. and Munday, M., 2011. Acceptance, acceptability and environmental justice: the role of community benefits in wind energy development, *Journal of Environmental Planning and Management*, **54**(4): 539–57.
Crase, L., 2007. Pipes and drains, rabbits and hats, politicians and promises, *Connections: Farm, Food and Resource Issues*, (Paper 59). http://www.agrifood.info/connections/2007/index_2007.html.
Crase, L. (Ed.) 2008. *Water Policy in Australia: The Impact of Change and Uncertainty*, Resources for the Future, Washington, DC.
Crase, L. and Dollery, B., 2008. The institutional setting, In *Water Policy in Australia: The Impact of Change and Uncertainty* (Ed, Crase, L.) Resources for the Future, Washington, DC, pp. 74–89.
Crase, L. and O'Keefe, S., 2009. The paradox of national water savings: a critique of 'Water for the Future', *Agenda*, **16**(1): 45–60.
Cropanzano, R., Byrne, Z. S., Bobocel, R. D. and Rupp, D. E., 2001. Moral virtues, fairness heuristics, social entities, and other denizens of organizational justice, *Journal of Vocational Behavior*, **58**(2): 164–209.
Cropanzano, R., Goldman, B. and Folger, R., 2003. Deontic justice: the role of moral principles in workplace fairness, *Journal of Organizational Behavior*, **24**(8): 1019–24.
Davidson, B. R., 1969. *Australia Wet or Dry? The Physical and Economic Limits to the Expansion of Irrigation*, Melbourne University Press, Melbourne.
Delingpole, J., 2013. *How Big Wind Blows Away its Opponents*, The Australian, Available at: http://www.theaustralian.com.au/national-affairs/opinion/how-big-wind-blows-away-its-opponents/story-e6frgd0x-1226665248198 (accessed 21 June 2013).
Denning, A., 1955. *The Road to Justice*, Stevens & Sons, London.
Devine-Wright, P., 2009. Rethinking NIMBYism: The role of place attachment and place identity in explaining place-protective action, *Journal of Community & Applied Social Psychology*, **19**(6): 426–41.
Devine-Wright, P., 2011a. Place attachment and public acceptance of renewable energy: A tidal energy case study, *Journal of Environmental Psychology*, **31**(4): 336–43.
Devine-Wright, P., 2011b. Public engagement with large-scale renewable energy technologies: breaking the cycle of NIMBYism, *Wiley Interdisciplinary Reviews: Climate Change*, **2**(1): 19–26.
Devine-Wright, P. (Ed.) 2011c. *Renewable Energy and the Public: From NIMBY to Participation*, Earthscan, London.
Dingle, S., 2013. *An Ill Wind, Background Briefing*, ABC Radio National. Available at: http://www.abc.net.au/radionational/programs/backgroundbriefing/2013-05-26/4705822 (accessed 20 June 2013).
DNR, 2006. *Background to Water Management in the NSW Murray and Lower Murray–Darling River Systems*, NSW Government, Department of Natural Resources, Sydney.

Dole, D., 2002. Managers for all seasons, In *Uncharted Waters* (Ed, Connell, D.) Murray–Darling Basin Commission, Canberra, pp. 23–35.

Dovers, S., 2005. Clarifying the imperative of integration research for sustainable environmental management, *Journal of Research Practice*, **1**(2), 1–19.

DSE, 2004. *Victorian Government White Paper: Securing Our Water Our Future Together*, Victorian Government, Department of Sustainability and Environment, Melbourne.

DSE, 2007. *Our Water Our Future: The Next Stage of the Government's Water Plan* Victorian Government, Department of Sustainability and Environment, Melbourne.

Edwards, G., 2003. Water policy: setting the scene, *Australian Economic Review*, **36**(2): 193–202.

Farm Futures, 2009. *New Group Strives to Tell Real Story of Agriculture*, Available at: http://farmfutures.com/story.aspx/new/group/strives/to/tell/real/story/of/agriculture/17/29182 (accessed 20 June 2013).

Filor, K., 2007. *City Meets Bush*, Department of Agriculture, Fisheries and Forestry Available at: http://www.daff.gov.au/__data/assets/pdf_file/0020/164081/contoursmarch.pdf (accessed 20 June 2013).

Finkel, N. J., 2001. *Not Fair! The Typology of Commonsense Unfairness*, American Psychological Association, Washington, DC.

Firestone, J., Kempton, W., Lilley, M. B. and Samoteskul, K., 2012. Public acceptance of offshore wind power: does perceived fairness of process matter?, *Journal of Environmental Planning and Management*, **55**(10): 1387–402.

Fisher, D. E., 2007. Delivering the National Water Initiative: the emergence of innovative legal doctrine, In *Managing Water for Australia: The Social and Institutional Challenges* (Eds, Hussey, K. and Dovers, S.) CSIRO Publishing, Collingwood, Victoria, pp. 113–26.

Fisher, J. and Brown, K., 2009. Wind energy on the Isle of Lewis: implications for deliberative planning, *Environment and Planning A*, **41**(10): 2516–36.

Folger, R., 1998. Fairness as moral virtue, In *Managerial Ethics: Moral Management of People and Processes* (Ed, Schminke, M.) Lawrence Erlbaum Associates, Mahwah, NJ, pp. 13–34.

Folger, R. and Cropanzano, R., 2001. Fairness theory: justice as accountability, In *Advances in Organizational Justice* (Eds, Greenberg, J. and Cropanzano, R.) Stanford University Press, Stanford, pp. 1–55.

Fortin, M., 2008. Perspectives on organizational justice: Concept clarification, social context integration, time and links with morality, *International Journal of Management Reviews*, **10**(2): 93–126.

Fraser, N., 2001. Recognition without ethics?, *Theory, Culture & Society*, **18**(2–3): 21–42.

Gardner, A. and Bowmer, K. H., 2007. Environmental water allocations and their governance, In *Managing Water for Australia: The Social and Institutional Challenges* (Eds, Hussey, K. and Dovers, S.) CSIRO Publishing, Collingwood, Victoria, pp. 43–57.

Gough, C. and Boucher, P., 2013. Ethical attitudes to underground CO_2 storage: Points of convergence and potential faultlines, *International Journal of Greenhouse Gas Control*, **13**: 156–67.

Greenberg, J., 2001a. Setting the justice agenda: seven unanswered questions about "what, why, and how", *Journal of Vocational Behavior*, **58**(2): 210–19.

Greenberg, J., 2001b. The seven loose can(n)ons of organisational justice, In *Advances in Organizational Justice* (Eds, Greenberg, J. and Cropanzano, R.) Stanford University Press, Stanford, pp. 245–71.

Greenberg, J. and Colquitt, J. (Eds), 2005. *Handbook of Organizational Justice*, Lawrence Erlbaum Associates, Mahwah, NJ.

Gross, C., 2007. Community perspectives of wind energy in Australia: The application of a justice and community fairness framework to increase social acceptance, *Energy Policy*, **35**(5): 2727–36.

Gyles, O., 2003. More water for irrigation and the environment? Some problems and prospects for worthwhile investments, *Connections – Farm, Food and Resources Issues*, **5**: 1–13.

Haggett, C., 2008. Over the sea and far away? A consideration of the planning, politics and public perception of offshore wind farms, *Journal of Environmental Policy & Planning*, **10**(3): 289–306.

Haggett, C., 2010. A call for clarity and a review of the empirical evidence: comment on Felman and Turner's 'Why Not NIMBY?', *Ethics, Place & Environment*, **13**(3): 313–16.

Haggett, C., 2011. 'Planning and persuasion': Public engagement in renewable energy decision-making, In *Renewable Energy and the Public: From NIMBY to Participation* (Ed., Devine-Wright, P.) Earthscan, London, pp. 15–27.

Harding, R., Hendriks, C. M. and Faruqi, M., 2009. *Environmental Decision-Making: Exploring Complexity and Context*, The Federation Press, Sydney.

Hart, H. L. A., 1961. *The Concept of Law*, Oxford University Press, Oxford.

Hindmarsh, R., 2010. Wind farms and community engagement in Australia: a critical analysis for policy learning, *East Asian Science, Technology and Society: an International Journal*, **4**(4): 541–63.

Honneth, A., 2001. Recognition or redistribution? Changing perspectives on the moral order of society, *Theory, Culture, & Society*, **18**(2–3): 43–55.

Hopkins, P., 2009. *'Ignorance' Threatens Australian Food Output*, The Age. Available at: http://business.theage.com.au/business/ignorance-threatens-australian-food-output-20090622-cu1t.html (accessed 21 June 2013).

Horbaty, R., Huber, S. and Ellis, G., 2012. Large-scale wind deployment, social acceptance, *Wiley Interdisciplinary Reviews: Energy and Environment*, **1**(2): 194–205.

Howe, C. W. and Ingram, H., 2005. Roles for the public and private sectors in water allocation: lessons from around the world, In *In Search of Sustainable Water Management: International Lessons for the American West and Beyond* (Ed., Kenney, D. S.) Edward Elgar Publishing, Cheltenham, pp. 25–68.

Huijts, N. M. A., Molin, E. J. E. and Steg, L., 2012. Psychological factors influencing sustainable energy technology acceptance: A review-based comprehensive framework, *Renewable and Sustainable Energy Reviews*, **16**(1): 525–31.

Hussey, K. and Dovers, S., 2007a. International perspectives on water policy and management: emerging principles, common challenges, In *Managing Water for Australia: The Social and Institutional Challenges* (Eds, Hussey, K. and Dovers, S.) CSIRO Publishing, Collingwood, Victoria, pp. 141–54.

Hussey, K. and Dovers, S. (Eds), 2007b. *Managing Water for Australia: The Social and Institutional Challenges*, CSIRO Publishing, Collingwood, Victoria.

Jacquet, J. B., 2012. Landowner attitudes toward natural gas and wind farm development in northern Pennsylvania, *Energy Policy*, **50**: 677–88.

Jones, C. R. and Eiser, J. R., 2009. Identifying predictors of attitudes towards local onshore wind development with reference to an English case study, *Energy Policy*, **37**(11): 4604–14.

Keane, S., 2012. *Case Study: The Landscape Guardians and the Waubra Foundation*, Independentaustralia, Available from: http://www.independentaustralia.net/2012/environment/the-landscape-guardians-and-the-waubra-foundation/ (accessed 14 April 2013).

Kerselaers, E., Rogge, E., Vanempten, E., Lauwers, L. and Van Huylenbroeck, G., 2013. Changing land use in the countryside: Stakeholders' perception of the ongoing rural planning processes in Flanders, *Land Use Policy*, **32**: 197–206.

Langford-Smith, T. and Rutherford, J. (Eds), 1966. *Water and Land: Two Case Studies in Irrigation*, Australian National University Press, Canberra.

Langford, K. J., Forster, C. L. and Malcolm, D. M., 1999. *Toward a Financially Sustainable Irrigation System: Lessons from the State of Victoria, Australia, 1984–1994*, The World Bank, Washington, DC.

Layder, D., 1998. *Sociological Practice: Linking Theory and Social Research*, Sage Publications, London.

Legard, R., Keegan, J. and Ward, K., 2003. In-depth interviews, In *Qualitative Research Practice: A Guide for Social Science Students and Researchers* (Eds, Ritchie, J. and Lewis, J.) Sage Publications, London, pp. 138–69.

Lerner, M. J., 1987. Integrating societal and psychological rules of entitlement: The basic task of each social actor and fundamental problem for the social sciences, *Social Justice Research*, **1**(1): 107–25.

Lerner, M. J., 1998. The two forms of belief in a just world: some thoughts on why and how people care about justice, In *Responses to Victimisations and Belief in a Just World* (Eds, Montada, L. and Lerner, M. J.) Plenum Press, New York, pp. 247–69.

Letcher, R. and Powell, S., 2008. The hydrological setting, In *Water Policy in Australia: The Impact of Change and Uncertainty* (Ed., Crase, L.) Resources for the Future, Washington, DC, pp. 17–27.

Lewis, D., 2006. Water thieves leave farmers parched, *The Sydney Morning Herald*, 16–17 December 2006, p. 21.

Lind, E. A. and Tyler, T. R., 1988. *The Social Psychology of Procedural Justice*, Plenum Press, New York.

Lind, E. A., 2001. Fairness heuristic theory: justice judgments as pivotal cognitions in organizational relations, In *Advances in Organizational Justice* (Eds, Greenberg, J. and Cropanzano, R.) Stanford University Press, Stanford, CA, pp. 56–88.

Lloyd, C. J., 1988. *Either Drought or Plenty: Water Development and Management in New South Wales*, Department of Water Resources New South Wales, Parramatta, NSW.

Lloyd, G., 2012. *Ill Wind Blows a Headache*, The Australian, Available from: http://www.theaustralian.com.au/national-affairs/ill-wind-blows-a-headache/story-fn59niix-1226508730334 (accessed 30 April 2013).

Locke, S., 2012. *Managed Investment Schemes – Costly or Savvy?*, ABC Rural, Available from: http://www.abc.net.au/site-archive/rural/news/content/201212/s3660101.htm (accessed 20 June 2013).

Low, N. and Gleeson, B., 1998. *Justice, Society and Nature: An exploration of political ecology*, Routledge, London.

Lupfer, M. B., Weeks, K. P., Doan, K. A. and Houston, D., 2000. Folk conceptions of fairness and unfairness, *European Journal of Social Psychology*, **30**: 405–28.

MacCoun, R. J., 2005. Voice, control, and belonging: the double-edged sword of procedural fairness, *Annual Review of Law and Social Science*, **1**(1): 171–201.

Mackellar, D., 1971. *The Poems of Dorothea Mackellar*, Rigby, Adelaide.

Magnani, N., 2012. Exploring the local sustainability of a green economy in alpine communities, *Mountain Research and Development*, **32**(2): 109–16.

Martin, W., 2005. *Water Policy History on the Murray River: A Handbook for Murray Irrigators*, Southern Riverina Irrigators, Deniliquin, NSW.

McComas, K. A., Stedman, R. and Sol Hart, P., 2011. Community support for campus approaches to sustainable energy use: The role of "town–gown" relationships, *Energy Policy*, **39**(5): 2310–18.

Mercer, D., Christesen, L. and Buxton, M., 2007. Squandering the future: Climate change, policy failure and the water crisis in Australia, *Futures*, **39**(2–3): 272–87.

Meyerson, D., 2006. *Essential Jurisprudence*, Routledge–Cavendish, Coogee, NSW.

Midgley, G., 2000. *Systemic Intervention: Philosophy, Methodology, and Practice*, Kluwer Academic/Plenum Publishers, New York.

Mikula, G., 1993. On the experience of injustice, *European Review of Social Psychology*, **4**(1): 223–44.

Mikula, G., 2005. Some observations and critical thoughts about the present state of justice theory and research, In *What Motivates Fairness in Organisations?* (Ed., Gilliland, S.) Information Age Publishing, Greenwich, CT, pp. 197–210.

Mikula, G. and Wenzel, M., 2000. Justice and social conflict, *International Journal of Psychology*, **35**(2): 126–35.

Mikula, G., Petri, B. and Tanzer, N., 1990. What people regard as unjust: Types and structures of everyday experiences of injustice, *European Journal of Social Psychology*, **20**(2): 133–49.

Miller, D., 1999. *Principles of Social Justice*, Harvard University Press, Cambridge, MA.

Miller, D. T., 2001. Disrespect and the experience of injustice, *Annual Review of Psychology*, **52**: 527–53.

Miller, D. and Ratner, R., 1996. The power of the myth of self-interest, In *Current Societal Concerns about Justice* (Eds, Montada, L. and Lerner, M. J.) Plenum Press, New York, pp. 25–48.

Minichiello, V., Aroni, R., Timewell, E. and Alexander, L., 1995. *In-Depth Interviewing: Principles, Techniques, Analysis*, Longman, Sydney.

Mobjörk, M., 2010. Consulting versus participatory transdisciplinarity: A refined classification of transdisciplinary research, *Futures*, **42**(8): 866–73.

Molle, F. and Berkoff, J., 2009. Cities vs. agriculture: A review of intersectoral water re-allocation, *Natural Resources Forum*, **33**: 6–18.

Montada, L., 2003. Justice, equity, and fairness in human relations, In *Handbook of Psychology*, Vol. 5 (Ed., Weiner, I. B.) Wiley, New York, pp. 537–68.

Murray–Darling Basin Authority, 2013. *About the Basin*, Murray–Darling Basin Authority. Available at: http://www.mdba.gov.au/about-basin (accessed 7 May 2013).

Musgrave, W., 2008. Historical development of water resources in australia: irrigation policy in the Murray–Darling Basin, In *Water Policy in Australia: The Impact of Change and Uncertainty* (Ed., Crase, L.) Resources for the Future, Washington, DC, pp. 28–43.

Nancarrow, B. E. and Syme, G. J., 2001. Challenges in implementing justice research in the allocation of natural resources, *Social Justice Research*, **14**(4): 441–52.

National Research Council, 1996. *A New Era for Irrigation*, National Academy Press, Washington, DC.

National Research Council, 2008. *Public Participation in Environmental Assessment and Decision Making*, The National Academies Press, Washington, DC.

National Water Commission, 2004. *Intergovernmental Agreement on a National Water Initiative*, National Water Commission, Australian Government. Available at: http://nwc.gov.au/nwi (accessed 21 June 2013).

National Water Commission, 2006. *Water Management in Australia: A Vision of a Positive Future*, Government of Australia, National Water Commission. Available at: http://www.nwc.gov.au/__data/assets/pdf_file/0014/11516/Water-management-Australia-vision-PUB-0906.pdf (accessed 21 June 2013).

National Water Commission, 2008. *Water Planning in Australia: National Water Commission Position*, Australian Government, National Water Commission, Canberra. Available at: http://archive.nwc.gov.au/library/position/water-planning (accessed 22 June 2013).

National Water Commission, 2013. *National Water Initiative*, Australian Government, National Water Commission. Available at: http://www.nwc.gov.au/nwi/objectives (accessed 21 June 2013).

Neales, S., 2008. $2 bn pipeline could bring supplies in from Tasmania, *The Herald Sun*, Available at: http://www.heraldsun.com.au/news/victoria/plan-to-take-water-from-tassie/story-e6frf7kx-1111116947778 (accessed 20 June 2013).

Newman, A., 2012. Creating the power for renewal: Evaluation of New South Wales' renewable energy planning law changes and suggestions for further reform, *Environmental and Planning Law Journal*, **29**: 498–514.

Norton, A., 2012. *Graduate Winners: Assessing the Public and Private Benefits of Higher Education*, Grattan Institute, Carlton, Victoria.

Nozick, R., 1974. *Anarchy, State, and Utopia*, Basic Books, New York.

NSW Government, 2010. *Compliance Policy: Leading Policy and Reform in Sustainable Water Management*, NSW Office of Water. Available at: http://www.water.nsw.gov.au/Water-licensing/Compliance/Compliance/default.aspx (accessed 22 June 2013).

Owen, M. and Akerman, P., 2009. *Rann to sink PM's Murray Deal in High Court*, The Australian, Available at: http://www.theaustralian.com.au/news/rann-to-sink-pms-murray-deal/story-e6frg6n6-1111119047853 (accessed 20 June 2013).

Parkinson, G., 2013. *Battle for King Island: Wind Energy Politics at 20 Paces*, Reneweconomy. Available at: http://reneweconomy.com.au/2013/battle-for-king-island-wind-energy-claims-at-20-paces-67046 (accessed 21 April 2013).

Pigram, J. J., 1993. Property rights and water markets in Australia: an evolutionary process toward institutional reform, *Water Resources Research*, **29**(4): 1313–19.

Platow, M. J., Wenzel, M. and Nolan, M., 2003. The importance of social identity and self-categorisation processes for creating and responding to fairness, In *Social Identity at Work: Developing Theory for Organisational Practice* (Eds, Haslam, S. A., van Knippenberg, D., Platow, M. and Ellemers, N.) Psychology Press, New York, pp. 261–76.

Pohl, C., 2005. Transdisciplinary collaboration in environmental research, *Futures*, **37**(10): 1159–78.

Powell, J. M., 1989. *Watering the Garden State: Water, Land and Community in Victoria 1834–1988*, Allen & Unwin, Sydney.

Ramadier, T., 2004. Transdisciplinarity and its challenges: the case of urban studies, *Futures*, **36**(4): 423–39.

Rapoport, A., 1985. Thinking about home environments: a conceptual framework, In *Home Environments* (Eds, Altman, I. and Werner, C.M) Plenum Press, New York, pp. 255–86.

Rawls, J., 1971. *A Theory of Justice*, The Belknap Press of Harvard University Press, Cambridge, MA.

Rawls, J., 2001. *Justice as Fairness: A Restatement*, The Belknap Press of Harvard University Press, Cambridge, MA.

Reis, H. T., 1984. The multidimensionality of justice, In *The Sense of Injustice: Social Psychological Perspectives* (Ed., Folger, R.) Plenum Press, New York and London, pp. 25–61.

Richards, L., 2005. *Handling Qualitative Data: A Practical Guide*, Sage Publications, London.

Rogge, E., Dessein, J. and Gulinck, H., 2011. Stakeholders perception of attitudes towards major landscape changes held by the public: The case of greenhouse clusters in Flanders, *Land Use Policy*, **28**(1): 334–42.

Rood, D., 2007. *Pipeline Opponents 'Quasi-terrorists'*, The Age, 23 November 2007, Available at: http://www.theage.com.au/news/national/pipeline-opponents-quasiterrorists/2007/11/22/1195321951537.html (accessed 20 June 2013).

Roper, H., Sayers, C. and Smith, A., 2006. *Stranded Irrigation Assets*, Staff Working Paper, Productivity Commission, Australian Government, Melbourne. Available at: http://www.pc.gov.au/research/staff-working/strandedirrigation (accessed 21 June 2013).

Rutherford, J., 1966. Integration of irrigated and dryland farming in the southern Murray–Darling Basin, In *Water and Land: Two Case Studies in Irrigation* (Eds, Langford-Smith, T. and Rutherford, J.) Australian National University Press, Canberra, pp. 125–259.

Samuel, G., 1999. *Adapting to change – towards a fair and efficient Australia*, Western Australian Chamber of Commerce & Industry Leaders' Forum, Perth.

Schlosberg, D., 2004. Reconceiving environmental justice: global movements and political theories, *Environmental Politics*, **13**(3): 517–40.

Schlosberg, D., 2007. *Defining Environmental Justice: Theories, Movements, and Nature*, Oxford University Press, Oxford.

Seccombe, M., 2012. *A Field Guide to the War on Wind Power*, The Global Mail, Available from: http://www.theglobalmail.org/feature/a-field-guide-to-the-war-on-wind-power/406/ (accessed 30 April 2013).

Sewell, W. R. D., Handmer, J. W. and Smith, D. I., 1985. *Water Planning in Australia: From Myths to Reality*, Centre for Resource and Environmental Studies, Australian National University, Canberra.

Shklar, J., 1990. *The Faces of Injustice*, Yale University Press, New Haven.

Simon, T. W., 1995. *Democracy and Social Injustice: Law, Politics, and Philosophy*, Rowman & Littlefield Publishers, London.

Skitka, L., 2003. Of different minds: an accessible identity model of justice reasoning, *Personality and Social Psychology Review*, **7**(4): 286–97.

Skitka, L., 2009. Exploring the "lost and found" of justice theory and research, *Social Justice Research*, **22**(1): 98–116.

Skitka, L. J. and Bravo, J., 2005. An accessible identity approach to understanding fairness in organisational settings, In *What Motivates Fairness in Organisations?* (Eds, van den Bos, K., Steiner, D., Skarlicki, D. and Gilliland, S.) Information Age Publishing, Greenwich, CT, pp. 105–28.

Skitka, L. J., Winquist, J. and Hutchinson, S., 2003. Are outcome fairness and outcome favourability distinguishable psychological constructs? A meta-analytic review *Social Justice Research*, **16**(4): 309–41.

Smith, D. I., 1998. *Water in Australia: Resources and Management*, Oxford University Press, Melbourne.

Snowy River Alliance, 2013. *Snowy River 2009: Fact Sheet*, Snowy River Alliance. Available at: http://snowyriveralliance.com.au/oldwebsite/facts.html (accessed 21 June 2013).

Steffen, B., 2012. Prospects for pumped-hydro storage in Germany, *Energy Policy*, **45**: 420–9.

Stoeckel, K. and Abrahams, H., 2007. Water reform in Australia: the National Water Initiative and the role of the National Water Commission, In *Managing Water for Australia: The Social and Institutional Challenges* (Eds, Hussey, K. and Dovers, S.) CSIRO Publishing, Collingwood, Victoria, pp. 1–9.

Strazzera, E., Mura, M. and Contu, D., 2012. Combining choice experiments with psychometric scales to assess the social acceptability of wind energy projects: A latent class approach, *Energy Policy*, **48**: 334–47.

Syme, G. and Nancarrow, B., 2005. Creating community consent through fairness judgements, In *Consent and Consensus: Politics, Media and Governance in Twentieth Century Australia* (Eds, Cryle, D. and Hillier, J.) API Network, Perth, pp. 371–87.

Syme, G. and Nancarrow, B., 2008. Justice and the allocation of benefits from water, *Social Alternatives*, **27**(3): 21–5.

Syme, G., Nancarrow, B. and McCreddin, J. A., 1999. Defining the components of fairness in the allocation of water to environmental and human uses, *Journal of Environmental Management*, **57**(1): 51–70.
The Land, 2009. *Farm Day Dispels Urban Myths About Agriculture*, Available at: http://fw.farmonline.com.au/news/nationalrural/agribusiness-and-general/general/farm-day-dispels-urban-myths-about-agriculture/1497927.aspx (accessed 21 June 2013).
Thøgersen, J. and Noblet, C., 2012. Does green consumerism increase the acceptance of wind power?, *Energy Policy*, **51**: 854–62.
Twomey, S., 2013. *Wind Farm Plan Splits King Island*, Stock & Land, Available at: http://www.stockandland.com.au/news/agriculture/general/news/wind-farm-plan-splits-king-island/2651519.aspx?storypage=0# (accessed April 21 2013)
Tyler, R. T., 2000. Social justice: outcome and procedure, *International Journal of Psychology*, **35**(2): 117–25.
Tyler, R. T. and Blader, S. L., 2000. *Cooperation in Groups: Procedural Justice, Social Identity, and Behavioral Engagement*, Psychology Press, Philadelphia.
Tyler, R. T. and Blader, S. L., 2003. The group engagement model: procedural justice, social identity, and cooperative behavior, *Personality and Social Psychology Review*, **7**(4): 349–61.
Tyler, R. T., Boeckmann, R. J., Smith, H. J. and Huo, Y. J., 1997. *Social Justice in a Diverse Society*, Westview Press, Boulder, CO.
Valentine, S. V., 2010. A STEP toward understanding wind power development policy barriers in advanced economies, *Renewable and Sustainable Energy Reviews*, **14**(9): 2796–807.
van der Horst, D. and Vermeylen, S., 2011. Local rights to landscape in the global moral economy of carbon, *Landscape Research*, **36**(4): 455–70.
Walker, G., 2012. *Environmental Justice: Concepts, evidence and politics*, Routledge, London.
Walker, G., Devine-Wright, P., Barnett, J., Burningham, K., Cass, N., Devine-Wright, H., Speller, G., Barton, J., Evans, B., Heath, Y., Infield, D., Parks, J. and Theobald, K., 2011. Symmetries, expectations, dynamics and contexts: a framework for understanding public engagement with renewable energy projects, In *Renewable Energy and the Public: From NIMBY to Participation* (Ed., Devine-Wright, P.) Earthscan, London, pp. 1–14.
Walter, G. and Gutscher, H., 2012. *Public Acceptance of Wind Energy and Bioenergy Projects in the Framework of Distributive and Procedural Justice Theories: Insights from Germany, Austria and Switzerland*, The Advisory House, Zürich. Available at: http://www.advisory-house.com/UserData/Publication_1360865860.pdf (accessed 26 April 2013).
Watson, A., 2007. A national plan for water security: pluses and minuses, *Connections – Farm, Food and Resources Issues*, (Paper 60).
Watson, A., 2008. *Watering Victoria: The Good, the Bad and the Ugly*, Watering Victoria Symposium, Centre for Public Policy at the University of Melbourne, Melbourne.
Wengraf, T., 2001. *Qualitative Research Interviewing: Biographic Narrative and Semi-Structured Methods*, Sage Publications, London.
Williams, J., 2003. Can we myth-proof Australia?, *Australasian Science*, **24**(1): 40–2.
Wissenburg, M., 1999. *Imperfection and Impartiality*, UCL Press, London.
Wolgast, E. H., 1987. *The Grammar of Justice*, Cornell University Press, Ithaca, NY.
Wolsink, M., 2007. Wind power implementation: The nature of public attitudes: Equity and fairness instead of 'backyard motives', *Renewable and Sustainable Energy Reviews*, **11**: 1188–207.
Wüstenhagen, R., Wolsink, M. and Bürer, M. J., 2007. Social acceptance of renewable energy innovation: An introduction to the concept, *Energy Policy*, **35**(5): 2683–91.

Index

Page numbers in *italic* type refer to pictures or maps.